Force of Nature

ROBIN KNOX-JOHNSTON

with Kate Laven

PENGUIN BOOKS

PENGUIN BOOKS

Published by the Penguin Group
Penguin Books Ltd, 80 Strand, London WC2R ORL, England
Penguin Group (USA) Inc., 375 Hudson Street, New York, New York 10014, USA
Penguin Group (Canada), 90 Eglinton Avenue East, Suite 700, Toronto, Ontario, Canada M4P 2Y3
(a division of Pearson Penguin Canada Inc.)
Penguin Ireland, 25 St Stephen's Green, Dublin 2, Ireland
(a division of Penguin Books Ltd)
Penguin Group (Australia), 250 Camberwell Road, Camberwell, Victoria 3124, Australia
(a division of Pearson Australia Group Pty Ltd)
Penguin Books India Pvt Ltd, 11 Community Centre, Panchsheel Park, New Delhi – 110 017, India
Penguin Group (NZ), 67 Apollo Drive, Rosedale, North Shore 0632, New Zealand
(a division of Pearson New Zealand Ltd)
Penguin Books (South Africa) (Pty) Ltd, 24 Sturdee Avenue, Rosebank, Johannesburg 2196, South Africa

Penguin Books Ltd, Registered Offices: 80 Strand, London WC2R ORL, England

www.penguin.com

First published by Michael Joseph 2007
Published in Penguin Books 2008

1

Copyright © Robin Knox-Johnston, 2007
All rights reserved

The moral right of the author has been asserted

Typeset by Rowland Phototypesetting Ltd, Bury St Edmunds, Suffolk
Printed in England by Clays Ltd, St Ives plc

Except in the United States of America, this book is sold subject
to the condition that it shall not, by way of trade or otherwise, be lent,
re-sold, hired out, or otherwise circulated without the publisher's
prior consent in any form of binding or cover other than that in
which it is published and without a similar condition including this
condition being imposed on the subsequent purchaser

ISBN: 978-0-141-03219-1

www.greenpenguin.co.uk

Penguin Books is committed to a sustainable future
for our business, our readers and our planet.
The book in your hands is made from paper
certified by the Forest Stewardship Council.

Contents

PENGUIN BOOKS
FORCE OF NATURE

Robin Knox-Johnston entered the Merchant Navy at the age of seventeen, obtaining his Master's Certificate eight years later. Of the nine starters in the *Sunday Times* Golden Globe Race in 1968, he was the only one to complete the voyage, after 312 days alone at sea, and won the trophy for the first single-handed, non-stop circumnavigation. Since then he has participated in many ocean races, including the Whitbread, and in 1994 co-skippered *Enza* with Sir Peter Blake to set a new record for circumnavigation. He has been UK Yachtsman of the Year twice, International Yachtsman of the Year in 1995 and was knighted in 1995.

Kate Laven (BA Hons) qualified as a journalist after a brief career in advertising. She started out at the *Daily Echo* in Southampton, where she became a specialist cricket and sailing writer despite being resolutely ordinary and inelegant at both sports. As a freelancer she was the first woman to cover county cricket for the *Daily Telegraph* and was appointed sailing correspondent for the *Sunday Telegraph*. She is a regular contributor to Telegraph Media Group as a writer and web broadcaster, as well as a host of other newspapers, magazines, websites and books.

List of Illustrations

Introduction
The Bay of Biscay – October 2006

The whole boat shuddered as a wave broke over the bow, sending torrents of water crashing down the deck towards me. I instinctively grabbed a handhold as the boat recoiled but was knocked sideways by the force. I then ducked as the wave swept over me and into the cockpit, flooding it to deck level.

This was one of the worst storms I had encountered in more than fifty years at sea. When we had sailed from Bilbao at the start of the Velux 5 Oceans race, just thirty-six hours before, there had been a gale warning, but none of the weather programs had predicted anything this dramatic. My instruments on *Saga Insurance* were recording wind speeds of 50 knots and gusts of 72 knots. The experts, who were now safely at home tucked up in their beds, had been caught unawares, and it was we sailors who were paying the price.

There were six of us within a hundred miles of each other, and all of us were battling against the storm. After leaving Bilbao we had been racing towards Cape Finisterre at the western end of the Bay of Biscay when the wind began to increase. We could see it on our instruments, and even in the relative calm of the nav station we could feel our boats beginning to pitch and yaw more urgently and hear the wind noise through the rigging increase.

Our Open 60 yachts were designed to survive the storms of the Roaring Forties of the Southern Ocean. They are tough craft, developed for single-handers, and built to take a broach or have a huge wave break over them. But usually they run before the wind and waves. Here we weren't running. We were battling into both.

Mine was the most exposed vessel in the fleet, since I was the furthest north and furthest from the coast. I had no protection from the land and there was nothing to temper the winds as they blasted straight at me from the south-west or the waves that were crashing in from the Atlantic.

I was also the least experienced in these boats. The others had owned their boats for much longer. I had not experienced a gale in this boat yet, let alone winds of this strength, and so was trying to assess how *Saga Insurance* was handling. Had I been in *Suhaili*, the little 32-foot wooden ketch that I had taken around the world thirty-eight years before, I would have known exactly what to do to make the boat and me safe and more comfortable in these conditions. But I had been sailing Open 60s for just five months, and despite having sailed 5,000 miles in *Saga Insurance*, I still had no idea what she was capable of or how she would behave when the seas turned angry.

This was a violent introduction, and there was no room for error.

I knew I had to get it right because if I didn't, and the boat became imperilled, my life would be threatened. I could draw on years of experience in handling boats from dinghies to monster multihulls, and sailing through both hurricanes and the maelstrom that can be the Southern Ocean, but it makes no difference how many years you have spent crossing the oceans. You never feel totally confident in your ability to survive a storm. There is always something you have not thought about, something that will surprise you. If you make a bad call, your life, your boat, everything is at risk.

A tried and trusted rule of the sea is to put the boat first. If she survives so might you. Put yourself first and both you and the boat are likely to be in trouble.

This is why earlier I had been watching the waves so carefully, watching how the boat was behaving. This is why I had been standing in the cockpit for a couple of hours, my feet as wide apart as I could stretch them and my face battered by the elements. I needed to feel her every movement and become a part of her. This is how I had done it before and this was how I was doing it now.

Rain squalls had been coming every half an hour or so, completely wiping out visibility and flattening the tops of the waves as if they were being doused in oil. *Saga Insurance* was comfortable most of the time, feeling underpowered and rolling easily with the increasing waves. Also I had sea room – there was no land to leeward for 250 miles, so I could always allow the boat to drift for a couple of days if necessary, more than enough time for the storm to move on.

The bow rose to another wave and crashed into its crest, sending spray flying everywhere. *Saga Insurance* rolled with the blow then slammed hard into the next wave. I didn't like this. The boat was fine when she was held up into the wind and her bow was pointing about 45 degrees from the direction the waves were coming from, but when she was knocked off and bore away, she speeded up and pounded heavily. I wasn't sure how much of this punishment she could take.

I ducked again as the wave came aft but there was nothing I could do. She was as comfortable as I could make her for the moment, so I climbed below, ate a Mars bar to keep my energy up, and lay down in my soaked oilskins on the navigation bench.

I lay on my stomach with my legs spread and my hands tightly gripping one end of the chart table. With the boat bouncing and crashing around like a trinket in a washing machine, this was the only way to keep myself from being thrown about. I must have been there for more than half an hour, wondering how long this was going to continue but being quite certain that the longer it went on, the worse it would get.

Any ideas of making headway on the race track and stealing a march on the five other skippers were long gone. In these conditions, where the waves were getting big, rising a good 10 metres high into thunderous skies, my instinct was to go into survival mode. If you look after your boat, it will look after you. With a voyage of 30,000 nautical miles ahead of me and a fractured coccyx already inhibiting my performance, I could not afford to take any chances.

And then she rolled. The force hitting the boat was not a blow but an overpowering surge, and *Saga Insurance* was heaved over onto her starboard side. For a moment I was vertical and disoriented, knowing that my body was no better than a rag doll and that if I fell back now it would be straight onto the side of the cabin and my healing tailbone could be fractured again.

Within seconds she swung upright again, and I climbed out into the cockpit to see if everything was all right on deck.

I emerged feeling slightly shaken but as far as I could tell unharmed. As I scrambled out on deck to check for damage, initially all I could see was that the windex, an arrowhead on a strut at the masthead to show wind direction, had disappeared, and the other instruments were showing crazy wind angles because they had all been dislodged.

As far as I could see, that was the extent of the damage. Down below, things were pretty orderly. Surprisingly, not much had come loose so it didn't take long to tidy up. But as soon as I finished, I rested again, this time on the cabin deck on the premise that if we were rolled again, there was less distance to fall.

The roll worried me, since it was a sign that the waves had got even larger and more powerful. Any more like that would certainly cause damage.

We were in unknown territory and I was left wondering what on earth I could do now. The option of turning and running before the wind and waves did not appeal one bit, since it meant staying with the system as it moved toward the UK. I wasn't sure how the boat might react if I streamed warps, which had served me so well with *Suhaili* when caught in similar strength winds in the Southern Ocean, or attached the anchor to a bridle astern, as we had done in *Enza New Zealand*.

I sat there for an hour. The conditions remained the same and I was waiting for daylight so I could make a more systematic check of the boat. I dozed off for a few minutes, and when I opened my eyes again the wind sounded slightly less ferocious. The instruments confirmed that the wind was down to 45 knots. It looked as if the 90-degree roll had been the climax to the storm. As so often happens, once the wind began to ease it dropped quickly, and by daybreak it was down to Force 4 and the seas were beginning to ease. The time had come to get racing again.

I went to hoist the mainsail but I immediately noticed a problem. A small section of track had torn away, about 2 metres above the deck. I persuaded the sliders as far as the first reef to rejoin above the break, but no further. I could not race like this, since I was unable to sail efficiently. I had to get the track repaired, and this was not a job I could do by myself at sea.

I looked at the chart. The nearest big port was La Coruña in Spain. Reluctantly I set a course and contacted race headquarters to tell them I had officially suspended racing. It was not a good start.

1. A New Beginning

At the start of the Velux 5 Oceans race in October 2006 I was sixty-seven years old. My whole life had been involved with boats and the sea, but recently my time had become consumed with matters of a more personal and painful nature. In 2003 my wife Sue died of ovarian cancer; for some time before that she had been very sick, and needed round-the-clock care at our home in Devon.

We had known each other for fifty-seven years, having first met when my parents moved me and my three younger brothers down from Heswall, on the Dee estuary, to Beckenham in Kent after the war in 1946. Her family lived opposite. There were only two years between us – I was eight and she was six – so we often played together. She was quite a tomboy. At around the time I joined the Merchant Navy, aged seventeen, we started going out together; she would come over to our place and we would listen to records, or we'd go to the cinema.

Sue was my first serious girlfriend, and as soon as I got my second mate's ticket and qualified for a marriage allowance, I asked her to marry me. I then promptly disappeared for a year to work on the company's ships in Asia.

We were married in January 1962. I was twenty-two and she was just twenty – which, with the benefit of hindsight, was probably too young. We honeymooned on the slopes in Kitzbuel in Austria and within a few days I left to resume my service with the British India Company, working as third officer on the ships carrying mail, cargo and deck passengers between Bombay and Basra.

Sue joined me in Bombay a few weeks later and settled in quickly, even though I was away three weeks out of every four. We found an apartment, and after fifteen months our daughter Sara was born. She arrived five weeks early and, as it happened, five hours after I had left Bombay for a three-week voyage. I had no idea we'd had a girl until a week later, when our third engineer had a letter from his wife, who was also in Bombay, telling us that Sue had had an emergency Caesarian and that the baby was a girl.

This was an odd way to find out I had become a father, but we had no family in Bombay and Sue was in hospital recovering so there was no one to write to me. Sara was three weeks old, very tiny and utterly adorable when I first saw her. I felt very protective, both of Sara and her mother, and right from the start Sara and I had a tremendous bond. We suspect the Caesarian must have caused complications for Sue, because we were never able to have any more children. We just had to accept that. We were very happy with the one we had so we just got on with it.

Although this was a time of great joy, we were young and ill equipped to cope with the upheaval of having a child, and my relationship with Sue started to change. The arguments revolved around a new boat that I was having built at the Colaba workshop with two colleagues.

My plan was that as soon as the boat was completed, Sue, Sara and I, along with my other two colleagues, would sail her home to England. It didn't occur to me that this might be dangerous. To me, a seaman by profession, this was just an extension of my work in a smaller boat. I knew people who had taken small children sailing and didn't see why we couldn't do it. But Sue was horrified. For her, taking a baby that young on such a long voyage was very far from being a sensible plan.

She was being protective, but I couldn't see that and wanted us to be doing everything together. Also, all my money was tied up in the boat, which by then we had named *Suhaili*, the name of the south-east wind in the Persian Gulf. If I abandoned her I had nothing, and I wouldn't be able to look after my family. If I got her back to England and sold her, I could raise the money for a house. But this cut no ice with Sue. She absolutely refused.

Looking back, I can see that she was being totally reasonable, but at the time I simply could not understand why Sue didn't want to come with me.

The situation led to a lot of arguments, and eventually Sue left. There was no ultimatum. She just upped sticks and went. All very sudden, but that was how she was. She had tremendous strength of character, which was why she'd been able to settle in India quite easily, when I was required to be working away from home most the time. That strength and independence was one of the things I liked best about her.

I was devastated when I realised our relationship was over. Maybe as some sort of knee-jerk reaction, I decided to take a year or so out from the British India Company and sail *Suhaili* home via Arabia and South Africa, with my brother Chris and a friend, Heinz Fingerhut.

We were away for eighteen months. We ran out of money by the time we reached Durban, and it was also late in the season for rounding the Cape of Good Hope, so we all took jobs, I as captain of a small coaster and later as a stevedoring supervisor, Chris with an insurance company, and Heinz back at sea as a radio operator. By the time I returned home to England in 1967, my divorce had been finalised. Although relations between Sue and myself were not good, there was never any dispute over Sara. We stayed in touch and I saw Sara whenever I could. Never at that time did I think that Sue and I would get back together again, and I even became engaged to someone else, albeit briefly.

After I sailed around the world in *Suhaili* in the Golden Globe race of 1968–9, my life changed. In the first place the British India Company, along with many other famous British shipping companies, was being absorbed into the P&O Group, and that was not a future I wanted. BI, as the company was known, had been my home from the age of seventeen and I could not envisage working for a new company. I decided it was time to leave the sea and, with some investors, set up Mercury Yacht Harbour on the Hamble in Hampshire, where I bought a house.

Then in 1971 I heard Sue wanted to travel to Lisbon to see her sister. I contacted her to say I was thinking of sailing there myself, and did she want a lift to save her the ferry fare?

She agreed, which I took as a sign that she wanted to try again, and our voyage laid the foundations for a second chance. I was now thirty-two and Sue thirty, and this time round our relationship seemed more mature. We were older and wiser and not so stubborn. Years later, Sue said that I had been 'bloody boring' when we lived in Bombay because I was always off doing things – canoeing, swimming, building *Suhaili* – and she would have liked me to have been less energetic.

We remarried in 1972. This was one of the smarter moves in my life and we had a good marriage, though I'm sure I caused her a lot of frustration because I was still pretty pig-headed. I seldom remembered her birthday or our anniversary, but she never seemed too concerned. She was always very supportive of my sailing and she had an instinct for people, good and bad. I relied on her a lot to make my personal judgements for me and she was invariably right. We liked the same people and enjoyed doing the same things. We had our ups and downs but by and large were a happy team.

The cancer was diagnosed very late, despite numerous trips to the doctor saying she had something wrong, and I didn't appreciate at the time that a late diagnosis is almost a death sentence. If you catch ovarian cancer early there can be a good chance of recovery; if late, the average expectancy is three years. We shared the nightmare of operations and chemotherapy. We watched the cancer recede, almost disappear, and then reappear a month or so later. I watched Sue slowly wither, desperately trying to find some cure which never came. I never consciously realised that I would lose her until three days before she died, when she was taken to the hospice. I thought we were there to sort out her feeding so we could build her up after another dose of treatment, but was told that she was dying. It came as a massive shock. She knew what was happening but I think she was worried I would insist on trying some other treatment so didn't tell me. She'd had enough.

I was with her when she died, surrounded by her family, but am not sure how much she was aware of this as she was well dosed with morphine. The fact that I was never really able to say goodbye still hurts me.

I went through the mechanics of the funeral, a job to be

done, but after it was over and everyone had gone home, I sat in the house, alone with the dogs, and tried to get to grips with what had happened.

We had had some tough times but had stuck together solidly through them. No decisions affecting me or my career were made without discussion, and after the disaster of Lloyds in the 1990s, which had completely wiped me out and made our lives utterly miserable for the best part of five years while I tried to pay off debts and secure our future, things were looking up financially. We were looking forward to a happy retirement, watching our five grandchildren grow up and taking time to visit the places we had always wanted to see. That dream had now been shattered and I felt bitter about it. What had Sue done to deserve this?

I tried going to church more often, looking for some sort of an answer, but became increasingly disillusioned. If God was so merciful why deprive Sue of the good years she had worked so hard for? A state of shock existed for almost two years. I did not socialise much, except with the family, and had no interest in female company; I missed Sue so badly that to embark on any new relationship felt almost like adultery.

But slowly the pain of the loss numbed, and I came to realise that I needed to draw a line beneath the past and get on with life and find a new purpose. I was still only sixty-four, and the longevity gene that has been so potent in our family – producing a handful of octagenarians and nonagenarians and, in my aunt Aileen, one centenarian – was showing no sign of fading. This effectively meant another lifetime for me to fill with new challenges.

During the time I'd spent looking after Sue my associations with boats and the oceans had fallen away, but sailing was my calling – and when this new realisation finally dawned, I found I was itching to get back on the water.

A voyage or even a race would be as good a project as any, I thought, and the Velux 5 Oceans was tempting. It was such a large proposition, it would allow little thought or time for anything else.

It was way back in 1969 that I completed the *Sunday Times* Golden Globe, the only finisher of nine starters all aiming to be the first person to sail solo non-stop around the world. I had left the Merchant Navy after that voyage and settled down to shore jobs, building a yacht harbour on the Hamble and developing St Katharine's Dock Marina in London before moving to Troon in Scotland and building a marina in the inner harbour there. I had continued to race, competing in six of the two-handed Round Britain races and winning two, two Admiral's Cup series and a Whitbread race. But with my remarriage to Sue in 1972, and with our daughter Sara away at school, at that time the thought of going away and sailing solo around the world again held no appeal for me.

Then one day in late autumn in 1979, as I was sitting in my house in Scotland, I picked up the phone to find Dave White, an American sailor who I'd met through the Observer Single-handed Transatlantic Race (OSTAR), at the other end. He was calling from the Marina Pub on Goat Island, Newport, RI.

'We were having a few beers at St George's Yacht Club in Bermuda after the Bermuda One Two Race and we've come up with an idea.'

Wait for it, I thought, knowing what those end-of-race sessions were like.

'We're planning a solo around-the-world race with stops from Newport and back to Newport. What do you think? Would you do it?'

'No', I replied unhesitatingly. 'I'd want a very, very good reason to race around the world solo again, with or without stops.'

Inevitably, though, the concept intrigued me.

Even before the Golden Globe race, four of us had decided we wanted to go one better than Sir Francis Chichester, who in May 1967 had returned from his solo around-the-world voyage, with one stop in Australia, to an astonishing reception in Plymouth. Around a quarter of a million people turned out on the waterfront to see *Gypsy Moth IV* come home.

The four comprised me, Bill King, the Frenchman Bernard Moitessier and John Ridgeway. Then in March 1968 the *Sunday Times* cleverly spotted a marketing opportunity and announced the Golden Globe. The rules were simple: competitors had to pass south of the three great capes of Good Hope, Leeuwin and the Horn; outside assistance was forbidden and no one was permitted to board the boats; the winner would be the first to return to their start point in the British Isles. Later, when the organisers discovered that we were all planning to sail at different times, a prize of £5,000 was offered for the fastest circumnavigation within these rules.

Those of us in the smaller boats had to leave early in order to guarantee reaching Cape Horn in the southern hemisphere mid-summer, so the rules were changed to allow boats to depart when they liked between June and October. None of us was really interested in the newspaper's race; what we all wanted was to be the first to complete a solo non-stop circumnavigation, and so we were going to sail when we were ready. Ridgeway was the first to go, on 1 June, Chay Blyth followed a week later and I sailed on the 14 June. Moitessier and King started two months after us.

The format of the race created a good amount of confusion that has persisted to this day, as Moitessier was in line to make the fastest voyage, but was running three weeks behind me geographically when he decided to pull out. People still say he was winning when he changed his mind about returning to Europe, and it is true that he was in line to post the fastest time, but both he and I agreed he would have been unlikely to have caught up with me before I got back to Falmouth, although I think the finish would have been close.

The race now being proposed by Dave White avoided this confusion because it would start on one day, with a designated start line, and the winner would be clear.

A voyage around the world has always excited the public's imagination. The first solo circumnavigation was made by the American Joshua Slocum in 1896 in his 35-foot sloop *Spray*. It attracted a lot of attention at the time, but it was some years before anyone else attempted it. By the time Francis Chichester set off in 1966 only four other people had completed the trip, but this exclusivity was about to change if Dave White could get support for his Around Alone Race.

Dave's gruff voice came back: 'Well, we'll keep you informed and maybe you'll change your mind'.

'No chance' I replied. 'But good luck.'

With a group of friends, Dave set up Goat Island Yacht Club to host the event. No other club would associate themselves with a round-the-world race for 'crazy' men, as the solo sailors were known. They sent out the Notice of Race and contacted all the sailing magazines in the world with details of the event. The response was extraordinary: within a few weeks they had received 400 enquiries from all around the world (though they later admitted that this number did include enquiries from a bunch of prisoners, who had written in presumably just to fill in some time). The entry fee was $400 and by January 1980 around twenty people – mostly friends of the race committee – had signed up and paid their fee. In the meantime Dave was struggling to find sponsorship, which created some uncertainty over whether it would go ahead.

One of the potential entrants, Richard Broadhead from the UK, approached the British industrial gas company the BOC Group. They were changing their name from British Oxygen to BOC and the company's head of corporate communications, Nigel Rowe, decided that although they were not interested in supporting any individual skipper, the event was a perfect vehicle for bringing together the various members of the BOC Group worldwide, including the USA, South Africa and Australia – all stopovers for the race.

He approached the race committee in Newport and found a willing audience who were more than happy to have a sponsor. The Around Alone, which was Dave's working title for the event, became the BOC Challenge, and Dave was able to focus on his original intention of being one of the competitors, which left the sponsors looking for someone to run the race.

My phone went again. Apparently I was the logical choice for the job of chairman of the race committee. I did not want to enter but was drawn to the idea of running this brand-new event, so flew to Newport with Nigel to meet the rest of the members and start to hammer out the final rules.

Much was already decided. The start date was scheduled to be in August 1982. There would be a two-class field with the maximum length being 56 feet (the length of Francis Chichester's *Gypsy Moth IV*) and the minimum length 32 feet (the same as my *Suhaili*). There would be compulsory stops in Cape Town, Sydney and Rio de Janeiro, and the rest of the rules were based on the Observer Single-handed Transatlantic Race, which had been running since 1960 and proving very popular.

This was the first solo around-the-world race since the Golden Globe fourteen years before, and the rules for that had been somewhat erratic. One of the lessons learned from that race was that all entrants needed to know their boats properly before they set out. The only way to get this knowledge is by having time at sea and putting a few thousand solo miles on the clock, so we introduced a rule that every entrant, in order to qualify, must sail single-handed in their boat across an ocean on a voyage of not less than 2,000 miles.

The race started from Newport in late August 1982 with seventeen boats, ranging from ex-IOR racers to solid heavy cruisers.

Right from the start, one boat stood out. Frenchman Philippe Jeantot's revolutionary 56-foot *Credit Agricole* was specially built for short-handed racing. She was wider than the others and shallower, with a plumb bow and a large and powerful rig. If this was the way things were going then no one else was on the same bus.

The race brought plenty of drama and highlighted the

importance of modern electronics in solo sailing, most
notably the ARGOS satellite position fixing system whose
merits were truly shown when it went over the side of one
of the boats but carried on buzzing for weeks afterwards
despite floating in the middle of the Pacific Ocean. Our sole
means of communicating with the boats was still by single
sideband radio, although a network of ham radio operators
gave a better coverage than had been possible for me.

Four skippers, including Dave White, pulled out in Cape
Town with equipment failure. On the second leg to Sydney,
the American Tony Lush discovered his keel was about to
fall off his yacht *Lady Pepperell*. He activated the panic button
on his ARGOS system to alert the race organisers and was
rescued twenty-four hours later by his compatriot Francis
Stokes, just moments before his boat sank. Desmond
Hampton slept through an alarm and ran *Gypsy Moth V*
onto Gabo Island, south of Sydney, where she was quickly
smashed to pieces.

On the third leg Jacques de Roux's 41-foot boat *Skoiern
III* was pitch-poled in the Southern Ocean 1,400 miles away
from land. In 60 knots of wind, it dismasted and the mast,
still held by rigging, knocked a hole in the boat. He activated
ARGOS and transmitted a distress signal, together with a
position, which winged its way around radio hams who
passed it back to Newport, where Peter Dunning, the marina
manager, coordinated a rescue. Richard Broadhead in his
boat *Perseverance of Medina* was 240 miles to the east of de
Roux, who was now pumping constantly to keep his boat
afloat, and as soon as Broadhead received the signal he sailed
back against the wind and sea to rescue him. Remarkably,
although his only indication of de Roux's position came
from ham messages, Broadhead found him within forty-

eight hours and picked him up, four hours before *Skoiern III* slipped several thousand leagues under the sea, never to be seen again. Broadhead later dropped de Roux with a French navy vessel, whose crew took him in exchange for rum, baguettes and camembert.

Jeantot finished in 159 days and the last man over the line, Kiwi sailor Richard McBride, arrived back in Newport in 264 days.

Although none of the ten skippers who completed that first race entertained any ideas of heroism, and most of them still hold to that view, a tradition for heroic acts was established.

At the prize-giving, BOC Group chairman Richard Giordano announced that as far as the Group were concerned the race had been a great success and they wanted to be involved again four years later in 1986. A loud cheer went up. The BOC Challenge would not just be a one-off, it would now become a regular part of the international racing calendar. Solo racing around the world had arrived.

For the 1986 race we made a few changes to improve safety levels. At the end of the first race I had called together all the finishers and we had spent half a day going through the lessons we had learned, and a number of recommendations were made. The first was that we should increase the overall length allowed from 56 to 60 feet. Class 1 was to be for boats between 50 and 60 feet, Class 2 for boats between 40 and 50 feet in length. The rescue of Jacques de Roux after his boat had been holed led to the proposal that all the boats should have three watertight bulkheads, so would retain enough buoyancy to float until rescue could be arranged without the need to pump for days. The final proposal came about because we were beginning to see drawings of potential boats that had no keel and would depend on water ballast alone for their stability; a monohull without a keel to balance its rig and sails when the tanks were empty or being changed was likely to capsize, and it was agreed that in future the boats could not heel more than 10 degrees on either side when all their tanks on one side were full and the other side empty. A boat without a keel would not be able to comply with this rule. Our objective was ensure safety at the same time as allowing as much freedom as possible for new ideas to be developed.

For the second race in 1986 there were five boats that showed strong similarities with the *Credit Agricole*, and these became known as BOC boats after the race sponsors. Their distinctive features were wide and shallow hulls, plumb bows and wide sterns.

Up to this point the races open to these boats had been the BOC Challenge and races like the OSTAR and Route de Rhum, but now Philippe Jeantot contacted me and said he was thinking of organising a non-stop solo race around the world. Of course he did not need my permission, but I thought it nice of him to·ask. I told him that as far as I was concerned it was a great idea and I would support him, and thus the Vendée Globe was born.

With more races to enter, more of the BOC boats began to be built. The rules for the boats were still being set by the race organisers at this stage, and Philippe Jeantot and I kept in touch to ensure we both used the same. In 1991 a number of French competitors created a class associ-ation, the International Monohull Open Class Association (IMOCA), which set up rules for the class. The most inter-esting innovation was a capsize test where the boat, without its mast, was pulled over until it floated upside down and then released. It had to come upright to comply. More recently the number of watertight bulkheads has been increased. But once rules are introduced there is always a pressure to introduce more. A minimum horsepower for the engine was decreed to be 27 hp. I could never find out why such a figure was introduced; a better system would have been to say the boat must be able to motor at a certain speed for a certain distance. Escape hatches had to be in the transom. This was the logical place, but I would have preferred a rule that stated the hatch must be clear of the water whatever the situation of the boat, to allow new ideas to come in. The IMOCA has certainly moved in the right direction; it has promoted safety and been quick to react to failures such as Tony Bullimore losing his keel in the Southern Ocean, and the result has been a boat with every latest safety feature.

No other class of boat in modern yacht racing has impacted so profoundly on the sport as the Open 60. It is interesting to see how closely the new range of boats built for the Volvo race resembles the Open 60s. Experience of round-the-world races, and in particular the need to survive in the Southern Ocean, has led to a standardisation in design. The single-handed scene has also produced a number of remarkable innovations that have transferred to yachts in general: two examples are self-steering and roller furling. Features such as rotating masts and canting keels may never transfer to the general cruising yacht but they are becoming more accepted for racing boats.

The route for the 1986 race was the same as four years previously and there were twenty-five entrants. Tragically, one of the most popular returnees, Jacques de Roux, fell overboard off the Australian coast during the second leg and was never found. This was our first fatality and reminded us that however experienced and talented a sailor is – and Jacques was a consummate professional – the risks in single-handed offshore yacht racing remained serious.

Sixteen of the original twenty-five starters finished the race, with Jeantot in a new *Credit Agricole* once more crowned champion, improving his time by a massive twenty-five days to 134 days, which was ten days faster than the fully crewed 80-foot *Great Britain II* in the first Whitbread race of 1973. Jeantot averaged almost 8.5 knots over the 27,100 miles, one knot faster than in 1982. It seemed enormously fast at the time.

I felt after this event that it was time to move on. The race was now firmly established and no longer needed my input. Indeed I felt it might be a good idea if someone else came in and introduced their own ideas so I returned to writing books and helping to set up the public affairs branch of the Royal Navy, prior to starting Clipper Ventures, a company organising round-the-world racing for amateur sailors.

BOC Group pulled out as sponsors after 1995 and the name of the race reverted to the Around Alone. The lack of sponsorship inevitably led to a decline in the event and by 2002 there was a serious possibility that the race, which was due to start in November that year, would not go ahead. It had taken a lot of time and hard work to establish the event and with the launch of the non-stop Vendée Globe by Jeantot in 1989, I felt it would be a great shame if the tradition of a solo stopping race were to be allowed to fall by the wayside. So I suggested to my fellow directors at Clipper Ventures that we pick it up ourselves and run it.

A few months before the start of the 2002 race we took

over responsibility for the race and set about securing its future. To begin with, we decided it would be run under IMOCA (the Open 60 class association) rules in order to attract more European Open 60s, even though we knew this move would not go down well with skippers such as the Kiwi Graham Dalton, who was building his boat to the original Around Alone rules and would now have to invest more to ensure it complied. We also decided it should start in the US as usual and stop in the UK – Torbay, just to be different – before going off to Cape Town, New Zealand, Salvador (Brazil) and back to Newport, a course of around 28,800 miles, which would make it the world's longest single-handed round-the-world race.

We thought we would have around twenty boats from across the world, though we knew the clash with the Route du Rhum would restrict our numbers, since so many French skippers had obligations to their French sponsors and to French events. Given the short lead time, finding a title sponsor proved an insurmountable task but we went ahead anyway, on a very tight budget, with thirteen entries from ten different nations. For the first time, we organised a fully crewed 'Prologue' race from Newport to New York, where the skippers and their crews took part in Sail for America, organised as a memorial to the people who died in the September 11 attacks the year before. There were three classes, 60 feet, 50 feet and 40 feet.

Entries included Emma Richards, who was aiming to become the first British woman to participate and the youngest ever person to complete the race; Kojiro Shiraishi, an inspirational young Japanese sailor who had been support crew to the legendary Yukoh Toda in the first BOC race; and Bernard Stamm, a pint-sized Swiss sailor made of grit and steel who, like me, came from a merchant navy background. Stamm was regarded as one of the most complete single-handed sailors on the circuit and duly went on to enhance his reputation with four convincing wins in five legs in our first race in 2002, which earned him the now coveted Around Alone title.

As soon as that race finished, the team at Clipper set about preparing properly for the 2006 event. The first thing was to rename it to mark its relaunch – and we chose 'The 5 Oceans' because the race comprised five major ocean crossings and we felt the name summed up everything we were trying to achieve with the event. It had a global feel to it, implied extreme challenge and worked well in French and English.

The next priority was to find a sponsor. Dozens of proposals were sent out and after months of discussions with a number of candidates, the Velux Company of Denmark signed up.

We had consulted widely on the preferred format of the race and the skippers especially had urged us to shorten the race so that their campaign costs could be reduced. A new route was chosen with just two stopovers, in Fremantle, Western Australia, and Norfolk, Virginia, and Bilbao in Spain was selected as the first non-USA start-and-finish port. Because the 2002 race had shown that by having 40-footers racing against 60-footers the larger boats spent long periods in port waiting for their smaller competitors to arrive, the 40-foot class was reluctantly dropped and the race restricted to Open 50s and 60s.

So far, although I was chairman of the company and the driving force behind the development of the race, I had taken no part in many of the early discussions, but watched with interest from the sidelines. All that was about to change.

As I became less interested in running the 5 Oceans race and more fascinated by the boats and the competition, it crept up on me slowly that I was beginning to think as if I was an entrant myself.

I mentioned this to one or two people and was told I was joking, wasn't I? I was reminded of an encounter in Cowes in 1968 when I was preparing *Suhaili* for the Golden Globe. A blazered gentleman came up to the boat, sniffed as he looked at her and enquired: 'Are you this Johnny who thinks he's going to sail alone around the world non-stop?' I answered I was going to have a go, and his response was so stupid, it made me laugh rather than get angry. 'Well, it can't be done and anyway you couldn't do it' – a nice vote of confidence from someone I had never met before, who knew nothing about me, and who I was never going to meet again.

But this time was I really joking, or was I serious?

As I shared my idea with more and more people, the reasons why I shouldn't be doing it mounted up. For a start, I had no experience of the Open 60 boats. This was a valid point and deserved some consideration, but all warnings about how fast and powerful they were and how their performance differed from other racing boats served only to stir emotions that had been dormant for some years. I had sailed large fast multihulls for years, winning the French 60-foot championship in 1986, and these boats were faster than the Open 60s. In any case, the best way to get experience, I thought, was to get a boat.

The comment that really grated, however, was that at

sixty-seven, I was too old. What had age got to do with it? We all age differently. Some are old and tired at fifty; some reach the same stage at eighty. Just because our bureaucratic masters have chosen sixty-five as the official retirement age does not mean that the instant we cross this threshold we become useless to society and a drain on the resources of the National Health Service. We are no more liable to instant heart attacks every time we climb stairs, and our brains do not all of a sudden turn to porridge, so why are we expected to slip into old age at this point and spend the rest of our lives with our feet up watching TV? I considered myself to be sixty-seven going on forty-eight, and so far had seen no reason to slow down or cease to continue the activities I had always enjoyed.

I have also noticed that when one reaches sixty-five, one is treated as a small child all over again. At sixty-four our experience of, say, living in the tropics might be considered useful and even valuable, but the moment we pass over that dreaded divide we come in for overly solicitous instructions to drink plenty of water, wear a sun hat and use plenty of sun cream if we venture out into the sun, as if we had forgotten everything we ever practised during our years spent in the tropics.

Passing the sixty-five-years mark means nothing except to the bureaucracy. If you are still fit, there is no reason why you cannot continue to lead an active and adventurous life. Indeed, you are probably in a better financial position to participate in adventurous pastimes than you would have been twenty years before, with children and other responsibilities to accommodate.

We are humans. We need stimulation. We get it from projects, and the more adventurous and exciting the project, the greater the stimulation. Projects that are tailored to our abilities keep us physically and mentally fit. Apart from that, if something is easy and simple there is no satisfaction in achieving it. The harder the challenge, the greater the feeling of satisfaction that comes with success.

My generation seems to be lucky in this respect, in that we are living more active lives for longer. Maybe it has something to do with rationing during the war, or perhaps compulsory games lessons at school. For me it was also my early years as a Merchant Navy apprentice, when we were worked extremely hard and fed very well, so developed strong bone structures and a robust constitution and lost any fear of hard work.

As I began to think seriously about entering the Velux 5 Oceans, I discussed it with William Ward, my partner in Clipper Ventures, whose opinion I trusted implicitly. If I were to take time away from our business it would increase his workload, as the company had grown substantially since we set it up in 1996.

We had never intended to have the company this long. Our initial objective was to send eight yachts around the world in a race being organised by someone else, but we found the race organisation impossible to deal with and were left, at short notice, with eight yachts under construction and many crew signed and paid up but no race. So we went ahead and organised one ourselves.

The Clipper race took a different route to any other – crossing the Atlantic, through the Panama Canal, the Galapagos, Hawaii, Yokohama, Shanghai, Hong Kong, Singapore, Seychelles, Durban, Cape Town and Brazil, then home. It gave a wide variety of weather conditions, but that would only help the crews become more experienced.

We aimed to take either complete novices or weekend
sailors and turn them into competent yachtsmen. Our training was determined by our race, not by any need to tick the
boxes on the Royal Yachting Association's syllabus. Some
journalists, who never came to see what we were doing,
slated us for not having a 'proper' race, which they never
actually defined beyond hinting that it required more than
eight boats. As usual they were taking a safe position,
pretending to authority without taking any responsibility.

In my view, there was no rule preventing us from de-
signing a race route that embraced some of the world's most
attractive places and which required a crew to learn more
about spinnaker handling rather than sailing a boat close-
hauled. Besides, spinnaker handling requires more skill.

Half the time yachting journalists need to be contentious
just to get space in their pages, so one should not be
surprised, but it certainly hurt us in our early years because
their criticisms put potential crew off. One magazine, having
never sailed on our boats, described them as Clipper
Clunkers, and four people withdrew from the race the day
after the magazine was published, so although I thought the
objections illogical I realised we had to take them seriously
and counter them.

Our first race in 1996 was a big success, both from the
crews' standpoint and commercially. The skippers and the
crews were very loyal and loved it, but certain sections of
the media, who still refused to come and see what we actually
did, remained sceptical. Their negativity impacted on the
second race in 1997, which wasn't so successful because we
did not fill all the berths. I had to remortgage my house and
William was hocking stuff just to pay the bills. The boats

had cost almost £3 million and we had daily provisioning costs which were not covered by our income.

But we were determined to get it right. We could not let such a potentially dynamic business turn to custard.

One day, while lying in the bath and thinking about the negativity of the national newspapers, I had the idea of trying to attract interest in the regions by getting cities from around Britain to enter boats in a competition similar to football, where towns and cities vied with each other. I felt sure that although the national papers did not support us, the regional papers would get right behind the race. Their circulations together were higher than the nationals and I felt they could be the perfect vehicle for us in raising our profile. The national papers would then have to sit up and take notice. I had learned a lot about press and publicity when I was one of the four people setting up the public affairs department for the Royal Navy, and I knew how powerful the regional titles could be.

I also decided to approach *The Times* with a sponsorship proposal as a means of securing coverage. Our timing could not have been better. The Millennium was approaching and they wanted to do something different to mark it, so were intrigued by our presentation. The city concept appealed to them especially, since our deals with the cities meant they were able to promote themselves at every stopover. There was no cash involved in these deals back then – our partners just agreed to support and promote the race – but the concept worked well. In 2000, our third race, we had eight boats representing eight cities and *The Times* were title sponsors, which proved a highly successful partnership.

In 2002 we introduced an international perspective with

three overseas cities: Cape Town, New York and Hong Kong. We followed that up by commissioning a brand-new fleet of boats, designed by Ed Dubois and built by the Double Happiness Yard in Shanghai.

In the last race, in 2005, we attracted ten entries from right across the globe – three from the UK and the rest from Australia, South Africa, China and America, where the interest grows markedly each year.

The Clipper concept had been successful because we had worked hard on injecting fresh ideas and evolving. In 1998 we took Clipper Ventures plc to AIM, the London Stock Exchange's international market for smaller companies, so that we could raise capital for further investment and give ourselves a value on our shares. This was an expensive exercise, and I'm not sure it was the right thing to do. Enabling people from the outside to have an input into how the company operated wasn't always beneficial, and those who tried to tell me how to run the boats were quickly booted into touch. It always amazes me how people with no experience of a particular business suddenly become experts when representing a shareholder and want to interfere. The exercise broadened both William's and my knowledge of business and commerce but, without question, made us slightly more cynical.

The City is only interested in how much money it can make from you. If you make them money, they are 100 per cent behind you, but the moment that changes, they turn against you. Having said that, the process of taking Clipper to AIM introduced us to some interesting people and enabled us to expand the company to the extent that my role was no longer pivotal.

This growth and self-sufficiency was now vital since it

meant that William would not be left high and dry if I decided to go off sailing. But what would he think?

His answer was typical. 'If you really want to do it, why don't you?' he said. 'I think it would be brilliant if you did.'

Sara just took the whole idea in her stride. She had grown up with me wandering off from time to time to go sailing, so I hadn't anticipated any objections.

I asked both William and Sara to keep the thought to themselves as there is nothing worse than people who get up and announce they are going to do something, but never do. I would only go public if and when I had put everything in place.

The first thing I needed to sort out was the money to buy a boat. I rang my bank and told them I wanted to borrow some cash for my retirement project. And what might that be? they asked, fully expecting my answer to be an olive farm in Italy or a golf time-share in Barbados. There was a stunned silence when I said it was to race single-handed around the world. Then delighted laughter. 'Only you could come up with something like that,' said my manager. 'I'll ask the partners what they think.' Within three hours, I was told the loan had been approved.

So with that hurdle behind me, I now needed a boat. It had to be an IMOCA Open 60 as the race was only open to them, rightly or wrongly. There were four in the UK, but the strength of the class lay in France. Fortunately, my French sailing colleague Bernard Gallay ran a yacht broker-age which tended to specialise in these sort of racing boats, so I asked his advice. Like everything it came down to price.

The Open 60 class had been developing and a ten-year-old boat would be out-designed and heavier than a new one. The difference in performance might be as much as 10 per cent, the equivalent of two weeks in a round-the-world race. There were eight on the market in total, but only two were really up to date and they were quite expensive.

Wanting to get a feel for what the market was offering, I drove over to France to look at a couple. As I was going to Lorient anyway, Bernard suggested I take a look at *Fila*, winner of Around Alone in 1998, when she was campaigned by the Italian Giovanni Soldini.

I looked at another boat in Lorient first, but, although cheap, it needed a lot of work and was never going to be competitive. *Fila* looked good even though she had been laid up for a couple of years. She was designed by the French company Groupe Finot, one of the accepted leaders in the field of Open 60s, and had been state-of-the-art when built in 1997, having both a hydraulically operated swing keel and a rotating mast.

I liked the look of her but she was beyond my budget. I drove on down to Les Sables d'Olonne and looked at another boat which was ready to sail, within my price bracket but older.

Bernard joined me that evening and we chatted it through. What did I think of *Fila*, he asked.

'Loved her, but beyond my budget,' I replied.

How about making an offer? he suggested. The only offer I could make would be considered insulting and I could see no point in making enemies, but Bernard was reassuring. 'OK, I'll tell him how much you have and see if he is at all interested'

I went away lecturing on the *Queen Mary 2* for a fortnight, but kept in contact by email. A week into my trip I received a message from Bernard saying my offer had been accepted.

My immediate reaction was 'What on earth have I done?'

But this was quickly replaced by excitement. I told Bernard to draw up the contract and wired the deposit.

That was it. I was back in the saddle and was raring to go. It had been a very long time since I had felt so euphoric and alive. The forthcoming year was going to be very far from ordinary, and the planning started in earnest at that very moment.

2. Messing About in Boats

Ever since I completed my first circumnavigation in 1969, people have been intrigued by my connection with the sea. Unlike some of the French sailors who routinely fill their logs with symbolism and poetry, my appreciation of the world's oceans is rooted more in a practical working relationship than in romance, though it would be true to say that I've had some of the happiest moments of my life while at sea.

All sailors are asked about their earliest associations with the sea, and for some that first encounter is like an epiphany, a momentous discovery. For me, I knew at the age of seven I wanted to make a career at sea. The calling was powerful and irresistible, but I have no idea where it came from. It is fair to say that my entire subsequent life was decided by a seven-year-old!

I was born in Putney, admittedly not far from the banks of the River Thames but not close enough to the sea for it to be accessible or important. My father's family were farmers in Northern Ireland, though since my grandfather was not the eldest son and therefore not in line to inherit the farm, he went into the Irish linen business.

There was a strain of Scottish Covenanter in the Northern Irish Johnstons which had come from our Presbyterian farmer forefathers, who fled the Scottish lowlands in the early seventeenth century. My father and his three sisters had a strict upbringing with the emphasis on education and social justice, and as a result all of them developed a strong work ethic. In my father's case this meant he was incapable of sitting and doing nothing. His attitude was that if you were not working, you were sinning, and although he was never evangelical about it, I think it rubbed off on all of us.

My mother's father was a barrister and all his brothers were lawyers bar one who became a brigadier in the Royal Engineers. There were a number of naval officers on my mother's side – including her cousin Captain Tom Cree, and the ship's padre on HMS *Royal Oak* who perished when it was torpedoed by a German U-boat in 1939. Another cousin, Donald Cree, was secretary of the Royal Cruising Club for forty years. He was a keen yachtsman, but surprisingly I never met him. He was still alive when I went round the world but unfortunately we never managed to meet up.

The only adventurer in our family, of this current generation at least, was my second cousin Giles Kershaw, who came to be regarded as the greatest aviator in modern Antarctic history. He was actually a commercial pilot with Cathay Pacific Airways, having taken up flying as a teenager but, like me, he had a real yearning for adventure so took time out from his day job to fly for the British Antarctic Survey. In 1990 he was flying an experimental gyrocopter over the Antartica ice, intending to use it for aerial photography, when he was hit by a gust at 200 feet and fell to his death. He was only forty-two.

Giles apart, there is no evidence from either side of the family of any great passion for exploration or discovery, though there was no shortage of family members who spent lifetimes pushing boundaries.

My uncle Arthur Irving crossed Russia in the 1930s, after taking a double first at Oxford. My aunt Aileen, Dad's older sister, went to the Royal Holloway College in 1928 – it was unusual for a woman to attend university in those days – and took a first in Modern History before embarking on a distinguished career with the British Red Cross in Washington. She still has one of the sharpest intellects I have ever come across, even though she is now a hundred years old. My other aunt, Maureen, was a schoolteacher who became a government inspector.

Some years earlier, my grandmother's uncle Bill Grout Williams was the only man in England to be making black crêpe at the time of Prince Albert's death in 1861, and he made a fortune flogging it to mourners. There was so much money swilling around, he rented Chequers, which is now the prime minister's country home, while he was waiting for his own house, Pendley Manor in Tring, to be built. My cousin Dorian Williams, the television equestrian commentator, established an adult education centre at Pendley in 1945 and also set up an annual Shakespeare Festival which, more than sixty years later, is still going strong.

All of them accomplished, yet none of them impassioned pioneers or explorers. No inveterate seafarers and not many victims of destiny, as I surely was.

My grandparents had both been born and brought up in Northern Ireland. He was from Coleraine and she from Lisburn, but they moved over to England in 1905 and settled in Berkhamsted, where my father and all of us, except Micky, went to school. My grandparents, who I lived with for three years while I was at school, were probably the biggest influences in my early life, my grandmother especially, even though she was very firm. When I earned my boxing colours at school and asked her to sew the badge onto my blazer, she left it in her workbasket for three weeks. Her attitude

was that gaining the colours was good, but she expected
no less.

She was a strong character but a nice person as well.
Throughout her life she religiously followed two main tenets:
'Do as you would be done by' and 'The Lord helps those
that help themselves'. Both have played a big part in the
way I have tried to live my life and at certain times, particularly when I was being tested during the first circumnavigation on *Suhaili*, the absolute truth of these principles has
become evident. 'It is no good lying in your bunk listening
to the rising wind and feeling the boat beginning to strain
and praying for God to take in a reef,' I wrote in *A World of
My Own*, my account of that voyage. 'No one but a fool
would expect anything to happen. One has to get up and
reef the sails oneself before the boat's movement will ease.
If the wind continues to increase, one takes in more sail
until eventually one has to heave to. When everything has
been done that you know you can do, you put your trust in
your Superior Being and just hope that what you have
done is right. This will probably seem obvious to everyone,
believer or otherwise, but there is a great deal of comfort to
be gained thinking that there is something out there that
can protect you. Because of this belief, throughout the
voyage I never really felt I was completely alone and I think
a man would have to be inhumanly confident and self-reliant
if he were to make this sort of voyage without faith in God.'

My father David Johnston (Knox was a forename that
somewhere along the line became part of a surname) was
also a major influence. Someone once asked me who I would
thank if I had to make a lifetime-award acceptance speech,
and it would have to be my father for all the sacrifices he
made for our education.

Money was short in our household. We had no television until after I had gone to sea. We never went abroad on holiday – our holidays were always in a caravan in Selsey, but we found that exciting because it was by the sea and involved a whole new set of adventures that Beckenham and Berkhamsted could not offer.

Everything in our house was second-hand. The washing machine and refrigerator were never new. Dad had a company car and Mum an old 1933 Standard Ten, which we regularly used to take to pieces. Our home in the Avenue in Beckenham was a typical Victorian three-storey house with four bedrooms on the first floor: Mum and Dad in one bedroom, our wonderful nanny Carrie Richards in the other, then the four boys in the two remaining bedrooms. There were two flats at the top of the house, which were let out to provide some income. There were no luxuries in that house.

My father worked on the shore staff of a shipping company – but I don't really know what he did. He never went to sea, though knew a great deal about ships, which I suppose influenced me. Once I showed an interest, he talked about ships a lot. During the war he volunteered and served with the Royal Engineers as a major with a dock company, and after he was de-mobbed that he went to work at my grandfather's Irish linen company.

Perhaps it was my father's shipping background that first excited my interest in the sea, but he was mostly away until I was eight, and by the time he came back from the war I had already decided that my future lay with ships and boats and the oceans. I remember attending an open day in Chatham but only have vague recollections of clambering around grey ships. I knew I wanted to go into the Navy but have no idea why.

Once I'd made my decision, all my interests focused on the sea, and by the age of fifteen I could give chapter and verse on every ship in the Navy – where it was built, what class it was in, what its armament was. Various friends had *Jane's Fighting Ships* and I would spend hours flicking through the reams of pages in each edition. I never owned one of my own because they were too expensive. I never begged my parents to take me to see any ships. It would have meant using petrol, and in those days petrol was expensive so we never went anywhere unless it was necessary.

I decided I wanted my own boat when I was eight, but there was never any spare cash in our household so for the next three years, I saved every penny that came my way to buy a 10-foot clinker-built sailing dinghy I had seen advertised for £17.10s. I cut that advertisement out and carried it around everywhere with me.

All my dreams revolved around getting that boat, and by the age of eleven I had saved enough money. But when I went to buy it, the price had gone up to nearly £30, which was way out of reach. I realised that the only way I was going to own my own boat was if I built one myself.

A dinghy was beyond my capabilities then, so I started with a canvas canoe on a wooden frame. It was put together while I was at school, in my grandparents' loft at their house on the outskirts of the town where I lived before I became a boarder. I worked alone on that canoe every Sunday – which was the only day I had free from school – for three months, using a set of books for reference. At 10 feet long and 2 feet wide it took a bit of manoeuvring to get it out of the loft, but eventually my aunt Maureen and I managed to lower it down and take it to the Grand Union Canal, where it was officially launched.

I hadn't put a deck on it so when my friend leaned over to grab it to pull it in and I leaned over to grab him, the boat capsized . . . So back into the loft she went. Eventually I got round to decking it and we took it on the top of Dad's car the next time we went on holiday to Selsey. I asked my brother Chris to sit inside, which he duly did, but when I let it go she immediately capsized again. I could not work out why she kept going over and, according to Chris, was much more concerned about that than I was about drowning my little brother.

I was very excited about having my own boat at last, not just because I had hankered after one for so long but because whenever I was paddling around in her, I experienced a real sense of freedom. For the first time in my life, I was master of my own boat and my own boss. That gave me such a buzz.

I would spend hours just paddling around, and I'm sure those early days spent idly on the water, stumbling across lessons in the wind and tides, boat-handling and the like, strengthened my resolve to sail. Later, I built a mast – a metal frame attached to a keel that was bolted on – and my mother made me a sail, and we turned the canoe into a sailing boat. It wasn't very successful but I was learning all the time.

Most of my memories of childhood revolve around making or fixing things. When we were very young, a friend and I used to make the most enormous Plasticine models of hills with fake tops. Then we made Plasticine soldiers to put inside. My brothers, who were always running around trying to join in, touched those models on a pain of death.

At Berkhamsted I rebuilt a little Austin 7, bunking off sports on Saturday afternoon to run home to my grand-parents' house, where this exquisite machine evolved in the back garden. I avoided cricket, said I was going to play tennis, left in the direction of the courts and then, when out of sight, belted up to my grandparents'. Michael Meacher, now an MP, was head of tennis and was very good about not mentioning my lack of attendance, although, if the truth be known, he was probably quite pleased as I was not a good player. At home in Beckenham I had my own little workshop in the cellar where I would disappear for hours on end making things, boats mainly.

This tendency to refashion and repair must have been in the genes. My mother was always doing things with her hands. She was a wonderful dressmaker and was making wedding dresses and upholstering furniture until well into her nineties. And my five spirited grandchildren, all aged under eleven, are already showing signs of being good with their hands – they are very interested in how things work and are gradually but determinedly taking over one of the rooms in their house for making models and painting soldiers.

My handiwork with the canoe was featured in the second issue of the junior edition of the *Daily Express*. There was a story and a picture with the canoe held aloft above my head. I was fourteen, and it provided my first lesson in the value of publicity: it got me free tickets for the second Boat Show at Empire Hall in Olympia in 1955, which was sponsored by the *Daily Express* publishers Beaverbrook. They sent me one ticket but I wrote back asking for more, since I had three brothers, so they sent me tickets for them too and the four of us went off from Beckenham Junction to Olympia. It was there I saw *Wanderer III*, Eric Hiscock's 31-foot Laurent Giles sloop in which he and his wife Susan had just sailed around the world.

I remember looking at this boat and saying, 'I'm going to go round the world one day. I'm going to do that.'

By then I was totally into boats. It was almost an obsession. While all my friends were getting comics or football or cricket magazines, I was subscribing to *Light Craft*. I read it avidly every month and soaked up every new detail about small boats and canoes, indeed anything that floated.

I would love to have joined a sailing club but it was difficult for a boy to join a sailing club on his own. You needed someone to take you there, take you out and encourage you, but I never had any contacts like that. I went sailing on Bletchley reservoir with some friends once, on their home-built wooden Heron dinghy with a mainsail and a jib, and that was the first time I had done any proper sailing. I loved it.

When I joined the Merchant Navy's cadetship *Chindwara* in 1957, aged seventeen, we were taught to sail in a whaler, as in those days lifeboats still carried sails and we needed to know how to use them. Later the ship was given two clinker dinghies and as far as I was concerned, one of them was mine. I took it out wherever we were and whenever I could and gained a reputation for capsizing the boat in every port east of Suez. The worst punishment they could possibly mete out to me was to stop me from sailing.

I don't think I was especially talented but I spent so much time on the water it was inevitable that I would improve, and although I was never an Olympic hopeful, it became quite normal for my watch to win the inter-watch sailing race which was held reach trip.

I enjoyed my apprenticeship. The British India (BI) Steam Navigation Company was one of the largest in the British merchant fleet and more than half of its vessels, cargo and passenger ships, were based east of Suez. Our trips on the *Chindwara* were to Africa, east and south, and I loved it. After three years I did one long trip to Japan and then returned home to take my Second Mate's Certificate. Everything about the sea and ships interested me. It was one of the reasons I joined the Royal Naval Reserve after I had passed my Second Mate's, because it was another aspect of the sea. I spent time on anti-submarine frigates and a short period in a submarine. Later I served on minesweepers, but missed the fun of hunting submarines. On rejoining BI I chose to serve out east and spent the next four years on small deck-passenger and mail ships running from Bombay to Basra, calling at just about every port in between in the Persian Gulf, which, in those days before oil income began to be invested, meant anchoring off. This was interrupted by flying leave home to take my Mate's Certificate and get married. It was an exciting and interesting run, spiced by a series of bombs placed on the ships as part of the rebel operations in Muscat and Oman which led to a sister ship being sunk with the loss of 400 lives.

This love of ships is still with me and even today I can spend a happy day wandering through docks, although the arrival of containers has meant that the cargoes are no longer visible. Its more efficient but less interesting.

In the space of the next ten years, I went from messing about with my chums in clinker dinghies in Indian Ocean and Persian Gulf ports to racing solo around the world in a ground-breaking race that would push boundaries both in the sport and in the levels of human endurance.

While serving out east and based in Bombay, I built *Suhaili* with a couple of fellow officers, our intention being to sail back to England once our contracts expired. Looking back, this seems ambitious, but in the Merchant Navy I was gaining knowledge, experience and confidence across all disciplines of seamanship and it never occurred to me that my credentials weren't up to scratch.

The design was not our first choice, but the company we bought the plans from in Poole sent the wrong ones out and we liked the solid seaworthy look. Much later I discovered that the plans were actually by the American naval architect William Atkins, a design called *Eric* he drew in 1922, and the Poole company had no right to sell them. She was all teak – keel, frames, hull and deck. The masts were solid, of Kashmir pine, which meant she heeled easily.

On arriving home I went back to BI, but Francis Chichester was just completing his one-stop solo circumnavigation and as far as I could see that left only one thing to be done – go round solo non-stop. The opportunity to be first at something was there, but it would not be there for long. If I wanted to be the first I knew I had to get moving quickly.

Suhaili was not my first choice of boat for the voyage. Colin Muddie designed a very clever 56-foot steel boat with schooner rig which would have been cheap to build and had sufficient length for speed. We got a quote to build the hull complete for £2,000 but I just could not raise the money. However, by that time I had become almost obsessed by the concept of a non-stop solo circumnavigation, so I took what I had. In retrospect it was the right choice. *Suhaili* was not a fast boat at all, but she was rugged and strong and I knew her inside out. It was this knowledge of the boat that was probably one of the principle reasons why I succeeded.

By the time I set out on the Golden Globe race in 1967, I had sailed 17,000 miles during the voyage back from

Bombay via Arabia and the Cape of Good Hope. In pure sailing terms, I was the second most experienced sailor in the race, a fact that was totally missed by the yachting journalists.

The only man who tipped me to succeed was Bernard Hayman, editor of *Yachting World*, because he had been in the Merchant Navy himself and knew how well we were trained. The Golden Globe was a race – all nine of us who set out wanted to be the first to complete the voyage – but it was also a pathfinding adventure and for that seamanship was primary.

Looking back, I would say that I was not bad at racing but always a pretty good seaman. I enjoyed the racing, the speed and the competition were exhilarating, but what I liked best about sailing was the sense of independence – being the boss and being free to do whatever I wanted.

I still have that today and am probably at my happiest when I am out sailing. The choice of where to sail is in my hands, to go where I want to go and do what I want to do. If I had to describe my perfect day, it would be to anchor up somewhere on the west coast of Scotland in a well-sheltered spot – though it would have to be more than 200 yards clear of land, so we didn't have the bother of the midges – where we could scramble ashore for long walks. I would have close friends for company and we would all enjoy a sundowner in the cockpit.

I had never really sailed in the UK until I teamed up with Les Williams in 1970 and won the two-handed Round Britain Race. Up to that point I had used yacht clubs around the Indian Ocean – Karachi, Bombay, Madras, Mombasa, Dar el-Salam – but I had no association with any yacht club in Britain.

When I first brought *Suhaili* back from India I tried to join the Royal Medway YC but was told there was a two-year waiting list and besides, I couldn't afford it. So in 1967 I joined Benfleet Yacht Club, because Dad knew a member, and we laid *Suhaili* up in Benfleet Creek while I went back to sea. It was a nice friendly club and has stayed that way, so I'm still a member there. That was the only British yacht club I had been exposed to so I had no idea what other clubs were like and was not aware that they could be a little snooty.

After I had sailed round the world, I borrowed a friend's boat while *Suhaili* was being refitted and sailed down to Lymington, where I had been invited to a dinner as guest of honour. I sailed up the river, moored at the Yacht Club and went in to see the secretary. He was incredibly patronising. First of all he told me not to make a mess, and then said I would have to move if any members came along.

Bloody hell, I thought. This wasn't like Mombasa or Durban. That was my first introduction to this aspect of English yacht clubs and I was surprised that they didn't welcome visitors as they did elsewhere in the world, where, by and large, they were very pleased to see you.

Now I have a better understanding of their difficulties. With so many yachts and yacht clubs around, I realise they can't have people pulling up willy-nilly or there would be no facilities for the members. The problem was that I expected them to behave like any other yacht club I had been to, and without asking or even giving it any thought I'd just tied up. It was a different yachting world, and not one I was used to.

That patronising Yacht Club secretary reminded me of certain officers in the Royal Navy, who tended to look down on men trained in the Merchant Navy and treated us like second-class citizens. It took them a while to realise that we knew our stuff. I didn't resent the way they treated us, I felt sorry for their lack of understanding. They had certain preconceived ideas and were not open to influences – not unlike those who think that anyone over sixty-five should be sitting at home in front of the TV, not setting out to sea in an open boat. They had an arrogance about them. I answered them back if I thought they were wrong.

I have never been very good at doing what others think I ought to do. I will listen to their comments, and go away and mull over them, but no one knows me as well as I do myself, so it's my opinion that I ultimately trust. In any case, those who rush to offer gratuitous advice are usually the least qualified to give it.

There are so many restraints in life, one of the greatest being peer pressure at school or in an office. But no one can see inside each of us to what we really are capable of achieving, what we are thinking and what we are challenging ourselves to do, and how we might in fact do it if we could escape the indifference of a cynical teacher, friend or parent.

I saw the effect that a little encouragement can have on young people when I was president of the Sail Training Association. A few words of praise when they had climbed the mast for the first time made those students stand taller. It was the beginning of self-belief.

It's pretty safe to be negative about some unusual project, and dangerous to be encouraging as there is a good chance of being wrong. Yet time and time again we see that young people, if encouraged, can achieve far more that they thought they were capable of achieving. Older people too. So if you want good advice, go to those whose opinions you rate, not those who rate themselves.

3. Grey Power

There were just five months from the time I bought the boat to the start of the Velux 5 Oceans. She had been laid up for nearly two years, so there was a great deal to be done to get her race-ready.

The first thing was to get the boat where I could most easily prepare her, which I decided would be Gosport, where the Clipper headquarters were. I arranged for her to be launched in Lorient, and towards the end of May four of us flew out to bring her home. We collected her from a pontoon beneath the forbidding concrete U-boat pens built more than sixty years ago which had proved too hard to destroy.

A quick handover and we were away in the gathering darkness, all of us complete strangers to the boat. I had very little experience of an Open 60. I had sailed with Alex Thomson from the Solent to Plymouth before he did the OSTAR in his Open 50, and later had an afternoon sail with him in *Hugo Boss,* his Open 60, but I had no real knowledge of what these boats were like before we slipped our lines in Lorient.

It was not an easy passage. The wind blew Force 6 for the first few hours from the direction we were wanting to go in, so we had a thankless beat under reefed sails.

Then the continuous furler on the jib decided not to function and began to allow the sail to unroll. This self-furling technology was new to me and however hard I tried,

I could not get the sail to wind up. I ended up with a very sad and butchered jib.

The experience gave me a pathological hatred of this type of furler, and nothing since has changed my mind about them, although I still have one. When it came to choosing furlers for the jib and solent during the refit, I went for the single-line barrel type and have never regretted that decision. I should have replaced the reacher furler while I was at it as well.

The next day, as we passed through the Canal du Four off Brest, we sent one of the crew aloft to cut away the lashing holding the head of the jib to the mast, and then we stowed the wreck.

During the second night, I received my first somewhat brutal lesson in Open 60 manners, and they did not emanate from any school of etiquette that I had ever known.

We were heading in towards the Needles and needed to gybe. The wind was a Force 6. These boats do not have fixed backstays like the normal yacht, but running backstays like multihulls. We hauled in the sheet but were totally unprepared for the way the boat heeled right over when the mainsail came across and luffed up into the wind. I was on the new lee side with the tiller hard over but just could not hold her. I yelled to the others to release the sheet as I slowly slipped down to the guard rails, which saved me from being flung out over the side into the choppy seas.

I hung on for dear life as water gushed over me. The motion set off my lifejacket, inflating it to twice the size, which made my efforts at recovery even more difficult. The others ran over to grab me and, between them, hauled me back into the cockpit.

No damage was done but it was a useful lesson in two respects.

The first was that gybing had to be done very carefully, as the boat pulled the wind forward so quickly –far more quickly than I was used to with normal monohulls. Gybing, like tacking, is often a matter of instinct rather than science, in the same way that reefing and changing sails is a matter of human judgement rather than any response to what a sailmaker has promised. But a new boat means a calibration of impulses and I was finding my feet, quite literally.

The other lesson from the gybe concerned safety aboard. Although I had a life jacket and safety harness on, I had not been clipped on because I was expecting to have to move quickly across the cockpit. Never again.

We reached Gosport around forty-two hours after leaving Lorient, having learned that this new boat of mine was a serious, no-nonsense thoroughbred that demanded respect.

An Open 60 has a clear deck, apart from a small stream-lined cabin top and the cockpit. From the cockpit a small watertight hatch leads down to the cabin below. This in theory is 14 foot wide by about 10 feet, but the working area is more about 6 feet square – quite small, really, but perfectly adequate. It doesn't bear much resemblance to a cruising cabin; there is no concession to comfort at all. Everything that adds unnecessary weight is removed. There are no lockers and no beds as one would understand them, just light aluminium canvas-covered frames. We do have cushions for these bunks but they are not very comfortable.

There is headroom only beneath the cabin top; through-out the rest of the boat you have to stoop. There are no floorboards, so you walk on the hull everywhere. The bulkheads, deckheads and deck are painted white to lighten the cabin as the black carbon fibre absorbs rather than reflects light. Running around this cabin are electric cables, connecting all the electronics and bringing in the power from the solar panels.

The only place to sit is in front of the navigation station, but you have to be careful when swinging your feet around that you do not catch a wire or hydraulic pipe. It is a stripped-out workstation. There are no frills, just all basic equipment needed to get on and race the boat.

Dominating the forward part of the cabin are two large hydraulic rams that control the angle of the canting keel, which is housed in a box in the middle of the boat. This box is watertight, as it is open to the sea at the bottom where the keel passes through the hull. The keel pivots at the bottom of the hull. The hydraulic pump that controlled these rams was electric, but I soon found that it drew so much power it was necessary to run the generator if I wanted to heel the keel across. The whole objective of the canting keels is to try and keep the boat more upright so the sails spill less wind and give more power as a result. They are a comparatively recent introduction, but are becoming quite commonplace in ocean-racing yachts.

My workstation was a chart table and an instrument panel which looked like the flight deck of an aircraft. Normally, most of the instruments were on, but not always. The Sat C system was always kept on as it would be used by race control to poll our positions in the race and it brought me basic weather forecasts. The Iridium satellite phone was left on when it was working, showing 'Ready' on the face. A Fleet 77 satellite system was fitted before the race, its distinctive dome dominating the stern deck, but I only switched it on when I needed it because it is expensive on juice.

The automatic pilot, with two separate controls, was fitted before the qualifier. It had its main controls in the cockpit but two repeaters at the nav station so I could control the course from there if necessary. Many of these instruments had alarms included which would go off if a radar signal was detected, for example, or the boat had gone off course, or one of the satellite systems had lost its link, or even if one of the information connections, like the GPS (Global Positioning System), went down. Some of these alarms were oversensitive: I once had four alarms going off at one time. They could become a hazard when I was tired as after a while I tended to sleep through them, which meant I might miss something that was important. To control all this equipment I needed two laptop computers, one that looked after communications and the other for navigation work.

The bench in front of the nav station was hinged so it could be made level when the boat was heeling over, and this was where I slept nearly all the time. I don't think I slept in one of the bunks more than five times during the whole voyage, as I liked to be close to the controls. Often I would just lie on it in my wet oilskins, because I knew I might have to jump on deck. This of course soaked the cushion, so on the occasions when I was dry I had to reverse it.

With so much electronic equipment about I never put my coffee or tea on the table because of all the danger of a spill. The provisions were stored in boxes lashed to the hull beneath the cockpit. If the boat went on its side the food would not fly all over the place, as had happened on *Suhaili* in a storm south of Cape Town, when I had been rudely awakened by my boat being on her side and all the stores, including a pot of jam that unfortunately opened, landing on top of me.

The rules of the race required us to carry 10 gallons of fresh water in containers for emergencies. I kept a 2-gallon container for normal use, topping it up from the electric water maker, or from rain in the sails, as necessary. I never ran short. There is more rain about than people realise, and provided the sail is clean this can be gathered and stored. On *Suhaili* I had lost all my fresh water in the knockdown and had to live on rainwater for the next eight months.

Most of the time, the hatch to the cockpit would be open. I prefer it open because I can hear the sea and if I have to get out I can do it quickly. In the Southern Ocean I closed it a couple of times because rain or hail was coming in or the cockpit was flooding and I didn't want the water getting below. On a couple of occasions it was closed to keep the cabin warm. I made a big effort to keep the interior spaces dry and when water did get below, either through the hatch or from dripping clothing, I sponged it up pretty quickly.

When these boats heel over, you have to have handholds to prevent yourself falling over and to get around. You swing round rather like a monkey, going from handhold to handhold but always holding on to something. If you lost your grip it could be a long drop, as I discovered on the way across to Halifax, when I fell and badly bruised an arm and knee.

These carbon-fibre boats are incredibly noisy. Some sailors even wear ear defenders to keep the noise down. Every sound seems to be magnified, and the first time you hear the sound of a rope tightening on a winch drum you wonder what has broken. You hear the sea going past, the hissing increasing as the boat speeds up, and then at about 12 knots certain vibrations start which disappear at 15 knots. I can lie at the chart table and be within half a knot of guessing the speed by the sounds I am hearing.

On *Suhaili,* you could hear the water swishing past the hull, but it was nothing like so noisy.

Hatches through the watertight bulkheads at either end of the cabin lead to the sail locker forward and the lazarette aft. Both have water ballast tanks in them that allow me to weigh down the boat when required – so that, for instance, when going to windward I would flood the upper forward one, or when going downwind I would flood one of the after ones to keep the bow higher and reduce the risk of nose diving. The connections between the rudder stocks dominated the lazarette, which was where the autopilot motors were, hydraulic on the starboard side and linear to port, which gave me choices and back-up if one failed. Most of the time these bulkhead hatches were left open so I could hear what was going on in the two adjacent compartments and I would crawl through when necessary. Both had hatches through the deck as well, but often these were firmly clamped closed to prevent water getting below. Of course if I wanted to take a sail on deck, or stow one below, the forward deck hatch had to be opened, and this did lead to water getting below on occasions.

There are two more compartments within the boat, both forward of the sail locker and sealed with watertight doors. I rarely went there. It was only necessary to go forward to work the hydraulic pump for the inner forestay, and we moved those controls to the cockpit in Fremantle anyway.

A week after arriving from Lorient, I sailed for America. This was in order to comply with the rule we had made twenty-four years ago about race qualifiers. The requirement had not changed. Every entrant must have sailed single-handed, in the boat they had entered, on a transoceanic voyage of not less than 2,000 miles measured on a rhumb line between the start and the finish ports. Having introduced the rule when I was race chairman, I could hardly excuse myself from it now.

The point of the rule was mainly to ensure that every contestant knew their boat and knew what they were letting themselves in for; it also served to discourage the romantics who might turn up for the start but then find that solo sailing was not to their taste after all. The bars of marina pubs and yacht clubs are full of people telling you what they are going to do. But you turn up a year later and they are still there, still going to do it, with the excuse that something wasn't ready so a window had been missed. But there would be another one next year and in the meantime, they would bask in the admiration of those who could not differentiate between dreamers and doers.

I needed to learn as much as I could about the boat as quickly as possible. There would not be much time for the final refit and if anything serious needed to be done, it was important I found out now. I have always believed it imperative to have time on the water before setting out in a new boat on a long race.

Before I started out on the Golden Globe, I had virtually lived on *Suhaili* for two years, either at sea or in port, and had been very closely involved with her build, so I was familiar, intimately so, with every nook and cranny of her structure and every facet of her performance. Such a thorough knowledge allowed me to improvise when there was equipment failure or breakage and made possible a series of gambles in manoeuvres that I would never have been able to contemplate had I not been so confident with her. This was the main reason why I was able to complete the course and establish the record.

Looking at the entry list, I was by far the least experienced of the entrants in the Open 60 class and had a great deal to learn very quickly. This 5,000-mile round voyage to North America would at least give me some time afloat. I would have preferred a longer voyage and more time but there was no point worrying about it. We had to fill our heads with how to make things possible and forget about all the reasons why reaching the start line would in itself represent a miracle.

I decided to sail to New York to meet the Clipper fleet, which was due to arrive towards the end of June as they neared the end of their race around the world. That was 3,000 miles, comfortably in excess of the race requirement. Because the boat was new to me and was still an unknown quantity, I took three crew for the outward journey so that if anything went wrong I had the manpower to deal with it. The return journey would be solo and would constitute my qualifier.

My crew comprised a group of guys who I had never met before. None of them had been on an Open 60 before but all of them were experienced sailors and all were connected with Clipper.

One of them, Kent Cassells, an American who had been scheduled to work on a Clipper training course, was quite surprised when I called him to see if he was available. 'Hello,' I said. 'My name is Robin Knox-Johnston and I wondered if you would like to sail across the Atlantic.'

He was a bit taken aback. That didn't happen to too many people every day, he said, but he agreed and within seventy-two hours we were pushing off from the dock.

There was no doubt that *Grey Power*, as I had renamed the boat in response to comments about my age, had lacked love and affection while she had been laid up. She had gone to seed a little and needed a good spring clean both above deck and below. The electronics at the chart table were French and some of the instruments were British, others Italian. There were notes on walls about what all the switches did – some in French, some in English, some Italian. I speak a bit of French but no Italian, so they weren't much help, and mostly we worked out what everything did by trial and error.

I thought 200 miles a day would be a reasonable average for a racing boat crewed by four able sailors but it was not to be. We ran straight into headwinds. These are to be expected in the Atlantic when you sail west in our latitudes, but they usually veer or back a bit. Not these ones. We bashed our way west, but the timing was not going to work out. Then one night we hit something, a whale we think, as it struck us on the port side forward and then near the aft starboard rudder. This all happened at 1.30 one morning and threw most of us out of our bunks. As we scrambled for wakefulness and torches, the watch on deck yelled, quite unnecessarily, 'We've hit something'.

We found that the impact had damaged one of the brackets connecting the rudder stocks to the self-steering. The rudders are linked and the linkage was gone. We fixed the linkage by means of lashing a spare sail batten between the two rudders, but the full repair would require the services of a carbon-fibre specialist.

We had seen a number of whales before the collision. We had counted six, some of them coming as close as 30 metres and some just conspicuous plumes of spray in the distance as they blew after a deep dive. I doubt we caused the whale much harm; it would have been more like a rude awakening.

But we were unsure about the damage the collision had caused, so a day later when the wind dropped I went overside to check the hull. There were no obvious marks or signs of damage to hull or rudders, which was very reassuring, although later we discovered a indentation in the hull aft that required cutting away the outer skin, replacing the core and rebuilding the hull.

I had never struck a whale before, though our first attempt on the Jules Verne Trophy was scuppered when *Enza* struck something as we were passing 160 miles north of the Crozet Islands in the southern Indian Ocean. We are still not sure what it was – a whale, a container, a tree or log or just fibre fatigue – but it forced us to put our record attempt on hold while *Enza* was repaired.

It seems collisions with whales are becoming more common. Maybe this is because whales are on the increase or perhaps we have more yachts making oceanic voyages and the opportunities for collisions have grown.

Clearly the whales are switched off, dozing or sleeping, as they do not seem to hear a yacht coming. It would be interesting to know how many collisions occur with motor yachts as opposed to sailing yachts, to see whether the engines put out sufficient noise to act as a warning. When I was first officer on the liner *Kenya* we lost about half a knot of speed one day and discovered a whale, its back broken, stuck on the bow – it had obviously not heard us, although we were a steam-turbine ship. Do echo sounders, left on, create a warning? In Canada we discovered a high-pitched moose warning system that is fixed to the front bumper of a car, and maybe one of these in the focsle might help. Short of fitting all whales with beacons and navigation lights, unless we can find out what will disturb a resting whale we are going to continue to see collisions with yachts, and not all may get away with as little damage as we sustained.

Everything we learned about the boat was positive. I had been worried that the keel would not get us across the Atlantic and although we had ordered a new one, we needed this one to stay the course, which thankfully it did. There were also issues with the engine, which again was due to be replaced once the qualifier was completed.

There was a big rumpus whenever we wanted to start the engine because we had to do it with a blow torch, blowing hot flames into the air intake. The cause was easy to identify by the cans of Easystart we found on board. If this is sprayed into the air intake it tends to remove the lubrication around the piston rings which wear more, reducing compression and thus making Easystart more necessary. We talk about diesel engines becoming addicted to the stuff and this is why. I threw it all away as I will not have it on a boat. While one person was wielding the torch, somebody else had to turn a key that was on the other side of the cabin and another had to whack the starter with a hammer. It was lucky we all had a sense of humour because sometimes, at three o'clock in the morning, it wasn't funny. The engine seemed to have a personality all of its own.

The stove was also playing up. Because it wasn't working well, we tried to burn diesel in it. Poor Colin, a Scotsman who had done one leg of the Clipper many years ago and had happily taken on the role of chef for our crossing, would come out of the hatch with a black face. Not just once or twice but pretty much every day.

With all these distractions, and the need to go somewhere where the rudder bracket could be repaired, we were losing time. We had to allow for a major refit between the finish of the qualifier and the start of the race, so I looked for a closer destination than New York.

I did not need 3,000 miles to qualify, only 2,000. St Johns in Newfoundland was just too short, but Halifax in Nova Scotia was 2,400 miles away. That would do.

We ended up staying in Halifax for five days because the repairs to the rudder stock bracket which connected the autohelm took longer than anticipated. Kent stayed with me after the others went and helped me get ready. He was the last one to step off the boat when I sailed away up the river. It was the first time he had seen the boat being sailed solo and later he told me she looked 'beautiful'.

It felt strangely lonely as I motored quietly away from the Royal Nova Scotia Yacht Squadron. The Yacht Club had been friendly and helpful and is definitely worth a visit, if anyone is sailing that way. I turned and waved goodbye for the last time and focused on the channel out from Halifax. I had not sailed single-handed since 1990, and the trip over with Kent, Colin and the fourth crew member Robert had taken twenty days and been comfortable and friendly, apart from too many headwinds. Now I was on my own and already missing their cheerful repartee, so it was time to get busy.

The motor gives 4 knots, the sails in excess of 9 knots, so once the channel had widened, I hoisted and started making my way eastwards. I was relieved to be getting underway on my own. It was the next phase in the plan and I was anxious to get the crossing under my belt. I also had deadlines to meet in London and various business pressures to contend with, so was balancing a range of commitments.

But even before I reached the end of the channel, the

visibility had clamped right down. This is a regular occurrence for the locals – the Grand Banks are notorious for fog – but for a visiting single-hander it is a nightmare. There are a lot of fishing boats, and I discovered that not all show navigation lights at night. It meant a constant watch on the radar until past Sable Island at the edge of the banks, some 150 miles away. That could take fifteen hours or two days, and I was not looking forward to it.

This was my first chance to really get to learn how I was going to manage this new machine alone. In effect, single-handers are only as good as their autopilots, because these do nearly all the steering. If the pilot reacts quickly, all well and good. If it is slow the boat will yaw around, perhaps as much as 20 to 30 degrees from the desired course.

This might not matter on a boat like *Suhaili*, where the relative wind movement was slight, but I soon discovered that on *Grey Power* the pilot needed to react very quickly as even 10 degrees of course change, which might bring the wind forward 15 to 20 degrees, made a vast difference to boat speed.

If the wind came forward she took off. If it went aft she slowed, but the difference could be as much as 10 knots of boat speed. Initially, I found the noise of the water passing the carbon-fibre hull unsettling and worrying. It sounded dangerous and it was always accompanied by some bone-breaking vibration that made everything above and below deck, including me, shake, rattle and roll. I soon learned that if I went on deck everything seemed less threatening, but it would take some getting used to.

Despite the occasional bursts of speed we did not have a very fast passage. We had not had time to do much to the boat before we sailed so there was a whole host of things that needed either a bit of tender loving care or replacing.

Also I did not trust the rigging, but that was more to do with my lack of experience with this style of rigging because I was unsure how much strain it might take. I was used to shackles and bolts holding my wire rigging to the mast and boat, but here the rigging was Kevlar rope and secured with lashings which looked puny. In fact the Spectra rope they use in this rigging system is stronger than steel but that concept takes a bit of getting used to, and since I tend to be cautious by nature, Spectra had to prove itself to me before I could fully trust it.

The concern over the swing keel had not gone away while we were in Halifax. I had been warned that it might be weak, so what with this and the doubts over the rigging, my approach on the way back was extremely conservative and we barely reached 16 knots. But I learned enough to lengthen the list of work to be done before I sailed her around the world and as the list got longer, so the time available for the refit seemed to become ever shorter.

It was a useful trip, and as I approached the UK I encountered busy waters and stiffer breezes which, since I had had only forty minutes' sleep in two and a half days, proved a challenge; but there were no problems and I felt rather pleased that I had handled the sleep deprivation as well as I had.

The Falmouth pilot vessel brought out crew to meet me once I had passed the Lizard – the English Channel with its heavy traffic is no place for a tired single-hander – and we headed for the Endeavour Yard in Gosport, arriving towards the end of July.

*

We had just six weeks before the boat had to be in Bilbao. We also had very little money, since most of the loan secured from the bank had gone on buying the boat. The sports marketing agency that negotiated the Velux sponsorship deal, Global SportNet, was also looking for a backer for my project, and shortly after I got back from Halifax they rang to say they had signed an agreement with Saga Insurance.

For an Open 60 campaign, we had estimated we would need £550,000 to pay for the boat, sails and equipment plus the salaries and expenses of shore crew. It meant me putting myself in the shop window, which I hate. I have no problem raising funds or profiles for others but I have always had difficulty presenting myself as a marketing opportunity.

We had drawn up a list of likely targets with Saga Insurance at the top of the list. Seven Seas, Thomas Cook and Prudential were also on there because, as the name of the boat, *Grey Power*, suggested, this campaign would, we felt, be particularly interesting to a certain age group. There had been a lot of talk about inspiring the over-fifties to get them moving, and we thought it would be appropriate if we targeted a sponsor who was strong in this market. There was a lot of interest, but we were approaching companies in April and asking for money for October and a number of them came back immediately with budget issues.

Saga said they were interested from the outset. From the first meeting, we felt they would go for it because it was such a good match, but they had never done anything like this before. Their sponsorship activity had been limited to the Chelsea Flower Show, so sponsoring me in this race represented a massive departure for them and would require a large investment in terms of cash and resources.

They were nervous about taking the full deal, so we worked out an arrangement where they paid less for reduced rights. I don't think they quite knew what they were getting into or how big a story it was potentially. David Stubley from Global SportNet conducted all the negotiations while I was busy with the boat. It proved to be a very tense time and took about three meetings between April and August to get all the detail worked out, but as soon as everything was agreed we unveiled Saga Insurance as our sponsors. As a consequence of the deal, the boat was rechristened with the sponsors' name.

There were other sponsorship deals. Henri-Lloyd had been my original clothing suppliers in 1968 and they came back in with some superb kit. Amlin provided the insurance and Aladdin's Cave some parts; Raymarine gave us new instruments, radar, plotter and autopilots, and Volvo provided a new and more powerful engine.

It was late, but their participation made a huge difference to what I could now do as far as getting the right equipment together. They were new to boat sponsorship and I was new to this Open 60 scene, so we were both on a sharp learning curve. This was a one-off arrangement, not like the longer-term sponsor deals that Alex Thomson and Mike Golding had, but that suited me. I did not intend to go back to being a professional racer again. I was doing this race and then thinking of getting a nice large sailing cruiser and heading off to see the parts of the world I had not visited thus far.

The fit between Saga and myself was obvious: they focus on travel and services to the over-fifties, and I was sixty-seven. One of their objectives is to promote an active retirement, and it is hard to think of anything more active than a solo race around the world. But this adventure had to be marketed to achieve the desired publicity. We did of course have the advantage that it was unusual for people of my age to be taking part in something quite so active, and I had a track record in the sport. Within a short space of time the publicity exceeded our wildest dreams. This was fortunate, because I had underestimated the costs. As it became obvious that we needed more support Saga rose to the occasion and increased their budget. The result was that I became more competitive as the race progressed.

The sponsorship business is much changed since the *Suhaili* days. Back then, you printed off a load of begging letters and sent them out to a random list of big-name companies, hoping one of them would land in the right place at the right time, preferably in front of an influential individual who both held the purse strings and liked sailing. Sponsorship was frowned upon in mainstream yachting: for example, Francis Chichester was criticised for having the wool mark on his boat when he went around the world in 1966–7. In those days, as an unknown Merchant Navy officer, hampered by being at sea and so not able to even visit anyone who showed interest, I did not stand much chance of obtaining sponsorship. I did manage to get a £5 voucher from Cadbury's and 120 cans of beer from Tennent's Brewery but that was it. The costs of that voyage were defrayed by advances on a book and newspaper and magazine payments.

The scene had begun to change after Eric Tabarly won the 1964 OSTAR and obtained huge publicity in France. The French media loved it, and sailing became almost a mainstream sport. With TV covering sailing, potential sponsors knew they could guarantee publicity if they supported a sailor, and the whole scene snowballed. It took longer to effect the British, mainly because TV in the UK could not get its head around sailing. It is still true to say that the best-known sailors are the single-handers, whereas gifted double gold-medal Olympians like Ben Ainslie and Shirley Robertson, though very well known and admired in sailing circles, are less well known to the general public.

The Open 60 circuit is never likely to attract the gifted amateur because it is just too expensive. A new boat will cost about $2 million alone, and the annual running costs come to close to half that, what with new sails and rigging, a back-up and support team to pay, hotels and transportation. So sponsorship is both essential and hard to obtain. The first thing to understand is that there has to be a good reason for a company to wish to pay out a large sum and it will be looking for a return on the investment. Publicity on its own is useful, but most companies will be looking to hit their own particular markets and will want the publicity to focus on where those markets are.

A racing yacht gets publicity if the race is well promoted, and fortunately the Velux 5 Oceans had the budget to do this. This is an important selling point for sponsors as it increases the exposure they will get from their participation. But this is likely to be general publicity, and they will still need to promote their own boat and skipper themselves to ensure their target markets are reached. This means they will have additional costs themselves.

From a potential sponsor's point of view a skipper seeking sponsorship needs to understand what the company does, what its objectives are, where its markets are, and how the company might benefit from the event. The skipper becomes a part of the marketing and PR arms of the company throughout their sponsorship arrangement. They need to be good communicators and always remember that their behaviour and performance reflect on their sponsor.

Then it becomes a question of how well the yacht is doing in the race, because the winner will always get more publicity than the rest of the fleet unless there are other features that are newsworthy. A tight finish or a close race will produce better coverage. A skipper who is already known to the public has an initial advantage as the media are more likely to cover their activities, but someone who is unusual can attract attention. For a while it has been much easier for females to get sponsorship than men, but as more of them take up the sport this will no longer be such an advantage.

Newcomers will have more difficulty persuading a sponsor that they are worth the large investment. A track record in a less expensive class, or experience in the Open 60 class in two-handed or crewed races, can help, but a company is going to need to be persuaded that a six-digit sponsorship is going to produce results and that is much harder for an unknown person.

I have never been really good at getting sponsorship. I have managed it occasionally, particularly when I already owned a boat and so was looking for less money as that capital cost was already covered. But in cases like *British Oxygen*, the 70-foot catamaran we won the 1974 Round Britain race with, and *Enza New Zealand*, we did not own the boat. When I sailed *Sea Falcon*, which I owned, it was much easier. The only success I ever had was with *British Airways*. But I had seen sailing as more of a pastime anyway, something I could combine with business, unlike the modern professionals who sail full-time.

Back in Gosport we hauled out *Grey Power* immediately and started work. Swing keels were new to me, and it took us three days to get ours freed so it could be removed. In the meantime I negotiated the purchase of a second-hand keel in France from PRB, which Groupe Finot said was in good condition and would provide the requisite stability. The life of these keels is about 70,000 miles if made of steel, perhaps almost half that of one made of carbon fibre, due to fatigue. Since a new steel one would cost £75,000, and a carbon one twice that, I had searched around for a second-hand one with sufficient life left in it for my forthcoming race.

There was a lot to do and I needed help so I put a note out to the Little Ship Club, a yacht club based in the City of London with members all over the country, of which I am president. Slowly but surely, the volunteers began to appear. Some jobs, like overhauling the hydraulic rams that controlled the keel's tilt, or fitting the new 40 hp Volvo engine which would be the charger for the batteries, were best left to experts, but the rest of the jobs – like cleaning, preparing for paint, fitting new hatches, removing all deck fittings, checking, greasing and reinstalling – were handed out to whoever showed up at the yard.

We were not experts with these boats, and although both Mike Golding and Alex Thomson's professionals were very willing to come and advise when asked, we missed that specialist back-up.

Skippers these days do little of their preparatory work, which was always something I enjoyed doing. Their job in this modern age of professional sailing is to promote themselves and their sponsors and ensure that they are up to speed with the latest technology – part sailor, part geek and part salesman. I worked on the basis that if I was involved with all aspects of the boat I would be in a better position to deal with things when they went wrong, a very Merchant Navy approach.

A new job had been created in yacht racing, and when I first heard the word I thought someone was having a laugh. The Preparateur. Apparently, the preparateur looked after the boat and ensured it was ready in all respects to race.

In some ways it was fortunate I was not convinced by the need to have a preparateur, because I had no budget for one. My cash was being spent on stores, sails, rigging and food. I was also chasing up contractors and equipment and trying to coordinate all our operations.

Most days there was a core crew of volunteers, and our ranks were bolstered by visitors who dropped by to help, many of them old chums of mine, family members, friends of family, friends of friends, Clipper crew past and future, and sometimes faces that no one had ever seen before. I was called the Pied Piper, rushing around the yard brandishing lists and a mobile phone and being pursued by a gang of helpers who demanded to be given jobs.

The days were long and there weren't any weekends off. I began to get tired, too tired for the good of my campaign, but there was no choice but to soldier on.

Time was running short and so much hinged on the efficient coordination of deliveries, and contractors and suppliers. The whole project was proving a little ambitious. When we needed the rigging, which was being manufactured in France and then dispatched to us via UPS, two of the five packages failed to arrive, which delayed stepping the mast. When we called to ask where the other two were we were told they didn't know, despite their boasts of a state-of-the-art computerised tracking system that could not fail. The packages were still in France, they said. Then they had left for the UK and now they were back in France. They'd had a receipt from the French manufacturer saying they had received them back.

The manufacturer denied having taken them back or signing a receipt. So where were they? This turned out to be a major mystery. In a depot in France? Or perhaps England? Or maybe lost? They helpfully told us that if the packages did not turn up within two days we should assume they were lost. The ineptitude was comic but we did not have the luxury of time to laugh.

If those items of rigging did not turn up it would be at least a week before new ones could be made and sent to us – and that would mean we would be late to Bilbao and face a large fine.

Richard Griffiths, one of the Little Ship Club members, is a barrister who had been helping me right from the start, and I decided that this was a task for a trained arguer. He took up the job with gusto and three hours later, having tracked down a director of the carrier and threatened I know not what, he came back with a satisfied smile to say the packages had been found and would be delivered the next day.

At the time, this was a very big deal and a totally unnecessary distraction, which says a lot about the tension within our camp. It cost us a valuable day when we still had many jobs to do that could only be done afloat and rigged.

The mast was set up just in time for the naming ceremony, which had been arranged for 22 September at Gunwharf Quays in Portsmouth. All the contestants had been asked to choose a theme tune, and I had selected 'Don't Stop Me Now' by Queen – besides having a rhythm I liked, its words expressed my attitude. I wrote to Roger Taylor and asked him if he minded my using his song and he came back saying he was delighted, so I followed up and got him to name the boat as well. 'Don't Stop Me Now' has now become a family favourite.

With a crew made up from my volunteers we had planned to sail to Bilbao with Alex Thomson in *Hugo Boss*, but once we got out into the Solent we saw that the mast had a nasty bend in it and I returned to Gosport to adjust the rigging. This gave me a welcome full night's rest before we set off the next day. The favourable winds that Alex had found had changed by the time we sailed and it took us five days to make the passage across the Channel to Ushant and then south to Bilbao. I did not realise it at the time but this weather was an omen of things to come.

4. Under Starter's Orders

Three weeks before the start of the race we arrived in Getxo Marina in Bilbao, where the Velux 5 Oceans fleet had gathered. At that time there were eight boats scheduled to be on the start line although two, Graham Dalton's *A Southern Man AGD* and Tim Troy's *Margaret Anna* were looking doubtful.

All the boats were lined up alongside each other in the marina and it was interesting to watch how the teams prepared, with some looking decidedly more organised than others. We still had plenty of preparatory work to do and immediately set about a jobs list that looked ominously long.

My team in Bilbao revolved around the same core group of five loyal volunteers that we had had in Gosport. Tim Etteridge, an American who wanted to help us out as part of his preparations for the Clipper Race 2007–8, had turned up at Endeavour Quay with a pair of willing hands and an apparent commitment to work through every waking hour. Huw Fernie was a young aerodynamics student who was taking time off from his studies to decide what he wanted to do with his life, and Dilip Donde, a commander in the Indian Navy, had travelled from the Andaman Islands where he was based to join my campaign as part of his preparations for a bid to become the first Indian to sail round around the world single-handed. Dilip's presence enabled me to start revising my Hindustani, learned from sailing with Indian crews in my Merchant Navy days, and although I don't think he found me a good student he became a good friend.

Julia Stuart joined us to help with my food arrangements. Nutrition is a vital part of any ocean voyage; having sufficient calories to provide the body with the energy it needs is fundamental. I had realised its importance on *Enza New Zealand* when we were dished up 5,000 calories a day per man, which had probably been a bit too much. My cholesterol was reading 9.8 at the finish and although I felt extremely fit and well, it had taken a dramatic change in diet to bring it down to 4.8 as quickly as possible.

Two months before we set out for Bilbao, we went through the choices and decided that 3,500 calories per day was probably enough for my purposes in the first leg. We then spent time sourcing easily prepared meals that would be nourishing and enjoyable; we ended up with a combination of freeze-dried meals from Expedition Foods, which just required boiling water to be added, and boil-in-the-bag meals, very similar to the Army's Compo rations used in field activities since the Second World War, which again only needed to be put in boiling water for a few minutes. I took a few tins so I could create my own meals from time to time, as I enjoy that, and quite of a lot of items like salami which are full of energy and can be eaten cold when cooking was not an option.

The final member of my volunteer team was Les Williams, a retired electrical officer in the Royal Navy, who I had first met in 1968 just a few months before setting out on the Golden Globe. We teamed up after I finished that race and enjoyed a series of successes, most notably winning the two-handed Round Britain Race in 1970 in *Ocean Spirit,* a 71-foot monohull, and the Cape Town to Rio Race the following year, when the meals for our crew of sixteen were cooked by the gastronome and broadcaster Clement Freud.

I had been introduced to Clement on *The David Frost Show* in America after I'd come back from my solo trip, and he had expressed an interest in yachting so we invited him to join us. This turned out to be a very good move, because we ate and drank extremely well. I remember one meal of Virginia ham with Cumberland sauce followed by mincemeat and brandy crumble washed down with two beers and half a bottle of wine. If he could see me prepare my dinners on board now – boiling water on a single-burner gimballed stove to rehydrate the contents of a plastic bag – he would have a fit.

Les and I were joined for that Cape to Rio race by a young gangly Kiwi named Peter Blake, who went on to be a watch leader with Les in the first Whitbread round-the-world race in 1973. He joined us again when Les and I were co-skippers on *Heath's Condor* in the 1977 Whitbread and then famously went on to run his own Whitbread campaigns, culminating in winning every leg in the 1989 race.

Peter and I teamed up again to win the Jules Verne Trophy in 1994 in *Enza New Zealand* in seventy-four days and twenty-two hours, by which time he was heavily involved in New Zealand's successful America's Cup challenges. The three of us remained friends until he was murdered in 2001 while on an expedition up the Amazon. I was having a quiet lunch with Chay Blyth when the news of his shocking death came through and neither of us could believe it, let alone understand it. It was a tragic waste of a relatively young life and a great talent.

More than three decades after I first met Les, he tipped up in Gosport to help me and spent four whole days stripping down and reinstalling a heater as well as a few other jobs on the electrics and electronics front.

There was no shortage of industry or enthusiasm among my team in Bilbao, but it soon became clear that we lacked essential experience in preparing one of these Formula One machines. I watched with envy as the professional teams working with Alex Thomson, Mike Golding, Bernard Stamm and Kojiro Shiraishi worked calmly and systematically through their lists. It was almost as if they were looking for jobs to do, since they spent all their time on boats on which most of the work had been done long before.

I had heard the term 'professional' bandied around in relation to the Open 60 campaigns but this was the first time I had seen first hand what it meant. The arrival of the professional sailor on the racing circuit has represented one of the most notable changes in ocean racing during the last forty years.

In the 1960s the only people being paid were the people who looked after the boats, the paid hands. The owners and their crews raced the boats but none were paid. In the 1973 and 1975 Admiral's Cup series, when I was racing on *Frigate* and *Yeoman XX*, the people who looked after the boats were not even in the crews; we were all racing because we wanted to race and none of us expected payment. This began to change during the 1970s, although our crew aboard *Condor* for the 1977 Whitbread race were all volunteers.

The other big change was in sponsorship. It had been creeping in for the oceanic and short-handed races since the 1960s, but it was not accepted in established circles then. When Clare Francis secured backing for her Whitbread entry *ADC Accutrac* in 1977 she was told to change the name of her boat to *That Boat* and remove her logos when she turned up at Cowes week the following summer. The no-logo rule was not changed for Cowes week until fairly recently. Skippers who wished to obtain sponsorship for the events that allowed the boats to be used for promotion were forced into boardrooms to try out their presentational skills. The role of skipper was acquiring a few extra new dimensions and people were beginning to realise that talents on the water had increasingly to be matched by commercial skills off it.

But there were commercial pressures growing in established circles to help defray costs and achieve a better performance. A boat that did well in a series fetched a better selling price at the end, and some owners began to hire well-regarded sailors to ensure a better performance. Once this process had started there was no way of stopping it. There was a downside: many of the people who had built boats for series like the Admiral's Cup found the costs escalating to an unacceptable level and withdrew, which led ultimately to a reduction in entries to the point that this wonderful series has ceased to exist.

Today there are sailors who are totally professional, and run campaigns similar to those on the motor-racing circuit. In the past decade or so, it has become possible to make a career out of yacht racing and the numbers of men and women making a living from full-time sailing have snowballed.

With this increased professionalism has come the need for qualifications. Boats that charge customers to go sailing now come under quite stringent Maritime Coastguard Agency rules for safety to protect the public, and these apply to the competence of those in charge. Forty years ago the only qualification available for yachtsmen was a Board of Trade Yachtmaster's Certificate; this has now been replaced

the boat out of the water by a crane to read its weight and then leaning it over 90 degrees and measuring the tension required to hold it there, it was Mike's project manager, Graham Tourell, nicknamed Gringo, who came along to supervise the operation for us, having done it before.

We were found to comply and in due course received our certificate. Unfortunately Tim's *Margaret Anna* did not measure up and he was told that if he wanted to make the start, he would have to add 300 kg of weight to the bulb of his keel. Despite his efforts , this proved too difficult in the time remaining.

My biggest bonus, however, was the unexpected arrival of two English preparateurs, Simon Clay and Tony Reid, both of whom were experienced in preparing Open 60 boats. Simon had spent four years with Mike Golding's *Ecover* campaign and was very familiar with the Finot design boats, which was invaluable, and Tony had worked on a number of Open 60s, most recently as shore crew with British yachtsman Conrad Humphries' *Hellomoto* in the 2004–5 Vendée Globe.

They had been summoned to Bilbao by the race organisers, who felt that both *Saga Insurance* and *Margaret Anna*, Tim's boat, could use some specialist help. One of the first things they did was to go through the boat front to back and make a list of the areas that needed attention. They were used to boats being cared for by full-time crews and Simon admitted to me later that he felt *Saga*'s state of preparedness was 'a little worrying'. He was judging us by the standards of the modern professional team, whereas I was looking at providing a safe boat first and a racing boat second. It was good to have experienced support like this, and my confidence was boosted as a result.

Lovely (as Simon Clay is known) was still working part-time for Mike Golding, so sadly we only had him for a week, but David Swete from the North Sails Loft in New Zealand, who had come over to check the sails and stay with us to the start, also brought some very useful expertise.

My priority was to make the boat seaworthy. I wanted to ensure *Saga Insurance* was safe to take to sea, and I would just have to master the new technology that was arriving once the race started. We didn't have the time for proper trials, which would have allowed us to check all the systems, but the boat was made ready to sail. Those who asked me how I thought I would do in the race were told I was at the bottom of a steep learning curve. The experienced sailors would most likely set off faster than me, but I would speed up as my knowledge increased.

Safety lectures and courses were arranged for all the contestants. This is quite normal before a big race and although we had all been through the safety equipment and survival techniques before, it was useful to be reminded how everything was operated so we could observe the proper safety procedures on our voyage.

One new feature was the course on survival in life rafts. None of us had realised that 85 per cent of all those who died in life rafts after abandoning their boats died within the first three hours. I had certainly never seen this information before. The reason is that the body will have drawn heavily on its glucose reserves during the lead-up to abandoning the boat and with all the additional stress and adrenalin, the blood sugar levels will have become dangerously depleted. When you finally make it into the life raft, there is a risk that you think you are safe and promptly relax and nod off – but if this happens, there is a good chance you won't wake up. The body is desperate for replacement sugar and liquid and if it does not get this quickly it will close down.

So we learned that it was essential to keep some high-energy drinks containing dextrose in the grab bag and start drinking them the moment you get into the life raft. In fact it was the most important thing to do, before even checking the life raft and its equipment. This talk was very useful and informative and we all went out and bought extra cans of high-energy drinks immediately afterwards.

We all carried quite extensive medical kits, and received a talk on what was in them and when they should be used. Having never carried anything more than Savlon and a few bandages, I found this instructive too, although I was surprised to find an instrument in the kit for inspecting the inside of my ear. Quite how I was supposed to get my eye round to look into it escaped me!

A week before the start, the worklist was reduced but we still had a lot to do and I was doubtful that we would be able to take part in the Prologue, which was a fully crewed race round buoys outside the harbour for all eight yachts entered in the Velux 5 Oceans race.

At the last moment, we threw caution to the wind and decided to get out on the track to trial various systems that had been installed during the week. I had yet to race against any other Open 60 and was anxious to see how our speed compared with theirs.

This was a chance for the organisers and our hosts in Bilbao to present the skippers and the boats to the Spanish public, and they made the most of the opportunity. We led the fleet from the pontoons with our theme song 'Don't Stop Me Now' blasting out over the loudspeakers, and received rapturous applause from the local Basque crowds, although obviously Unai Bazurko, the local hero, got the biggest cheer by some margin.

Not many people outside of Bilbao had heard of Unai Bazurko before the race started, but his family were well-known throughout the Basque region for their sailing exploits. He was following in the footsteps of the other Bilbao legend Jose Luis Ugarte, who by competing in the BOC Challenge in 1990–91 had become the first Spaniard to record a solo circumnavigation. This adventure had sowed the seed of a dream in Unai that fifteen years later was about to be fulfilled. His boat *Pakea* was brand new, built in Australia by another veteran of the race, Kanga Birtles, with whom he teamed up to win the Trans Tasman race in 2003.

Unai's campaign was well funded but, as is often the case with newcomers to a class, and that included me, there were aspects of the project that were challenging to his lack of experience. One of those aspects was clearly the design and development of the boat, so we were all interested to see what his money had bought and whether his Open 60 would prove to be a real contender once he got out on the track. He had participated in the 2003 Figaro race before going to Australia to get involved in the building of his boat and had sailed *Pakea* back to Spain from Australia, so he already had 15,000 miles on the clock, but, like my own, those miles were not racing miles so neither the boat nor the skipper had been tested. This was in stark contrast to Mike, Alex and Bernard, who inevitably were tipped as more likely to win than Unai, Koji or I.

For the Prologue, my crew was a mix of volunteers and

friends, and we headed out straight into a fresh north-easter which, we felt, was not very welcoming.

We stayed clear of the rest of the fleet on the start line at the offshore end, which was the windward end, while Koji got stuck 200 metres behind, trying to repair a damaged traveller block on *Spirit of Yukoh*.

Alex on *Hugo Boss* crossed the line first, with Tim Troy's *Margaret Anna* second, and Bernard and Mike immediately behind. The course took us north-east towards the Cape Villano headland, then four miles along the coast from Getxo. At the first tack we were lying third but not making the speed of Alex, Bernard and Mike. By the time Alex rounded the windward mark for a second time, he was well in front and neither Mike nor Bernard could close the gap for the 3.5 mile run to the finish line. He was going great guns, which was exhilarating to watch, and seemed to have the race in the bag. Then, just before he made his last big surge to the finish, he shocked all of us by ducking out and sailing past the committee boat on the wrong side, so he never actually crossed the finish line.

He later claimed he was superstitious and that winners of pre-start races or prologues were always jinxed in the main event, but I had never heard of that superstition and was convinced that he had missed the finish line due simply to poor navigation and then made up the line about being superstitious just to wind Mike up.

Mike, who seemed to share the superstition, was livid. He boycotted the prize-giving and voiced his disgust with both Alex and his tactics to the press, which of course they lapped up.

I was unaware of any hostilities between the two of them

prior to that day, but one couldn't fail to notice the rancour after that. Both of them have an eye for the headlines, but I felt there was more to it than that.

Mike served his apprenticeship in yacht racing with the Challenge Business, the company set up by Sir Chay Blyth in 1992 for amateur sailors to race around the world. In the first race, the British Steel Challenge, he skippered *Group 4* into second place, then returned four years later, with the same sponsor, Jørgen Philip-Sørensen, who owned Group 4 Securicor, to win it.

Alex earned his stripes with Clipper Ventures, the company I established in 1995 which created similar opportunities for novice sailors. Although there was a healthy competition between the two companies, the rivalry occasionally spilled over to staff, clients and supporters, creating two distinct but loyal camps.

My contact with Mike before this race had been sporadic, though I obviously followed his career with interest. In 1994, as he was setting a new world record for a solo non-stop round-the-world race against the wind, we passed each other off Tasmania, him going one way on *Group 4* and me going the other on *Enza* in our bid for the Jules Verne Trophy. We spoke on the radio but apart from that brief exchange, we had not really come into contact very much

In 1998 he was the first Briton to build and campaign an Open 60, ahead of Ellen MacArthur by a few months. He entered the 1998–9 Around Alone race and had built up a considerable lead when he hit a sandbank off New Zealand in the second leg and was forced to withdraw, leaving the Italian Giovanni Soldini to claim victory in the race in his boat *Fila*, which ten years down the line of course is now *Saga Insurance*.

Mike twice competed in the Vendée Globe, but victory in a round-the-world race had always evaded him, despite an excellent record of either winning or finishing in the top group in other races.

In the same way that Mike was a successful product of the Challenge Business, so Alex Thomson was one of Clipper's great success stories, having become the youngest skipper to win a round-the-world race in 1998.

I first met Alex when he applied to Clipper for a job. He had been working for Britannia Sailing, a sailing school in Hampshire, and although he was only twenty-three, felt he had what it took to be a skipper. I wasn't sure. The job of skippering a boat of paying amateurs requires man-management skills of a high order in addition to sailing and seamanship ability. I decided to test him out and offered him the job of Mate to me in a sailing and climbing expedition to Greenland that we had organised for paying customers on two Clipper boats, *Ariel* and *Antiope*. He joined me and spent the next seventy days over the summer as mate on the boats, learning about seamanship, celestial navigation, negotiating, shifting and even anchoring to icebergs, as well as cooking chicken balti, spaghetti balti – or any balti for that matter – and a whole lot more besides.

Despite the thirty-five-year age gap, his approach was similar to mine. Seize the moment, have some fun and sort out any problems as and when they occur. We got to know each other very well and I came to understand how talented he was. He seemed to be able to get an extra knot of speed out of the boats whatever the conditions. I was also impressed by the way he adapted – his background was in racing, after all, but this was an expedition that required many qualities, other than sailing ability, of the crew. They needed to be competent all-rounders throughout every quarter of the boat; they needed to be good with the clients and comfortable with responsibility if something happened on their watch. Alex impressed on all fronts, though it was not until five weeks before the start of the Clipper race in 1998, after he had passed his Ocean Yachtmaster exams, that we told him he had been selected as a skipper.

Until then, he hadn't been particularly ambitious, but as soon as he was appointed skipper he set out his stall at the start of the race and declared his intention to win not just the race, but every single leg.

He saw the Clipper race of 1998–9 as a ten-month training course comprising sixteen different races where he could learn about fleet racing, crew management, routing, weather and different navigational scenarios. And he prepared well, studying the routes and talking to skippers from previous races, leaving no stone unturned. By then, because of the Greenland trip, he also had more than 8,000 miles on his clock, so despite his youth he was becoming quite experienced.

He was given enormous responsibility but told to get on with it, which was a gamble on our part. He loved it, saying that if he didn't win the race he would give up sailing. He did win it, convincingly, and I was very proud of him.

The following year he won the fully-crewed Criterion Round Britain & Ireland Race on an Open 50, *Sail that Dream*, breaking the old record set by myself in *More Opposition* in 1976 by more than a day, and his time of ten days still stands. In 2003 he was introduced to his sponsors Hugo Boss when he was sailing captain on a Farr 65 they had chartered for the Rolex Fastnet Race, and it was at that point he diverted into short-handed sailing, which is always a better bet for big spending sponsors wanting to maximise their return.

Since then he has competed in every single major short-handed race, coming second in the Transat Jacques Vabre with Roland Jourdain on the Open 60 *Sill* and third in the Defi Atlantique solo transatlantic race on the Open 60 *AT Racing*, setting a new twenty-four-hour world speed sailing record for solo monohulls of 468 nautical miles.

With Mike and Alex reared in opposing stables and going head to head on the solo race track, it was inevitable there would be some rivalry. Theirs had become good sport in the run-up to the race, with Mike calling Alex a 'bit of a prick' and the pair of them being likened to a 'pair of randy bulls in a very small paddock' by the race director, David Adams. Inevitably, all these comments found their way into the papers.

This wasn't the first time two competitors had fallen out so publicly. The professional circuit attracts some highly competitive characters, who can be gracious and friendly up to the point where the start gun fires, the gloves come off and a mist descends.

Take the duel between Ben Ainslie and the Brazilian Robert Scheidt at the Sydney Olympics in 2000, for example. Ben is laid back and charming ashore, but slap a number on his back and put him in a race and his character is transformed. It is this ability to make the switch that distinguishes winners from losers.

Sailing rivalries also have a dimension that few other sports have – namely, the life-and-death dimension, which makes relationships more complicated than most. The guy who you would happily biff one day on the dockside in Portsmouth will inevitably be the one who, some weeks or years later, puts his life on the line in the Southern Ocean to save you from certain death. It is a reality that underpins most relationships and, irrespective of all the posturing, guarantees an implicit respect.

After the Prologue in Bilbao, Mike and Alex were clearly at the 'biffing' stage, and their relationship would come under even more pressure a few weeks later.

In the days running up to the start, it was complete madness. Each morning we would meet on the boat at 6 a.m. and rarely leave before 7 p.m., working throughout at a frantic pace. But things were starting to take shape.

With two days to go, my navigation station was looking a bit spartan since most of my communications equipment and suite of vital weather and navigation software programs had still to be installed. There wasn't much I could do apart from wait for the various representatives and engineers to come onto the boat, fit the equipment and talk me through the various pieces of kit. I just hoped it would be fairly straightforward.

On the Friday before the start, in the space of a few hours, they loaded both MaxSea and Ocen, the two principal weather programs, into my laptops. Then the TV guys put on a program for sending back video and another one for sending back still photographs. I had three laptop computers. One carried all the communication programs, the other all the navigation information and weather programs, and the third was the reserve in case either of the ones in use failed, to make sure I could still access this important data.

There were three satellite communications packages, for the very same reason.

The Iridium system is now widely used by yachtsmen, navies and shipping and oil companies because it allows communication in remote areas via a network of low earth-orbiting satellites. The Inmarsat Fleet 77 package, which comes with the transceiver, antenna, cradle and handset, allowed me to make phone calls, send faxes, use the internet, send emails and even do live video conferencing. The third system was known as Sat C. It could do emails, but its main purpose was to receive navigation warning messages and the general shipping forecasts as text, and it was used by Race Control to poll our positions on a regular basis. This is a far cry from the *Suhaili* days, when satellite communications did not exist and I depended on a single sideband radio with limited power and range, which made the business of keeping in contact a hit-or-miss affair. Back then I seemed to spend a lot of time writing – all my logs and letters were recorded using pen or pencil rather than the ubiquitous keyboard that now rules our lives.

Computers have caused a dramatic change to our communications and navigation. In 1968 everyone used paper charts for navigation – published by the Hydrographic Department of the Admiralty, these were reliable works of art developed over more than a century. When computers came on the scene the Department started to produce programs of computerised charts. These had enormous advantages, most notably the speed with which the corrections, which were published weekly, could be applied to the charts. Previously, these corrections had kept navigators the world over slaving over their charts for hours each week to make sure they had the very latest information . . .

Another advantage of the computerised charts is that when interfaced with the GPS, another new invention since

1968, a small icon appeared to show exactly where the boat was on the chart, which cut down the time spent firstly on taking bearings and then plotting them to find your position.

We still carried paper charts as back-up, but there was no longer a need to carry so many. Most of us took the large-scale charts of the oceans we were going to traverse, plus the smaller scale ones of the ports we knew we would visit, plus some for potential funk holes should we need to pull in. When I left Falmouth in 1968 on *Suhaili*, I carried only twenty-four different charts covering all the regions around the world I would be passing through from Falmouth harbour and back.

With all the communications via satellites now controlled by computers, it was vital to have good ones and back-up. The long hours spent tuning in a radio were gone. Now, you just selected the program and pressed a button and the computer linked with the satellite and established communications – in theory at least.

My navigation was backed up by a Raymarine plotter, again linked to GPS, which showed the Admiralty charts and my position on them. I could also overlay the radar picture on the screen, which I found incredibly useful, particularly when approaching land, and it made it much easier to work out what other vessels were doing. This plotter was in the middle of the chart table, so I could glance below from the cockpit and check my position without leaving the helm.

On top of the new communications equipment and the Raymarine plotter and radar, I was also having to learn how to use a tracking and emergency system that was being fitted especially by the RNLI.

During that last Friday, as my new equipment and new

programs were being installed and as one engineer was replaced by another, rushing through to show me how each system worked, I found I was struggling to process all this information, some of which seemed contradictory. I was tired from the weeks of work on the boat, tired from the discomfort of a fractured coccyx, tired from the constant interruptions by the media, which were particularly bad that day, and tired because the Spanish don't start eating until nine in the evening, so if I wanted an early night, which I did every night, I was forced to go hungry. This was not a clever way of preparing for a hard race.

In the end it proved too much. I had to tell everyone that they were lobbing too much new information at me too close to the start, and I could not take it all in. The engineers who arrived to talk me through the systems were helpful and well meaning, but even for an IT geek this would have been a tall order. My frustration with computer programs had become a cause célèbre in the Clipper office at Gosport; the staff there were well used to my anger bubbling over when things didn't go as smoothly as I would have liked, or the computer crashed, which seemed to be a fairly regular occurrence. Now these engineers were rushing through the instructions and expecting me to become fully conversant with all the wiles and wizardry after just one demonstration. But one needs time to get the hang of these things and that, for me anyway, means using it to the point that things start to happen automatically.

I'm a seaman, and this is a hands-on profession, and I like to work with things for a while to maker sure I fully understand them. We wouldn't give a youngster of seventeen the keys of a car and a driving licence after having just pointed out the gear lever, the brake, the steering wheel and

the instruments. We make learner drivers go out and prac-
tise. But computer people rush through their instructions
then disappear, leaving you to find your way around their
programs mostly by trial and error.

If they wanted me to have all this new equipment they
should have given it to me much earlier, so I had time to
learn each system and get used to its foibles. One thing you
can be certain of is that a computer program will throw up
inconsistencies, and you need time to find out what these
will be and learn how to deal with them. But we never had
time for that. There was not a lot we could do about it – I
just had to accept that most my learning would have to be
done on the job and I was hopeful that, barring catastrophes,
I would be able to master it before long. It couldn't be that
difficult, could it?

The evening of the Friday before I left was spent with
friends and family. There was an official reception at the
Guggenheim Museum for all the skippers, the sponsors,
press and various VIP guests, but working late with the
program engineers meant I had to give it a miss. I was
exhausted, but my daughter Sara was arriving with her three
eldest children, Florence, Oscar and Xavier, and I was desperate to spend time with them before I went off. I picked
them up from the airport and a group of us went and had
dinner, which helped enormously in distracting me from the
last-minute preparations. At least I was able to relax for a
few hours.

On Saturday morning I awoke worrying about what was
left to be done, having lost the previous day to the media
and computer people. We still had a lot to do to be ready
by 3 p.m. on Sunday. At breakfast I told the press office

that interviews had to stop, or else I would still be on the pontoon when the rest of the fleet had packed up and gone. That would give them a good story, but not one that would show them in a good light.

I have had a difficult relationship with the media ever since 1969, when one daily newspaper tried to stitch me up, but I tend to go along with their requests because they have a job to do and our sponsors require it. This time, the cameras seemed to be everywhere. They even wanted to come into my hotel room the morning I was leaving, but that was too intrusive for me and my family so I told them, without apology, to bugger off.

My brother Mike and daughter Sara were both furious at this pressure. When we got down to the marina they took it in turns to stand at the end of the pontoon glowering at any journalist who tried to approach me or the boat. It worked for a while and I was able to check a few more things, but I never did get time to stow everything myself so that I would know where everything was. And I never found time to sort out my clothing for the voyage properly. The time had already been lost, to be honest. It was my own fault. I had been too accommodating, and instead of appreciating that I was simply trying to be cooperative, people took advantage and piled in more and more requests. It was another lesson learned, and I became much less available in subsequent ports as a result.

The final day went by in a flash. There was more meaningless instruction from the computer engineers, and I also made my first bid to go up the mast, to test out the harness and jumar clips, which worked a treat.

Les spent time down below helping to sort out the electronics while another old friend, Robin Aisher, who I raced with in several Admiral's Cup events, was on deck checking the rigging and the sails. Their help and moral support were invaluable even though neither had much experience of Open 60s, if any.

All my food, cigarettes, wine and whisky were stowed – four bottles of whisky and half a dozen of some very fine Spanish wine – and Sara and I then disappeared to the Harbour Master's office to pay some last-minute bills and sort out a few domestic items. My daughter has an excellent business brain so I'd entrusted all my finances and personal affairs to her, though with five young children to look after her days seemed as long and complicated as mine.

It was October, but she arrived with Christmas cards for me to sign, which impressed me no end, and while in the office I grabbed the chance to look at the weather for the following day. I didn't like what I saw: a gale was on its way towards the Bay of Biscay. I commented to Sara that if I didn't have to go out in those conditions, I would be very happy.

My final evening was again spent with family and friends. We ate steak and Spanish omelette, as per the Knox-Johnston family tradition on big occasions. Everyone was in great spirits, though Sara had a moment just before we all turned in and briefly became upset. Our relationship has always been special and we have become closer since her mother died, so the farewell this time round seemed that much harder. I did my best to reassure her. I didn't have any doubts that I would be OK. Whatever the sea threw at me I was confident of getting round safely. As far as I was concerned, I was just going to sea again.

The send-off at the Puerto Deportivo marina in Getxo, Bilbao, was unlike anything I'd ever seen before. There were hundreds of people, loads of TV cameras and a big stage with a silver-tongued MC who gave the skippers their last chance to deliver a final pithy soundbyte. When the interviews were finished, we walked through the crowds one by one to the backing of our chosen theme song and ventured down onto the pontoons to join our boats.

The noise was tumultuous and there was a real buzz to the place. Race starts are always a mix of apprehension, excitement and relief, though this one didn't bear any relation to the one in Falmouth when I started the Golden Globe.

On that day – Friday, 14 June 1968 – I spent the morning paying bills and renewing annual subscriptions and insurance premiums, went shopping for a Bible with the port chaplain, the Revd David Roberts (who I discovered later was Huw Fernie's grandfather), and had a final beer and a Cornish pasty with friends and family at the Chain Locker. Then I jumped down from the quay onto the boat and cast off. Ken Parker, my book editor, and Bill Rowntree, a photographer from the *Sunday Mirror* came with me along with Gus, our Labrador, until the moment I was ready to go, when I just told them all to jump off.

I started up the engine and motored out of the harbour, closely accompanied for about six miles by a boat carrying my mother and father. Saying goodbye to them was not easy. Dad was totally supportive, but I knew how sick with worry my mother was, and would be over the ensuing months. It was one of the hardest things I've ever done, and since then my farewells have been deliberately low-key. In 1994, when we set out on our second attempt to race round the world in under seventy-nine days for the Jules Verne Trophy, my wife Sue did not come to France for the start. She never liked farewells either. It was difficult for her because two days before a start, I would switch off and focus totally on what lay ahead. It made her feel surplus to requirements, so in the end she used to stay behind, saying, 'Look after yourself, see you soon, give me a call.' Some might find that strange but it worked for us. There was no lack of support from her, but she knew that I was best left to get on with things. She certainly would not have cared for all the fanfare and pizzazz in Bilbao.

It was strange going off again and had I not been so utterly exhausted and uptight during the final few days, I would have been able to reflect more meaningfully on what it all meant. As it was, I couldn't wait to depart. In the last minutes before the gun sounded, Sara and the children drew alongside to wave their final farewell, and she knew from the expression on my face that I was happy to be back on a boat and on my way.

The start was spoiled for me as I got into irons five minutes before the gun, which meant I crossed the line in last place. There were six boats on the line. Bernard Stamm from Switzerland, who had won the previous race, was back again in *Cheminées Poujoulat*. Alex Thomson was on *Hugo Boss*, Mike Golding on *Ecover*, Kojiro on *Spirit of Yukoh*, Unai Basurko in *Pakea* and me on *Saga Insurance*. Tim Troy was still in the throes of trying to comply with the IMOCA rules at that stage and Graham Dalton, campaigning *A Southern Man AGD*, the only 50-footer in the fleet, was not ready and would leave nearly a week later. Perhaps, in view of what was to come, I should have stayed behind as well.

The forecast at the start on 22 October 2006 was for a gale but no more than that. From Bilbao we set off along the north Spanish coast, a nice fine reach to start with.

The gale was due the next day. The Open 60s are designed to be tough enough for the Southern Ocean, so a gale is manageable if uncomfortable.

The light ESE wind died about mid-morning on the 23rd, but soon the wind rose from the south-west. Within three hours of the change the wind was gusting 42 knots – which is a severe gale, Force 9. I reduced sail rapidly in those three hours to just the storm jib. In retrospect I wonder whether I should not have tacked, or worn round and headed back in towards the coast to reduce the fetch (the distance travelled by waves with no obstruction) on the waves, but I held on to a slightly north-of-west course so I could take better advantage of the north-westerly winds that were expected to follow later.

The Bay of Biscay has a nasty reputation. Sometimes she is known as the Bitch of Biscay, depending on her temper. The Bay is wide open to the Atlantic, and when the winter storms start to roll in it can be a very dangerous place.

5. A Learning Curve

After the storm had passed – after I'd clamped myself to the navigation bench as *Saga Insurance* was tossed by the waves, clinging on even as the boat rolled and then righted itself, and then emerged shakily into the clearer air – what was glaringly obvious to me from the moment I saw the broken track was that with this handicap, the boat was not in any way fit for the Southern Ocean. She needed attention.

As I tidied up, my mind went into overdrive, trying to work out what my options were. Getting a new section of track was the priority. I knew I could sail without the wind instruments if I had to, but my speeds would be severely compromised. Stamm had gained a significant lead, but this race was on elapsed time, so I still had a chance of closing the gap if a new track section could be fitted quickly. Reluctantly, I decided to head for La Coruña in Spain.

Even at this stage, just hours into the race, all the whining, dinging and buzzing of the electronics were beginning to get on my nerves, so when I fired off a message back to my team telling them I was coming in, I also wrote: 'If someone can work out how to stop the Sat C alarm tweeting all the time and the depth alarm going off I would be eternally grateful.' All that din made sleep almost impossible, and there were other alarms, like the radar and Active echo transponder that warned me of approaching ships, that really were important. Bloody electronics. I'd spent more time on them than on sailing. This was meant to be a sailing race, not an electronics obstacle course!

I wasn't the only one to be forced off the race track by the storm. Both Alex and Mike had headed into port, Mike to La Coruña with damage to three of *Ecover*'s mainsail batten boxes and Alex to Gijon, between Bilbao and Coruña, his jib completely shredded from the knock-down *Hugo Boss* suffered in the storm. Unai Basurko also headed back, and of course Graham Dalton was still in Bilbao preparing to start following his delay with rudder, rigging and mast problems. Tim Troy was also trying to get to the start.

At one point, then, just a couple of days into the race, six Velux skippers were in port sorting out their boats and only two – Bernard Stamm, who was defending his 2002 title on *Cheminées Poujoulat*, and Kojiro Shiraishi on *Spirit of Yukoh* – were still out on the water, making gains while we were making repairs. Mike, Alex, Unai and I all had to take a forty-eight-hour penalty for returning to port, but all of us thought we could make that up over the 12,000 nautical miles leg to Fremantle.

It took more than a day to get to La Coruña. The wind had gone light and with just a fully reefed mainsail our progress was painfully slow

I arrived on the 25th to find Mike Golding already moored up there and nearly ready to set out again. Alex had already left Gijon after taking delivery of and setting up a new headsail. It is standard practice on the Open 60s, where the headsails are on roller furlers, to lash the top of the headsails to the mast instead of having them on a halyard. It means that if they are damaged you have to climb the mast to undo the lashing but it's one less halyard to worry about. Unai had returned to Bilbao to carry out repairs to *Pakea*, Graham

Dalton had still to leave Bilbao and was waiting for the race director to finish scrutineering, while Tim Troy was heading to La Rochelle in France to carry out some modifications to his keel which he hoped would allow him to pass all the safety tests and join the race later, but he was running out of time.

Koji and Bernard had come through the storm relatively unscathed. They had stayed fairly close – about 20 miles – to the coastline around the north-west tip of Spain towards Cape Finisterre and had had some lee from the waves as a result, though inevitably they had some small repairs to make. Bernard was amazed when he found out he was in the lead since he felt like he had been just 'sailing' rather than 'racing' and had no idea the rest of the fleet had taken such a hammering.

When I arrived in La Coruña, I was met by Mike and also by Matt Pryor, the sailing correspondent of *The Times*, who I knew from his days as a 'legger' on the Clipper race. He immediately spotted that I had no one waiting to help me carry out the repairs to *Saga Insurance*, unlike Mike Golding and his back-up team, and his report the following day, which said my campaign was running on a 'shoestring budget' and that I had been dependent largely on goodwill due to a lack of support from my sponsors, led to a flurry of worried phone calls back at the office. Together with David Stubley, who had been responsible for putting together the sponsorship deal and who was a Clipper director, I released a statement putting the record straight. I would not have been able to start without the support from Saga and I was grateful to have it. To have that support questioned in a national newspaper just two days into the race was not especially helpful. In any case, Simon Clay was working on Mike's boat and as soon as Mike was ready Simon came across to give me a hand.

As soon as I stepped off the boat, I immediately started sourcing people able to secure a new piece of mast track. I had a spare section in the container I shared with Kojiro which was due to leave Bilbao that day, so I called through to get it to me urgently.

It was driven from Bilbao overnight and work started at once on bolting it to the mast. It was not an easy job as the bolt holes did not coincide with the original ones, so new ones had to be drilled in the carbon-fibre material. Two volunteers appeared from British yachts which were moored up in the harbour and helped me with other jobs that had exposed themselves in the storm. The Real Club Nautico de La Coruña very kindly provided me with a cabin while I was there, though most of my time was spent on the boat.

It was two more days before I was ready to go again and during this time I must have completed more than a dozen media interviews. The story of the storm had made the six o'clock national news in England, so media appeared from everywhere to see the boat and ask how we had survived, which was great for our sponsors because it planted the Velux 5 Oceans race right at the forefront of the British public's consciousness, not just those who followed sailing or sport but those who were captured by tales of adversity and adventure.

Whether we like it or not, it is sailors' misery, misfortune and sometimes their heroics that the general public find most captivating. It is no coincidence that two of Britain's better-known solo sailors, Tony Bullimore and Pete Goss, rose to household prominence after they were involved in dramatic ocean rescues. In the Vendée Globe 1996–7 Tony was deep in the Southern Ocean when his keel broke off on his 60-foot ketch *Exide Challenger*. The boat capsized and he famously survived for five days in an air pocket in the upturned boat eating chocolate and sipping water before an Australian navy vessel and helicopter arrived to end his nightmare.

He was amazingly lucky to survive, as was the Frenchman Raphael Dinelli, who in the same race was rescued by Pete after his boat *Algimouss* capsized in Force 11 winds and his mast smashed a hole in the deck. In big rolling seas, Pete turned back and risked his own life by sailing 150 miles in sixty hours to pick up Raphael, who by then had spent a few hours in a life raft. Both these stories generated front-page headlines and top-of-the-hour lead items and in both cases delivered a public profile that enabled them to move on to bigger and better things.

There is no easier way to get sailing on the front page of a newspaper than a disaster or dramatic rescue . . . The fact that, as with any ocean rescue, it was only by the grace of God that a life was not lost adds another dimension to what is already a compelling sport.

Yacht racing produces all manner of memorable contests, and not just in America's Cup or Olympic competitions. Ellen MacArthur and Frenchman Michel Desjoyeaux locked horns in the final stages of the 2002 Vendée Globe and, after racing 25,000 miles over more than ninety days, finished within a few hours of each other to make for an unforget-table and dramatic finale.

Races against time are also memorable, as we discovered on our successful bid for the Jules Verne Trophy in 1994 on the catamaran *Enza* and as Ellen showed us on *B&Q*

back in 2005. And unlike most sports, yacht racing is played out against a thoroughly hostile backdrop of some of the most inhospitable environments on the planet, and this inevitably brings mortality into the equation. One hopes there won't be a fatality in any race but they do happen – Jacques de Roux, Harry Mitchell, Gerry Roufs and, most recently, Hans Horrovoets all lost their lives in round-the-world racing, but the dangers are part of the appeal both for the sailors and the audience.

The French believe the British media obsession with calamity in sailing, rather than with the sport itself, is mystifying. Bernard was surprised when he started to follow Ellen MacArthur's round-the-world record because he said her reports focused purely on the drama and not on the racing. He came to the conclusion that this was the only way to communicate the story in England, but it served to conceal a major achievement.

I did not consider my life was particularly in danger during the Bay of Biscay storm – it never occurred to me to set off an EPIRB to say I was in trouble and needed assistance, for example, because I wasn't. My boat was fine – slightly damaged, true, but not in any way that affected her seaworthiness. She might have received more damage if any more large waves had arrived and repeated the roll, but they didn't. There was nothing anyone could have done until the wind and seas subsided, in any case – but to most people, it would have been seen as a brush with disaster.

With the new track in place I headed out to sea again and rejoined the race. There was still a problem with the wind instrument – there was only apparent wind but no compass or log input so I could not get it to provide the true direction and force, but that was better than nothing, so I decided to sail anyway. I had lost too much time already.

I was now four days behind the leading two boats, which could amount to 1,000 miles for an Open 60 where averages of 10 knots are normal. A gap this size meant I had to sail a good knot faster than the leader, Bernard Stamm, all the way to Fremantle, which was never going to happen. I had to adjust my own expectations, and felt that a podium place would be a respectable enough result given the circumstances.

But to achieve that I had to get moving, and quickly. The trouble was I had been tired when I set out from Bilbao after two months of round-the-clock preparations, the storm had taken more energy, and then I had been working hard on the boat in La Coruña. I was utterly exhausted. What I needed were a few days of predictable weather and consistent boat performance to get a routine established and start to take some rest, and that was not going to happen for a couple of days, until I could get clear of the shipping lanes. It took me around four or five days to settle in, though I managed to make a bad weather call during that time which cost me more miles. In part this was due to my being rusty but I was also having difficulty with the Maxsea weather program, which had suddenly decided I was not licensed to use their weather GRIB files (GRIB – gridded binary – is the format used by meteorological institutes to manipulate weather data). I struggled to remember how to get the other weather files downloaded onto Maxsea so it could use the information to predict a best course, which was one of the features that had been promised.

Once you have gone to sea, it's not exactly easy for an engineer or repair man to drop by. Out of sight, out of mind, and we never did sort out the license problem. I had to use the Ocen weather in order to get any benefit from the Maxsea system. We tend to blame computers for these problems, but here was an example of a poor program and no one available to deal with my queries.

After rounding Cape Finisterre, the north-west corner of Spain, I headed west to get clear of the shipping lanes and then turned south, but too soon. Normally in this area the weather tends to be dominated by the Azores high-pressure system, so you start to pick up a northerly wind, known locally as the Nortada, which will drive you down into the trade winds, but this time it wasn't cooperating, a depression was dominating the weather to the west and the winds were from the south-west instead. These south-westerlies, would, I thought, be replaced by the northerlies sooner or later when the high re-established itself. But it did not happen and I found myself having to tack out to the west again, which was not reducing the miles to go at all, to get a more favourable wind angle for the boat. I was hit by several squalls and winds that were pretty chaotic – gusting up to around 49 knots, veering as much as 60 degrees – which meant regular sail changes and no good long sleep.

I kept the sail area down during the squalls as I didn't like seeing a foot of leeward deck under water, and indeed when the boat was heeled that far I was discovering that taking in a reef did not lose any speed. This was part of my steep learning curve with these boats. With 30,000 nautical miles in front of me, my instinct anyway was to nurse the boat. I didn't want to overpress her because the margin of safety would be reduced, a risk particularly applicable in long-distance racing, where damage can mean a call into a port and huge loss of time, as I had already found to my cost.

It is better to sail at 95 per cent of capacity and have a 5 per cent margin for squalls or rogue waves than sail at 100 per cent and have no margin. This applies even more to single-handers, where you cannot be monitoring everything all the time. So many times in races I have watched people rush off with great élan but within days they have broken a mast or some vital piece of the boat and their race is over. Being forced out of a race because of damage is losing a race.

Part of the learning curve with *Saga Insurance* was learning to deal with the noises the boat made when carving through the waves. Carbon fibre amplifies noise, and at only moderate speeds I felt like I was in a rattling old underground train being blasted by an artillery of high-pressure hoses.

I would hear the noise build up, decide the boat was being pressurised too much and climb on deck to reduce sail, only to discover that everything there was fine. I would watch for a bit and then go below, noting that that particular decibel level was acceptable. Some sailors use earplugs to prevent themselves worrying about this noise but I didn't have any. In any case I thought I had better get used to it pretty quickly. If nothing else, it meant we were moving fast.

By this time, Graham Dalton had crossed the start line and was making good speeds, level with Unai Basurko. Tim had given up the unequal struggle to comply with the IMOCA rules and decided to withdraw, which was dreadfully sad for him. It had been his ambition to sail solo around the world and he had spent two years preparing his 60-footer *Margaret Anna* and trying to raise enough sponsorship to get her to the start line, but the costs and time required to sort out his stability problem put the project beyond reach, this time anyway.

Saga Insurance is a reaching machine, she likes the wind from the beam and when it complies, she picks up her skirts and flies. All these Open 60s, rather like the clipper ships of previous centuries, are best going off the wind or downwind.

But a succession of depressions from as far south as the Canary Islands continued to upset the usual trade winds in the eastern part of the North Atlantic, and everyone in the fleet was slowed down. At least this meant the front runners had not moved too far ahead.

I was looking at a 700-mile gap between myself and Bernard Stamm, which sounds a lot but I knew the leading pack would slow as they reached the equator, which would give me time to catch up. But then the gap would open up again once they got into the South Atlantic unless I got lucky in the doldrums. When you are so far behind, you have to be optimistic and think that at some point, the luck will change and start working for you.

Meanwhile, the sea and winds calmed a bit and the squalls disappeared and I was able to catch up on some rest. Even if the winds were contrary, the autopilot could hold the course for me. I had been sleeping in the cockpit for the first few days so I could deal with things quickly and keep a better lookout. It was not as comfortable as a bunk and sleep mostly took the form of catnaps, which was ideal because it meant I would get up and check round the horizon at frequent intervals in case a ship was in sight. When I set off in *Suhaili* in 1968, I slept fully clothed in the cockpit for the first few days with a flare in one hand and foghorn in the other just in case any ships came too close. This time

I had all this equipment to warn me if one came close, so I went inside and for the first time gave my fractured coccyx some relief by sleeping on a little round cushion that Sara had given me before I left. I slept a lot, in short bursts of up to ninety minutes, as much as my body needed. My batteries needed recharging and while conditions allowed, I took full advantage.

My coccyx was improving, despite all the demands on my body over the previous week. There was a slightly sore feeling when I sat awkwardly but I was gaining confidence as the pain progressively eased. I always seem to start races with some condition or other. When I left in 1968 I had a small attack of jaundice and took things easy for a couple of weeks.

I like to establish a routine as soon as possible on any voyage, though my routine on *Saga Insurance* couldn't have been more different than on *Suhaili*. Back then, I tried to get to sleep at around 10 p.m. if conditions allowed and I was clear of shipping lanes, and apart from a check at 2 a.m. I would sleep through to 6 a.m., when I would get up and make my rounds of the deck. This sleep could be interrupted at any time, of course, and usually a change in motion of the boat if the wind changed was enough to awaken me. But if I had had a quiet night, as soon as the deck check was completed I would fry up some eggs for breakfast and, if the weather was fine, sit out on deck with a mug of coffee and a cigarette. That early morning was always one of my favourite times – everything was fresh and new and no job, however onerous, seemed too big at that time of the day. Thirty-eight years down the track, my routine was very different

Now there were the media commitments to fit in to my

routine, which had not been possible forty years before. This was proving very difficult. The system had worked in the Bay of Biscay but now refused to connect, so I was unable to do a video call. I was only able to get through on the Iridium phone from time to time, it had decided it did not like its battery charger, and using it was frustrating anyway as the circuit kept being broken, so even a short conversation might require six separate calls. Much is made of this equipment, and when it works it is very helpful, but it seems to require an awful lot of work to make it operate effectively. More time to iron out problems would have helped, but the equipment proved to be very fragile. I was beginning to think its time requirements were not cost effective.

After two weeks I was only within 80 miles of the Canary Islands, which was painfully slow progress. Then for a couple of days I got reasonable trade winds and shot south, 265 miles in one day. I took 100 miles out of Alex in a couple of days, some 15 degrees further south by this time, but although this was a great encouragement it was too good to last. I knew he was in a different weather system as he came into the doldrums, but anything that closed the gap between us was a positive and good for my morale. The wind eventually shifted round to the north but eased to a Force 2 to 3. The direction was good, the strength too little. Ideally I wanted a wind on the beam, at the usual average of Force 4, say 15 knots, as that would have allowed me to wind the boat up much more easily, whereas what I had was the wind behind and at only 8 knots. If it was behind I had to harden up, which meant coming closer to the wind and so coming away from the course I wanted.

This area around the Canary Islands is usually one of my favourite sailing areas. The trade winds are normally there, the sun is usually shining and the sea is blue, but this time round the south-westerlies, followed by light northerlies, were creating frustration.

When we took the Jules Verne record in *Enza*, we went from Ushant to the Canaries in three days, but we had been able to choose our start time and had waited until conditions allowed us to sling-shot ourselves out of the Bay of Biscay straight into the trade winds. We had crossed the equator in less than eight days, a record that stood for some years.

The Canary Islands are the point at which the ocean routes divide. If you are crossing the Atlantic, they are your departure point, since the trade winds blowing westward are usually just a little south of here. If going south then I have usually found it best to leave the Canaries to the east because the wind, in my experience, has seemed steadier there, but the weather moves about a bit so this is not always the right thing to do. It can be dangerous going through the archipelago as there are huge wind shadows to the leeward of the islands where you can get stuck for days. Christopher Columbus found this out during his first voyage in 1492, when he was delayed in the Canaries for four weeks.

Almost five hundred years later, I had also stopped there on *Suhaili* while attempting to retrace Columbus's route across the Atlantic using Renaissance navigation methods and, as far as possible, his original log. We called in at San Sebastian de la Gomera before setting off west, using just an astrolabe to take the height of the sun at noon, and a 'Dutchman's Log' to calculate the distance travelled. Of course in Columbus's day it was not possible to calculate longitude because this required accurate timepieces which did not exist then and were not available for a further 200 years, but they could work out their latitude as the Portuguese had tabulated the movement of the sun, known as its declination, seven years previously.

When Columbus arrived in the West Indies he could work out how far north or south he was – although he got that wrong – but not how far west. That was dependent upon watching the speed of the boat through the water and estimating the distance travelled. When I arrived in San Salvador in the Bahamas, after 3,000 nautical miles and thirty-five days, I was only 8 miles out in latitude and 22 in longitude, and that gave me an awful lot of satisfaction, but showed the capabilities of the navigators 500 years before.

In recent years navigation has been revolutionised by satellites. Everyone uses the Global Positioning System (GPS), which provides a position to within a couple of metres plus the speed and direction every three seconds. So as well as a position it backs up the compass and speed log.

In the 1960s and 70s we were navigating with the same instruments as Captain Cook had used 200 years before, namely a sextant for measuring altitudes of selected heavenly bodies, a chronometer, which is an accurate clock, plus mathematical tables necessary to resolve a spherical triangle. It took ten minutes to work out a sight and that would only give you a line on the chart which you were on, not a position. To obtain a position it was necessary to take a succession of sights and then plot all the resulting lines, and where they crossed was roughly where you were. I say 'roughly' because the accuracy of the system was to within a mile or so. This took time, time spread throughout the day, and sometimes in rough weather you could be trying to get an accurate altitude for half and hour or more. And, of course, you could only take sights when you could see your datum, the horizon, so at night it was not possible. GPS has removed the need for the skills one developed and the time taken to work through the calculations. Modern sailors do not need to be navigators, until a fuse blows, but neither do they get the satisfaction from making a good landfall which we used to derive when the accuracy was down to our skills.

The Columbus experiment in 1989 was my last single-handed voyage. Now here I was again, alone and becalmed.

During this light period around the Canary Islands I continued to get to know the boat and her wardrobe. I spent a day taking a look at some previously untested light weather sails and trying to get to grips with the new video equipment I had been given.

The main wardrobe of sails on *Saga Insurance* was new. A new main, staysail, jib, big spinnaker and big reacher, which all cost $90,000, but the first sail I chose was the new 350-square-metre spinnaker, weighing in at 60 kg, which is equivalent to a lightweight racing dinghy.

The contrast with *Suhaili* was enormous. Her entire wardrobe cost me less than £500, but the sails were all Dacron, not Kevlar and Carbon, except for the spinnaker which was nylon. The largest sail was the mainsail at 28 square metres. I had five headsails, the largest being 20 square metres and that was a light-weather jib. The spinnaker was slightly smaller and had originally been made for a Navy whaler. You might think that this made them a lot easier to handle, but in fact they could be just as difficult as I did not have the modern systems and furlers to control them. It was not helped by any headsail on *Suhaili* having to be set clear in front of the bowsprit, which meant they could not be hanked to anything, so I had to pull the headsails in by hand rather than rolling them or snuffing them. On one occasion it took me an hour to get the 20-square-metre headsail handed as it kept billowing out to leeward and getting into the water. Dacron is more resilient than the modern materials and easier to repair as it can be sewn, but those sails needed to be tough as they had twice as long exposure to use. Even so the mainsail came back with more hand stitching in it than its original machine stitching where I had had to make constant repairs.

I had only been at sea for a fortnight and my strength had not yet built up, so I was finding the huge sails much too heavy to heave around on deck and was having to winch them up through the hatch onto the deck. But there was only one way to build up the muscles that had weakened as a result of my coccyx injury – and that was to try and lug the sails around. So I laid out the spinnaker bag, cleared its snuffing line (it is in a sock which you pull up to release the sail and pull down to snuff it), tacked it on, fastened the sheets and hoisted the sock.

But the snuffing line got caught around the sail, so I lowered it and released the tack. Then the wind caught it and off it flew, and it was a few moments before I was able to get the tack under control once more. In the process, the snuffing line went loose and was dangling close to the boat's side.

To pull it in, I had to swing on the boom guy and snag it with a winch handle. This worked a treat, so I cleared the snuffing line, re-attached the tack and hoisted again. I rolled the jib, pulled the snuffer up and out came this lovely sail.

It looked magnificent and I would have loved my sponsors to have seen it at that precise moment – ambling along with their name, Saga Insurance, filling the skies. Shame there were no snappers around. It would have made a great shot.

When I got it to pull, however, we accelerated and this pulled the wind round so rapidly that the boat could not respond quickly enough. When this happens you need to bear away to keep the sail full. If you don't, it starts to flap. I steered for three hours and reached 6 knots on one exciting occasion, but most of the time the foot of the sail was in the sea and we were making 2 knots, so clearly this was not the right occasion to use it.

Never mind. I had seen it and was happy about handling it in future. I snuffed the sail and hauled up the next one, which was the reacher. These can best be described as being halfway between a jib and a spinnaker. Cut fuller and larger than the jib, they are ideal when you are between being close-hauled and sailing with the wind behind the beam. They are a powerful weapon in the sail wardrobe, and since they can be rolled up on a furler are easily managed by a single person.

But right now it did not matter particularly which sail I used, I just needed one that would stay filled and remain steady. Even the best sails need wind. Over the next four hours, I did not make much progress but I learned a bit about these new sails. Then I set the medium reacher, which was the one sail that came with the boat that was worth keeping and I liked it.

Had our preparations in Bilbao been of the textbook variety, I should have started the race with all this knowledge, but as luck would have it, the winds in the run-up to the start were too strong and so unsuitable for testing light sails. This was a wasted opportunity since David Swete, the service manager from North Sails New Zealand, was on board during that time and it would have been useful to have tried them with him around.

So up went the reacher. It had a peculiar roll in it which took a bit of ironing out but then it set, which brought the boat under control and built my speed to a steady 4 knots for a while, on the right course too, which was a bonus.

By the time I had tried those two new sails out and set the older reacher, there was no time to master the complexities of the video camera. That would have to wait until another day, I thought, as I set about cooking dinner.

I made some additions to the current stew, adding two potatoes from my dwindling stock as they were going a bit soft and needed to be eaten, plus quite a lot of garlic, some of which was showing signs of sprouting. I love to have fresh food aboard, particularly onions and garlic, which usually last longest. Root vegetables like carrots and potatoes keep quite well but start to go floppy after six weeks, and brassicas like cabbage and lettuce will only survive a week. This combination was not a great success, and the next day I put in a tin of corned beef to make it more interesting.

After my dinner I sat in the cockpit, steering by hand in the very bright moonlight, listening to *The Gondoliers* by Gilbert and Sullivan. I was perfectly happy and relaxed but still thinking about the course and the gybe angle under the current sail configuration. Eventually, at midnight, when I had given up on any sleep thanks to the recurring strains of garlic, I decided it was time to change tack.

I rolled up the reacher – gybing these sails tends to create all sorts of tangles – then gybed the main and unrolled the reacher. We set off on the new tack. Neither the course nor the speeds were perfect at first but, with the gybe completed, I felt more relaxed and was able to sleep in patches. Things began to improve during the night as the wind veered.

While I was struggling with light winds in my efforts to make progress south, Bernard was crossing the equator and entering the Southern Hemisphere. It had taken him just seventeen days to cover 4,000 nautical miles, which meant he was averaging 10 knots. Koji, lying second, was 240 miles behind and putting in an impressive performance. Mike and Alex were making up for their lost time and snapping at Koji's heels, and it was difficult to see him holding them off for long. I was some 1,000 miles behind this leading group.

I had stowed some excellent wine in the hold – or rather Jose Ugarte, the Spaniard who was the inspiration behind Unai's endeavours, had stowed twelve bottles of some excellent wine – and since it was warm, around 25 degrees, that evening I poured myself a glass of Chateau Ugarte, recovered some pickled olives from a jar that unfortunately had cracked and stretched out in the cockpit.

This is a little tradition of mine. I like a bit of time to think about how things are going, reflect on the weather and consider my tactics in a relaxed manner. So towards evening I will usually have a glass of whisky or wine and just sit quietly in the cockpit, or below if it is wet, and wind down for a while.

Like most professional seamen I drink alcohol frugally at sea. When you might have to carry out some complicated evaluation at any moment, the last thing you want to do is dull your senses and reactions. On *Suhaili*, I left with twelve bottles of whisky and twelve of brandy and came home with one whisky and two brandy. On that trip, I also took 120 cans of Tennent's lager, but most of that remained when I returned to Falmouth as I had kept it as a liquid reserve in case I was unable to obtain drinking water from rain. I had consumed fourteen bottles of spirits between 14 June and 14 January, which works out at about half a bottle a week. In seven months, I had also smoked the best part of 3,000 cigarettes, which is fourteen cigarettes a day. In fact by 14 January, after seven months at sea, I was down to 110 cigarettes and knew I was going to run out, which I duly did in the South Atlantic forty days before reaching home. Giving up smoking, I was soon to discover, was just a matter of willpower!

As the leaders crossed the equator I could see from the position reports that they were all moving faster than me and the weather downloads, which were now working, showed they were getting better conditions, while my area continued to show light winds. It was as if the doldrums had moved north.

Our daily average speeds were around 7 knots, but it was an improvement on the previous week when, with headwinds, I had been averaging 6 or less along the route I needed to take.

There was nothing I could do to speed up and I was losing time. I began to worry that if I continued at this slow average I might have to start rationing, and I started to check on my supplies to see how much I had left.

I had used a gallon a day of fuel since La Coruña, which was slightly worrying since I had taken 55 gallons. The Volvo engine was not really strained when running with the generators, and even when I transferred the engine charge to the main batteries it made little difference. Maybe we needed a larger alternator, but again that was something we did not have time to find out before I started. All I knew was that I needed to get a shift on if we weren't going to have to divert to restock.

Little domestic problems were starting to achieve an importance far greater than they deserved. The top came off the washing-up-liquid bottle and most of its contents spilled. I mopped it up with a sponge and, not wanting to waste it, took the opportunity to have a wash. Not having a lot of fresh water, I used seawater for both washing and rinsing. Seawater tends to keep the skin fresher anyway.

Then I went looking for another bottle of soap but somehow, in the rush to get away in Bilbao, it had not been stowed aboard. I now had a cupful of soap left to see me all the way to Fremantle.

So clothes washing was now out. Rinsing only was a possibility, and I usually did this by tying an item of laundry to a rope and letting it drag astern. It might not come out much cleaner but it was certainly fresher, although a good rain squall was necessary to get the salt water out of the cloth. When there were no rain squalls, my body would have to make do with a hard scrub with salt water and no soap until we got close to the finish. This was an issue because now, three days after passing the Canary Islands, we had reached 17 degrees north, so the temperature was rising to about 30 degrees in the cockpit and more than 35 down below.

There was little shelter to be had from the sun except in the stifling cabin, so to keep cool I gathered up buckets of seawater and just tipped them over my head.

We were in flying-fish waters, and the movement of the boat frequently disturbed these little fish and sent them sashaying over the sea to safety. They don't literally fly – they glide, using their tails to push them along, though they cannot keep this up for too long as their wings, which are just extended pectoral fins, dry out. I usually found a few on deck each morning, where they had landed during the night and failed to get back into the sea. They were quite small, and not worth eating. They need to be about 10 inches long before the effort of cooking them is worthwhile, as they are very bony. The best way to eat flying fish is to boil them so the flesh falls off the bones and then make fish cakes or fish pie, though they do have rather a strong fishy smell which lingers long after the meal has been eaten and the washing-up finished.

The only other things found on deck were squid. Again they were very small, but they needed to be handled carefully as they were prone to discharge a nasty black inky substance which acts as an effective stain if you are not careful.

I was still being pressured to get through to APP, the TV company that was sorting out all the onboard images and video footage. So far, I had made just one successful connection and that was on the second night of the race when we were still in the Bay of Biscay. In the three weeks since, the whole system had turned out to be a disaster, and my frustration was not helped by the difficulties of working in a cabin that was like an oven.

To attempt a call I first had to top up my fuel tank, and it was always difficult to avoid spillage when the boat was bouncing about. I would then have to mop up the spillage, getting my hands covered in diesel which, of course, had to be washed off before I went back and touched anything else.

Then I would start the engine and run it for about two hours to build up the voltage, since the Fleet 77 needed a minimum of 12.5 volts. There would always be a couple of squalls to divert my attention before I attempted my first call on the satellite system, which would require at least two reboots of the computer and a string of invective as I grew increasingly irritated. By the time I had reached this stage, the cabin was like a furnace from the heat of the engine.

I tried and tried to get through to them. I could feel their frustration coming through in emails asking me to call at certain times. I kept attempting this, but to no avail.

I just could not get the system to connect through from my transmitter, although I was doing nothing different to what I had done just after the Biscay storm. These difficulties were blamed on my lack of understanding of computers, but I am not quite the Luddite they thought me to be. When someone from the suppliers decided to check the instructions they had given to me for making this connection, it was discovered there was a mistake. I got through fine after I was given the correct information, though no one could explain how I had got through once before using the 'wrong' directions.

This whole business made me extremely angry. I had spent hours and hours trying to get it to work, using up valuable time that should have been spent on making the boat go faster. As far as I could see, it could easily have been avoided if only someone had taken the time and trouble to go through the instructions to make sure they were correct. I was working 24/7, with a multitude of tasks to deal with, and they were working nine to five for five days a week with just this one task to focus on, but they had still taken three weeks to sort out a simple problem.

After we sorted out the problem with the live video connection, they asked me to edit and transmit some film I had taken, but I was reluctant to waste any more time on a system that seemed unreliable and that no one seemed interested in sorting out in a hurry. Being on my own with a heightened sense of 'me versus the rest of the world' may have deepened my resentment, but I felt that people were forgetting that I was trying my damnedest to win this race. That was the reason I was there. Racing was my primary objective and these other requirements were secondary.

This incident, more than any other, summed up for me how different things were today compared to the first time I went round the world in *Suhaili* in 1968.

Back then I had a single sideband HF radio with limited power, and getting through to a shore station or another vessel was difficult and often not possible. For eight out of the ten and a half months that voyage took, the radio would receive but not transmit, which was why so many people spent a few months thinking I was missing.

My poor father was reminded most evenings in the pub that my silence was ominous, but he never lost faith and waited patiently until I was able to get a message through. I managed this off Australia: when I came within reach of the pilot vessel off Melbourne, I threw them a package containing letters and film canisters and whatever else needed to go off. I saw some fishermen off New Zealand a fortnight later and then no one for four and a half months.

I had no back-up team to call on, to help deal with problems or emergencies. I was entirely on my own, doing jobs, making repairs, reading books – I took 105 books, nine Admiralty Pilots and twenty-four charts with me – and listening to my Sanyo cassette tape recorder. If anyone had told me then that in a future yacht race I would be sitting at my chart table downloading weather information from a computer, sending and receiving electronic emails to anywhere in the world and talking directly to a presenter on the

BBC Radio 4 *Today* programme, to be heard by two million listeners, I would have laughed.

Satellites have changed everything. Nowadays, if we have the time and money, we can spend all day on the phone or surfing the internet irrespective of whether we are in the English Channel or in the desolate wastes of 49 degrees south. Email is a terrific boon. In one month I had sent and received more than 500 emails; it would have been a lot more if we hadn't established a new email address before I sailed, so I would not be inundated. All normal emails to me were vetted, and only those considered important to the race were passed on.

Using email I was able to send off all my various logs and blogs as they were completed. At times, it was quite therapeutic to sit down and describe my day and know that within minutes, quite literally, anyone who was interested would be able to share it. My log in *Suhaili* was religiously written up every day but no one got to see it until after I came back.

The misleading video-link instructions apart, I enjoyed having the ability to make contact with family and friends, but I used it sparingly. In fact if the satellite phone rang I tended to treat it as a nuisance, an interruption in my little world. There were a number of alarms and sounds that could distract me but one in particular I listened out for was the echo-radar alarm, which alerted me to the radar of another vessel and sent a response so the other vessel knew I was nearby. This is a vital piece of equipment and I trained myself to respond to its alarm.

One night, early on in the journey, this radar picked up a merchant ship long before I could see its lights, which was just as well because it passed about a mile ahead, the sort of distance that starts making one nervous. The speed of *Saga Insurance* was more than twice that of *Suhaili*, and merchant vessels are also faster these days. The result is that vessels on reciprocal courses close with each other much faster. The time between a vessel appearing on the horizon and being within a boat's length of your bow is alarmingly short.

Increasingly the congestion in the shipping channels is becoming a problem, and the blatant disregard for rules and regulations among seamen driving these big boats a major concern. Dee Caffari said after her round-the-world voyage in 2006 that the most dangerous part of sailing round the world was contending with the shipping lanes, and I agree with her.

How many vessels have I passed at sea which have ignored my presence or failed to answer a call on the VHF when they have been bearing down on me? Far too many is the answer. Rule 17 of the International Code for the Prevention of Collision at Sea states quite clearly that when collision cannot be avoided by the action of the giving-way vessel alone, then that vessel shall – not may, *shall* – take action to avoid a collision.

A collision at sea is seldom, if ever, just one vessel's fault. If I hit a large merchant vessel they would not notice, but if they hit me I would probably be finished, so it is in my interest to keep a close watch, by whatever means at my disposal, to protect myself. On the large vessels they are being paid to keep a lookout and maybe failing in that duty, but there are no authorities who are prepared to take action on this until, of course, a collision occurs. If it involves a small yacht, the chances are a collision will not be noticed.

A collision can be avoided by a yacht provided it has been plotting the other vessel and has the means to get out of the way, but if the yacht has no engine and there is no wind, it can do little. At least five collisions involving small yachts have been reported in British waters alone since 1999.

When I was in the Merchant Navy we were expected to keep a lookout throughout our watch, and woe betide us if we didn't. On one occasion, as we were heading towards Karachi, I was working out my mid-morning sight on the table at the front of the bridge where I could keep an eye ahead when the captain, Jack Hamilton, appeared. 'Everything all right, Third?' he asked. 'Yes, sir,' I replied. 'Nothing to worry about, then?' he enquired. 'No, sir,' was my response. 'Then what the hell is that?' he almost shouted.

I looked astern and there was a Pakistani destroyer coming up on us at 25 knots. I received a deserved bollocking. It did not matter that the destroyer was the overtaking vessel and thus had to avoid us. What mattered was that I had not seen it.

Captain Hamilton and I sailed together later, when I was chief officer and we had a new third with us. Going up the Irish Sea, I went up to the bridge to see how the new chap was getting on and to my horror saw a seagull standing up in the water ahead of us, as if it was stood on a reef or a sandbank. I asked the third where we were and he did not give a convincing answer, so I called Jack. Both of us went through all the motions, working back from the last fix, checking the radar and echo sounder. There was no land in sight but visibility was not good. We watched the seagull and, as it came closer, saw that it was standing on a piece of discarded wood, not a sandbank as we had feared!

Many of the most valuable lessons I have learned in my life were learned during my time in the Merchant Navy. I was just seventeen when I joined, and itching to get on with my life. School had never held much interest for me, because I was only ever interested in maths, history and geography. Other subjects held little or no appeal, but I was very good at the ones I liked.

My school reports had a recurring theme: they always said I could do better. In the subjects I enjoyed, I worked hard, though my maths master once said: 'Knox-Johnston, if you ever go to sea, I'm going to emigrate to Switzerland.' The next piece of homework came back with just 'by air' written on the top. I liked his sense of humour and probably learned more from him than most of my teachers because of it.

I passed eight O-levels, though failed French three times. I'm sure if the school syllabus had featured more practical subjects, as it does these days, my schooling would have been a little more distinguished. I was always better at making and doing things than thinking or studying.

I still keep in touch with a couple of people I was at school with, even though it is more than fifty years since we were there. Clive Jacobs, who became a BBC broadcaster and journalist, was one of my friends, and together we hatched big plans designed to test the limits of our masters' patience, not always with great success. We once tried to rewire the dining-room bell. We spent hours, in the middle of the night, crawling around with a tiny torch, laying new wires across the floor and into the walls, which when connected were supposed to make the bell ring at our table rather than at top table. There was a good deal of industry and giggling but the big switch-on came to nothing and from that point my electronics artistry, or lack of it, has been the source of much amusement in some quarters.

I was small and wiry at school, with blond curly hair. I was never difficult but I was a bit different. I would like to have excelled at sport but was only ever good at boxing and long-distance running. I liked the idea of being able to defend myself, and being a decent boxer meant you didn't have to worry about being bullied. Even in those days I tended to be a bit of a loner; I never worried about being in an in-crowd.

Perhaps because of that, I have always had an inner self-belief, which has meant I rarely contemplate failure. If I think I can do something I won't be persuaded otherwise.

We are all the products of our childhood and when I look back at mine, I can see aspects of my upbringing that definitely shaped my character.

I grew up in a disciplined environment but we had a lot of fun. With four boys born in eight years, ours wasn't exactly a quiet household and all of us developed our own interests early on. I was into ships, Richard was a good cricketer and Chris enjoyed his amateur dramatics – he was so gifted he should really have chosen that as a career, but with our background acting was not a realistic option. My youngest brother Mike went into the hotel business.

As soon as I was able, I sat the Civil Service Commission examinations so I could join the Royal Navy. I came out very high in aggregate marks – twenty-seventh out of 1,200 – but unfortunately was one mark short in physics. If I had wanted to join the Army or Royal Air Force, this wouldn't have mattered, but it was required by the Navy, so I missed out. At the time I was disappointed, probably more than I let on, because by then I had spent ten years dreaming of a life in the Navy and had never contemplated any life other than that of a naval officer.

But when I look back on those days, and the person I then was, I realise that failing the exam was one of the best things that happened to me. With my father's full support, I promptly applied to join the British India Steam Navigation Company as an apprentice. It was a tough, practical training. The Merchant Navy does things because they are necessary, and there is little time or inclination for non-essential activities. Some officers in the Royal Navy tended to look down on us merchant seamen but no one understood how thoroughly we were trained and how professional we were. When I got on a Navy frigate, I was streets ahead of the naval officers in navigation – I was a qualified navigator and none of them were. I was also a better watch-keeper because I had done more. I dealt with the men differently, and they liked it – not shouting at them but asking them to do things, because that's how you do it in the Merchant Navy, and that's what I still do today.

I thrived in that environment. In the first year, with hard physical work and plenty of good food, I grew 3 inches and put on 14 kg, none of it fat.

The other great formative and abiding influence on my life, of course, was my marriage, and remarriage, to Sue. We had hardships and difficult passages – as will occur on any long voyage – but in the end we came through. Without her, it was perhaps only my fresh engagement with the sea, in which my old Merchant Navy training and experience could once again be put into practice, that was propelling me forward now.

6. Casualties

The doldrums are infamous for their calms and squalls. They are the result of the winds in the northern hemisphere from about latitude 30 north heading south-west, and those of the southern hemisphere from about latitude 30 south heading north-west. Where the two meet the air rises, creating a large area of low pressure. This lack of anywhere to go but upwards means that winds are far from consistent and there is instability. So this is not an area of flat calms, although sometimes you can experience no wind for hours.

As I worked round the Cape Verde Islands, I was mentally preparing myself for this unstable region. I would have preferred to have gone west of the islands, which would have been the usual course, but was still in south-westerly winds and according to the weather files the wind appeared to be stronger to the east. I am not sure that it was. I was at 23 west longitude and I wanted to be between 28 and 30 degrees west when I reached the Inter-Tropical Convergence Zone, where the doldrums are to be found, as that is where the chances of a fast passage through are greatest. This had been discovered a century ago by the German Flying P line, who made a study of all their captains' logbooks and noted the faster passages down the Atlantic and round Cape Horn to Chile when their vessels crossed the ITCZ in that area. The discovery benefited them enormously, and their ships averaged one and a half round trips a year as a result instead of the normal one.

Because the ITCZ hovers close to the equator it is always hot. The zone moves north and south, following the sun, and it can jump quite quickly so you think you might have got through it only to find it has jumped ahead of you and you have to work your way through it again. In this zone you are constantly watching for clouds as you know there will be wind, and sometimes thunderstorms too with torrential rain beneath them. Boats caught unready for one of these squalls can end up being knocked over or have their sails damaged.

South of the Cape Verde Islands the wind died on me completely for a while. In those circumstances all you can do is sit, with the sails slapping from side to side, and try and coax some movement. This is where a canting keel does come in handy – swinging it out on the leeward side and heeling the boat over away from the wind helps the sails to flop into an aerodynamic shape. It is then just a case of being patient. Any movement that causes a breath to pass the sails can help to very slowly create forward motion.

This period was agonising. Once again I was losing time on the leaders. There had only been two days in the whole run down from Spain to the Cape Verdes when I had kept up with the boats in front, and this was when the north-east trade winds had appeared and I had got the big spinnaker out. I had been encouraged by that – at least we had shown we could hold them when we had good winds – but where were the winds?

That was the only opportunity I had to put the boat in its best sailing configuration. I have sailed that route to the equator five times and have never known the trade winds to be so reluctant to appear. I had bought a new reacher for this sort of work but it only came out of its bag once.

I was beginning to consider myself in a separate event to everyone else. While I was crawling round the Cape Verdes at 7 knots the four boats ahead of me were already across the equator and streaking away at 12 to 14 knots with easterly or north-easterly winds. Bernard was leading, but now Mike Golding had moved into second place; Koji was 400 miles behind and Alex was next, 650 miles astern. The gap between me and this group had widened considerably: Bernard was now 1,800 miles clear. Dalton was 300 miles behind me, and 300 miles further back was Unai; both were closing, with good trade winds. I assured myself that as they got closer to me they would get the same weather and so slow down, or they would bring better weather and I would speed up. It was about the only consolation I had in what was an increasingly frustrating situation.

The temperatures were now becoming very high as we approached the same latitude as the sun. Twenty minutes in the sun's direct glare in a day was enough to burn the skin. I opened the watertight doors and deck hatches to create a slight draught through the cabin, but it wasn't enough to make a real difference. I regretted not having a small awning I could rig over the cockpit, which at least would have provided some protection. These boats are designed to with-stand being thrown about in the Southern Ocean and, if necessary, to survive upside down for days, so there are minimal openings and certainly not any ventilators. Even the deck hatches are considered vulnerable, and I carried pre-cut pieces of plywood in the event that the glass of a hatch broke, or was blown out, which I have seen happen. There has to be a large market for the person who invents a totally safe ventilator that will let air in but not water. The standard Stephens-designed Dorade works well on an upright or heeled yacht, but would not seal if immersed. I sheltered in any shadow on deck, but my main relief, apart from a bucket of seawater thrown over my head, did not come until nearly midnight, when the cabin had cooled down. I was frequently tempted to dive in for a swim as I used to do on *Suhaili*, but our speed was never quite slow enough to make it a sensible option. I think the sun has got sharper during my lifetime, or my skin is less able to take its rays. We used to work on deck all day without shirts in the tropics, and provided we started out carefully, we never burned but just went nut brown. I cannot do that these days.

In the middle of this I decided to change the steering ram from the hydraulic to the electronic one. I switched over, but the control box came up with a bewildering array of messages and refused to work. This was not good. I didn't want to be racing halfway around the world with just one ram working and no spare. I got out the instructions and checked the wiring, and discovered that two wires were missing from the ram. Fortunately I carried a spare, and when fitted this worked fine for a while before abruptly switching itself to standby. I flicked on the other pilot, which took over. Later I switched back and the new ram worked fine again. Quite what the cause of this was I had no idea, but it was worrying. The pilots were going to be vital in the Southern Ocean and if they started to become unreliable I could put the boat and myself in danger. I was able to play with the pilots because we weren't moving anywhere, the wind had disappeared, and the race headquarters even called to check I was OK as they said I was drifting north. Well, my GPS gave me stopped and not drifting anywhere, but it was good to know they were keeping an eye on us.

In the heat I did not feel like eating very much. My diet was largely made up of freeze-dried meals and boil-in-the-bag recipes. When I got bored or felt imaginative I created 'pot mess'. You tip a few selected tins into the pressure cooker and boil them up. I use a pressure cooker because it uses less fuel, and also if it falls off the stove the contents don't spill out all over the place. The pressure cooker was small, but could take enough for two meals; in practice I usually added a tin or two after one meal, which changed the flavour and took advantage of what was already well stewed. It may not sound very appetising, and I would not cook it at home or offer it to friends, but I find most crew appreciate it at sea. I did not bring enough tins with me on this leg to have pot mess very often, something I put right on the next leg. Because you cannot have fresh vegetables in any quantity it is necessary to supplement the diet with Vitamin C; I also take yeast tablets, which tend to keep the blood clean and prevent an outbreak of those annoying little boils known as salt-water sores.

The freeze-dried and boil-in-the-bag meals are a real boon to racing yachtsmen. They are good quality and nourishing. Again, conditions had been very different in 1968, when tins were the only choice. My pot mess then was based on tins of either stewed steak or corned beef, with other tins added to suit my mood. I took 212 tins of each – what we used to call a gross and a half, before we were decimalised. It kept me healthy and nourished. In fact I came back from that voyage 7 pounds heavier, but a lot of that weight was due to increased muscle. At the end of the voyage my chest measurement had increased two inches, the same as my upper arms. My legs, on the other hand, had lost a lot of muscle and when I first arrived ashore, after 312 days at sea,

I found I could not walk more than 200 metres before my ankles began to hurt. It took time to build them up again.

There was good news on 12 November, when Sophy Williams joined the team as Press Officer. This took a lot of pressure off me as I now had someone ashore who could sift through all the media requests and arrange them so they fitted in with my schedules. Not that my schedules were complicated – I wasn't going to be 'out' – but there were certain times when it was more convenient. I had also decided that I needed more professional back up. I did not have anyone monitoring my progress, sorting out the spares I would need when I reached Fremantle and acting as team boss, so I took on Simon Clay. This was another good move, which I never regretted. He had only ever upset me once – when, in La Coruña, he had said '*if*' I got to Fremantle, to which I had answered firmly, '*When* I get to Fremantle . . .' He had yet to learn that when I said I was going to Fremantle, that was where I was going!

And then there was bad news. During the night of the 12th we crossed the ITCZ, the wind veering east and later south-east, but as we were adjusting to these changes a heavy squall hit, the autopilot switched itself to standby and we had a ferocious Chinese gybe as a result. This is where the mainsail crashes across from full out on one side into the running backstays the other side. I might have seen the squall coming but I was busy below trying to make a connection to a TV station, and the system as usual was being difficult and refusing to connect. Had I not been told that this inability to connect was nothing to do with the equipment, but down to me, I probably would not have tried so hard. But I only had myself to blame for that. I should have been more robust in refusing to use the equipment until someone had worked out what was going wrong with it.

The force of the impact was sufficient to break every single batten in the sail. These battens are what help the sail to hold its shape. On the Open 60s, like multihulls, there is a huge roach – that is, an area of the sail which is outside a triangle formed by the leading edge on the mast, the luff, the foot, and a line drawn from the end of the boom to the masthead. The only way to hold this roach is by means of battens, so if they are broken the sail creases and ceases to be so effective. To add to my difficulties I had the reacher up at the time, and as I tried to furl it, the furler jammed with the sail still half set. It took almost an hour to get the reacher under control and down on deck and stowed away. I set the Solent to give some power and then turned my attention to the mainsail. Initially I just wanted to reef it so I could examine the damage, but bits of broken batten had come out of their pockets in the sail and caught around the Lazy-Jacks, lines that go from the boom to the mast, supporting the boom and keeping the mainsail from flopping onto the deck when lowered. I had to cut the Lazy-Jacks to get the sail down and put two reefs in it. Then I removed the lowest four battens, took them below, and started to stick them together using a splint held in place with epoxy. This solution lasted less than twenty-four hours, when all the repaired battens were broken in another squall.

On the 15th I had an easterly wind, perfect for the direction I wished to sail, and which I should have been able to turn into 12 to 14 knots of boat speed, but with all the damage I was unable to take advantage of it – I could not set all the mainsail, and so lacked power. As a result, my days runs – the distance travelled from noon to noon – were less than 6 knots for two days, and down to 4 knots one day. This wasn't racing. I was now 2,400 miles behind Bernard and 1,400 behind Alex. But the last two were closing rapidly to within 80 miles in the case of Dalton, and 130 for Unai. To make matters worse the ITCZ moved south for a while and we were becalmed again. I was beginning to wonder what else could possibly go wrong.

I crossed the equator on the 16 November, twenty-five days after the start and a pretty slow passage. Nevertheless, I declared a 'Headland', which means I had a drink to celebrate.

The Headland policy goes back to the 1986 two-handed Round Britain Race. Billy King-Harman and I were lying fourth in my 60-foot catamaran *British Airways*, and were approaching Lerwick in the Shetlands with a decreasing wind. Eventually we almost stopped completely and found ourselves drifting into a small bay. We tried to tack three times to get clear but the boat would not go through the wind. Looking anxiously at the approaching rocks, I reckoned I had just enough room to try and wear her round, which is to go downwind to change tacks. We got perilously close to the rocks, positioning the anchor at the ready just in case, but she came round and very slowly we sailed back into open water. I said to Billy that when we passed the headland of the bay we should celebrate with a tot and the Headland policy was borne. To give it structure, we decreed a 'Headland' had to be declared by three voting members, namely the owner, the skipper and crew collectively – though funnily enough, in all my years of voting I cannot recall one single incidence of dissent.

The normal winds to expect as you enter the southern

Atlantic would be south-easterlies slowly turning east and then north-east, but this time they stayed stubbornly south-east, right down to 20 degrees latitude south. The only good thing about the weather was that the two boats behind had been closing in with the north-east trades as the wind reverted for them, but once they got close to me they encountered the same weather, so I was able to open the gap up a small amount. Having competitors this close proved invigorating. I knew I had the faster boat but it was up to me to prove it; this gave me something to race against, and perked me up no end. Up front, the rest of the fleet were effectively on a different race track, and it was getting harder to see them as competitors.

I tried putting splints on the battens, which seemed to work, for a while anyway, and with the wind blowing at Force 5 to 6, about 20 knots, I did not need the full mainsail, which meant it was easier to keep its shape. I then turned my attention to the autopilot. I went right through all the wiring and removed anything extraneous to the actual pilot, such as GPS, wind and speed; the latter were not working reliably anyway. With the pilot's computer now receiving nothing but course instructions and feedback from the actual ram, I thought I might remove whatever gremlin was causing the problems. This proved to be the case – almost. The control panel stopped sending me incomprehensible messages, but the system still threw itself to standby on occasions and I had to be very quick to respond. But at least we were now beating to windward so the worst that could happen was that she might tack herself if the pilot failed. I have used these units for about thirty years and never had a problem before. It is beyond belief that I should suddenly get two bad units, but it appears that is exactly what I'd

The four brothers
at Selsey, 1952

Berkhamsted School boxing team, 1955

Apprentice in the British India
Company, 1957

Royal Naval reserve P61 course, HMS *Nelson*

The Kuwait Consul in Bombay christens *Suhaili*, 1964

Sir Francis Chichester on RKJ's return to Falmouth, 22 April 1969

A family together again, after our remarriage, 1972

Starting Sara out sailing, Chipstead Lake, 1970

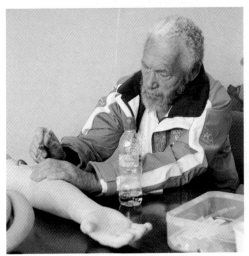

Medical training before the off

Velux 5 Oceans skippers. *Left to right*: Bernard Stamm, Graham Dalton, RKJ, Unai Bazurko, Mike Golding, Alex Thomson, Kojiro Shiraisho and Tim Troy

Saying goodbye to my daughter Sara and grandchildren Florence Xavier and Oscar

In formation with the Clipper fleet in the Solent

My nav station, *Saga Insurance*

Saga Insurance alone and at one with the planet

Saga Insurance approaches Fremantle at sunset

Robin and friends: my Fremantle team. *Left to right, top*: Tom Green, Dilip Donde, RKJ, Pete Cummings, Dave Swete, Lovely; *bottom*: Julia Stuart, Katie Cummings, Tim Ettridge, Huw Fernie

Saga Insurance on her side, twelve hours before the restart in Fremantle

Cold, wet, tired and very alone

Bernard Stamm and Kojiro Shiraishi celebrate with me in Bilbao

Celebrating at the finish

Doing the rounds of the media in Bilbao

been landed with and it made me nervous about the rest of the passage.

To reduce the pounding into the headwinds and seas I ballasted the forward port tank to provide a bit of stability. Light ships, such as these Open 60s, can be very lively in heavy weather; they become less likely to be thrown about in the same conditions if they are heavier, and the weight of a ton of water on the weather side helped to bring the boat more upright. It may seem perverse to load a racing yacht, which has been pared down to save weight, with ballast, but there are times when additional weight, in the right place, can be advantageous, increasing speed and safety.

Saga Insurance has four ballast tanks. Two are in the sail locker up front and two in the steering flat aft. They take the form of double-bottom tanks, and each one holds roughly about a ton of seawater when full. Filling and emptying them is easy and takes around ten minutes using four valves, one for each tank, in the bottom of the boat. You don't have to use a pump. By pushing the appropriate valve down, so its end is sticking out below the hull, and then turning the valve – so that its opening points forward when filling the tank, and aft when emptying – you use the water pressure created by the boat's forward movement to fill the tanks and a Venturi effect to empty them.

If the wind is coming from the port side, for example, I want weight that side to give added stability but I also want the front of the boat to be heavier to reduce the amount of bashing into the waves and make her go faster, so I fill the forward port ballast tank full.

When running downwind, these boats tend to bury their bows, so to check that I would fill one or both aft ballast tanks, which has the effect of lifting the bow. It makes life altogether more comfortable and, in theory, improves our speeds, which would be fine if the other gadgetry on board did not contrive to sabotage those benefits.

By the 21st I was increasing my lead over the two boats behind, but *Saga Insurance* was feeling sluggish. I went forward to do a check and found to my horror that we had a good 3 feet of water sloshing around in the sail locker, with the sails floating around. There was too much water for the pump, so I opened the hatch and began to bucket the water out. We were still sailing well and there was plenty of water coming over the deck, but I managed to remove water faster than it came in through the hatch.

Baling is one of those dull monotonous jobs where progress initially seems so slow you begin to wonder if there is another leak somewhere, because the compartment seems to be refilling as fast as it is emptied. But then you notice the sail bags are not quite so mobile. Next, they go aground, and then you are heaving them out of the way to get to the water at a lower level.

I spent an hour and a half bucketing around a ton and a half of water out of the locker before I was down to the bilges. There was no obvious leak, so my suspicions fell on the ballast system. The next morning there were 60 bucketfuls to remove, which is more than would be expected from water being absorbed by the sails, a possible source. I was finding this bucketing water an unnecessarily active part of an active retirement!

The average winds shown on the weather charts are just that, averages. They cannot be relied upon to give more than an indication of what to expect. Although the averages suggested that we should be enjoying a more favourable wind from the south-east, slowly backing east and then north-east as we progressed south, this did not happen until we reached 19 degrees south on the 21st. This was slowing the boat down and increasing the gap between me and the leaders. This was very frustrating: the more gains they made now, the more difficult it would be for me to claw back the advantage, not just in this leg but in subsequent legs too, because the Velux 5 Oceans Race is run on time and all leg times are carried forward.

I was pushing as fast as I thought was safe, although I would be the first to admit that my understanding of what was safe and what was not was still patchy. At all times, the boat was heeled over at 25 to 30 degrees, with plenty of spray coming over. This made climbing around a rather precarious activity, but by this time I was scarcely aware of the injury to my coccyx. It felt as if it had repaired itself, and my muscles were hardening up. I was, at last, getting racing fit.

When the wind eventually backed to the east I was able to speed up, and for four days we averaged 10 knots. It could have been faster, but the broken battens I had repaired kept breaking again and I had to lower the mainsail to get at them to make further repairs. It was in this area of South Atlantic high that I had made a mistake thirty-eight years before: I turned for the Cape of Good Hope too early and found myself on the wrong side of the system which served up strong headwinds for two whole weeks, day in day out, and cost me a lot of time. This time, determined not to make the same mistake, I continued to take a course nearer south than south-east. Ahead of me Alex had done the same thing. He had headed south rather than south-east in the wake of Bernard and Mike and so taken a wide loop, but it had paid off as although he had sailed a greater distance he had sailed faster. By the 21st he was in second place, 50 miles ahead of Mike and 700 behind Bernard, and gaining slowly.

What a difference time has made. Now, subject to accuracy of course, I had regular weather information and a pretty good idea of where the high was centered, which meant I could plot a course to its west and avoid the unpleasantness and the resulting loss of speed and therefore time. It is this availability of weather data that has transformed offshore yacht racing in recent years and given rise to the succession of new speed records. Getting to the equator in *Suhaili* from Falmouth, for instance, a distance of 3,500 miles, took forty-three days, which is seven days less than the current entire round-the-world record time set in 2005 by Bruno Peyron and his crew of thirteen on the maxi-catamaran *Orange II*.

In 1994, on our catamaran *Enza*, we went from the imaginary line between the Lizard and Ushant, the recognised start line for round-the-world attempts (although it is biased in favour of the French end), to the equator in seven days, four hours and twenty-four minutes at an average speed of 18.71 knots. That was eighteen hours faster than the time recorded by Peyron's first *Orange* catamaran in 2002, even though he knocked ten days off *Enza*'s round-the-world record of seventy-four days.

In 2003, Olivier de Kersauson and his crew of eleven reached the equator in six days, eleven hours and twenty-six minutes on the trimaran *Geronimo*, while Ellen, sailing alone, set a new solo record of eight days, eighteen hours and twenty minutes on *B&Q*, also a trimaran, in 2005, before going on to set a new solo round-the-world record of seventy-one days.

My time of twenty-six days from Bilbao to the equator in this race seemed laboured by comparison. But this wasn't an attempt on any speed record, and although I was enjoying having weather information to speed things up, from a performance point of view I was still finding my feet.

Without properly functioning autopilots, I began to worry whether it would be safe to head into the Southern Ocean for Fremantle, let alone around the world. I had to give some serious consideration to diverting to Cape Town to get the autopilots sorted out and collect some new battens. The pilots caused me enormous worry. Suppose they failed in a storm in the Southern Ocean?

Alex Thomson phoned and said he thought I ought to go in for repairs, but I wasn't certain whether this was a new, cautious Alex or he was genuinely concerned for my well-being! The battens were taking up a huge amount of my time, when clement weather windows allowed me to work on them, and the mainsail had developed a terrible shape. But to divert meant losing a minimum of six days – two to get there, two in penalties for making the stop, and two to get back to the right position to race again.

Eventually, with some trepidation, I decided not to lose the six days but press on, but it was not with any great confidence.

You cannot run one of these boats as you might a professional racing car. In addition to being the driver, you have to double up as the team mechanic and turn your hand to any part of the boat that ceases to function, large or small. So when my stove fell to bits, I had to sort it out or there would be no more dinner, or breakfast or lunch for that matter. I had not installed this equipment so it took half an hour to work out what was wrong and put it back together again. Job done, burner back.

The bilge pump also jammed, but I knew this type so it took only fifteen minutes to fix. One of the reasons I like to be right in the middle of a refit with my sleeves rolled up is so that I become familiar with all the equipment. It saves so much time and worry if a solution is found quickly and easily, especially if equipment failure results in an emergency.

But if I thought I was having problems, at least they were something I could deal with and were not life-threatening. Alex Thomson and Mike Golding were now neck-and-neck and closing in on the leader Bernard Stamm in a potentially thrilling chapter of the race when Alex suddenly called in to say he had a serious problem with his canting keel.

The top seemed to have sheared. Race control put Mike and Kojiro on standby as the nearest boats, but within a couple of hours Alex reported to race headquarters that he could no longer control the situation and needed to abandon his boat.

The section attaching the rams to the keel had sheared off, and the thing was swinging wildly. It was difficult to imagine what it must be like to have an uncontrolled keel swinging from the bottom of the hull causing unknown damage, but one thing was for certain: the situation would get much worse.

Mike had been closing the gap on Bernard, speeding along at a blistering pace. He had broken his own personal record for a top speed with 32 knots, and in the previous twenty-four hours had clocked up an extraordinary 446 miles. As the nearest competitor to Alex, however, he did not need to be told what was required of him. He turned back immediately and started heading towards Alex's stricken boat.

Giving assistance at sea is not voluntary. It is an international obligation and takes precedence over all racing
rules. Indeed, if someone refused to go and assist they
would, subject to a protest being made, be disqualified from
the race and possibly receive a longer disqualification from
the international body that governs sailing.

To ensure a level playing field in these sorts of situation,
procedures have been introduced to allow for redress. There
was no question that Mike would be compensated for the
time he lost in the rescue, so that his race did not suffer
from a competitive point of view.

In this situation, because there was an official Race Control, it was the race director, David Adams, who called the
shots. He knew where everyone was and who was best
placed to assist. The rest of us were not needed and carried
on sailing, but our minds were very much on our friends.
How was Alex doing overnight in a boat with an ungovern-
able keel? How would they work out how to transfer Alex
safely from *Hugo Boss* to *Ecover*? Once safe, where would
they head? Would there be enough food on the boat to get
to Fremantle with two aboard, or would they have to divert
to South Africa?

At the end of the day you have to trust the people involved
to get things right. Alex and Mike are both professional
yachtsmen who make their livings out of sailing boats, and
despite the dangers we were confident that they would
handle this rather unusual situation effectively. When people
called me up to ask if I was worried, I said that I wasn't.

Mike had to cover just 90 miles to reach Alex. If he had
been sailing downwind it would have taken just a few hours,
but as it turned out the journey was to prove one of the
most frightening and gruelling of his life, forcing him to

summon every ounce of courage, patience and determination that he could muster. Mike later wrote his own account of the rescue, and the drama is best told as he experienced it himself.

Two days ago, on the 23 November, the first sign of a change came with the 1020 hrs position report. Over the previous 48 hours Ecover *and* Hugo Boss *were making some of the fastest speeds of the race so far with 24-hour runs around 450 miles.*

On Ecover *we were seeing regular speeds in excess of 30 knots and our averages were around 20 knots. This is the most stressful sailing humanly possible – the speed is electrifying and the Southern Ocean is the most fearful location. Here the wind and waves have been uninterrupted by land for 15,000 miles and this makes it the best place for high-speed sailing but also the most terrifying for the sheer hostile and uncontrolled power exerted by the elements.*

But for us, huge strides were being made on Bernard Stamm's lead, all indications were that within the next few days the race, and the challenge for overall pole position, would be firmly up for grabs. But on seeing this particular position data file, with Alex and Hugo Boss *making only 8 knots to my 19, I sensed that things were about to change radically.*

I called the race office and asked them to find out what was happening. Minutes later they confirmed that there was indeed a problem on Hugo Boss *though Alex had not at this time requested any assistance. I told the race office that it was my intention to slow until such time as we could confirm that Alex was indeed OK. I would not normally do this, but something here was not right and at the speeds* Ecover *was doing, we were rapidly putting a big and difficult distance between each other. If I did need to turn around, the job of getting back was getting much harder by the minute.*

I put the deep reef in the mainsail, slowing the boat measurably but still averaging over 16 knots – then waited. Fifty minutes later David Adams called to tell me things had changed dramatically on Hugo Boss. *The keel head had snapped, the keel was swinging uncontrolled in the boat, which was now taking in water. It was just a matter of time before the situation turned from a dangerous one into a potentially fatal one. Alex was now asking for assistance and* Ecover *was the closest to render it.*

I put the phone down and looked at the B&G, which was showing that the wind was 42 knots. I climbed into the cockpit just as we screamed off a huge wave at 25 knots and I set about rigging the boat with storm sails to turn around. Twenty minutes later Ecover *was crashing through freezing waves at 9 knots on the reciprocal heading. Alex was 90 miles away and we had five hours before darkness set in.*

Ecover *did not enjoy this massive change of direction. The Fleet 77 sat com packed up immediately. Next the engine got up to its tricks again and with the batteries now desperately needing a charge, I was once more buried in the engine bay, covered in diesel as the boat lurched and crashed back to where we had just come from to the west. This time I had to fix the problem in a fully reliable manner since the engine would be needed to manoeuvre Alex on board.*

I ditched all advice, and rigged a jerry can filled with diesel as a gravity feed direct to the HP pump on the engine, skipping the fuel pump and secondary filter. The engine ran – and it now ran reliably. At last I could concentrate on preparing the boat and myself for the job of collecting Alex safely.

The wind moderated and headed me as I closed the distance. The sea state did not. If anything the waves got steeper and it became harder and harder to make progress so eventually I ended up with full sail as the ridge passed, then began reefing again as the breeze built back to 25 knots.

We were still not going to quite make the rendezvous in daylight but with accurate and regular information coming through my project manager Gringo from the race office we moved closer.

In the final few miles, Alex and I made contact over satphone and radio to make last small navigational adjustments.

Finally out of the blackest night imaginable, a flare shot into the air and in the glow I could see firstly Hugo Boss*'s mast then its masthead strobe light and finally its deck-level nav lights.*

I realised a transfer was too dangerous during the night. There was no question about that. If I lost sight of him during the transfer even for a moment – he would be gone. I dropped sail and tried to match his drifting course and speed.

While Alex slept, I fretted and tinkered with my engine, tested the controls and gathered my rescue kit, coiling down throw lines into buckets and in the end playing Solitaire on the PC. I was nervous about the transfer. At some point, it was clear that Alex might well end up in the water and in 5-degree C temperatures there would be no time for a screw-up.

Sunrise was at 0259 GMT and I called Alex to wake him. We both ate some food and generally got our acts together before he rigged in his survival suit and set himself up for me to come close.

The plan was that he would inflate his raft on his leeward side and jump in, taking some emergency supplies with him. He would then send a line across to me with his rocket-line thrower before casting himself adrift from Hugo Boss*. This was a good basic plan which meant he would never be unattached.*

I manoeuvered Ecover *under engine towards* Hugo Boss*. The controls were stiff because they had not been used for three weeks but otherwise all seemed OK. I experimented to see if I could drive the bows through the wind and waves. Nope. She would not go. I gunned the engine and – Bang!!! – the shear pin between the engine and drive leg failed. Now I had a reliable engine but with no ability to drive the propeller.*

I called Alex and just stopped him from jumping into the raft. Then I did possibly the quickest shear-pin change in history, even reducing the chance of a further failure by pushing the broken piece of pin into the slot and taping it up to give the whole thing twice the strength. Then we began again.

The first part went OK. He jumped into the raft and let a painter out so that he was 50 feet behind his boat. I positioned myself to leeward of both the raft and Hugo Boss. *Bringing the boats together would be a full-on disaster in the steep waves. He aimed the rocket thrower. I ducked – it looked like he was aiming at me! But the rocket line did not work. I grabbed my first pre-coiled down line and ran to the rail and did possibly the worst line throw imaginable. I turned and went around again.*

This time it looked better. I got a line to him but the throttle/gear control now would not work and I could not kill my speed or control the gearbox for ahead or astern. We dropped the line and I pulled some sail out to make another pass. By now he had dropped his line to Hugo Boss; *he could see the danger we would be in if the boats came together and realised that I needed some room to manoeuvre around him without getting any lines in the prop.* Hugo Boss *slowly headed away to the south looking low in the water but otherwise perfect – a deeply sad sight.*

Then I unfurled some headsail and we had another go. This time I got a line on him and he secured the raft but in the process the bows blew down and Ecover *began to sail too fast. A big wave threw us into a surf. Alex clung on desperately, injuring his hand in the process and crying out in pain and fright as the raft was being towed at 5 to 6 knots with the rope twisted around his hand. Looking for all the world like a doughnut skier, he moved his weight to the back of the raft but it still flooded with water. We dropped the line and round I went again.*

Perhaps the most bizarre image – which will stay with me – is the sight of Alex alone in his raft with Hugo Boss *a quarter mile distant, and in the steep seas the world's largest albatross sitting in the water just feet from Alex. This could have been almost funny but to me it began to look like a vulture moving in for the kill. This was just not happening . . .*

This time I took off most of the sail and used the engine which was now stuck permanently in 'ahead', leaping below to adjust the throttle setting under the sink and in the very last moment killing the engine completely with the kill switch in the nav station.

My approach was near perfect. The raft arrived on my bows and bounced down the hull which meant I was virtually able to pass Alex the line, which he fastened. I killed the engine and winched him back into the leeward side. Thank God. We had him!

We hugged as I welcomed him aboard and apologised for my shabby pick-up. 'I probably would have failed my Yachtmasters on that one,' I said. But we had him. What a fantastic feeling!!!

We took a couple of photos, grabbed his luggage out of the raft — we are not going to starve — and chatted and then chatted some more. The relief from both of us was tangible. As we talked, Hugo Boss, *now a mile away, disappeared from view. The boat was taking in water and this morning (25th) we heard that the Sat C had stopped transmitting —* Hugo Boss *had gone forever.*

Slowly we set about getting Alex sorted. I cut away his glove and we cleaned and dressed his hand injury which was painful but not too serious. He climbed out of his survival suit, we tidied up, drank some coffee then drank some more. Then we slowly set about getting moving. I unrolled some headsail and hoisted some mainsail, aiming the boat back towards Fremantle. Over the next two hours we cruised, talked, drank lots of tea and coffee — in 24 hours we had both been through the mill and back. Alex was deeply upset by the loss of his boat — but the main thing was he was safe.

I was not about to immediately charge back into the race full throttle — we had enough adrenaline in the past 24 hours to last us a good time

*yet and the race seemed distant and somewhat less important than
what we had just done. Alex was safe.*

No doubt there will be those who will say, with the benefit
of hindsight, Mike should have handled it differently, but
they weren't there. Mike was the man on the spot with a
very difficult task to undertake. It does not matter how he
did it. The only fact that matters is he did it.

Inevitably there needs to be a post-mortem when a boat
is lost. This was the first Open 60 to be lost for some years,
and then, as now, the problem was with the keel. Early
versions of the Open 60 design featured lead bulbs on the
keels that were dangerously light – about two tonnes, or
about a tonne lighter than the modern versions. This flaw,
that only a few naval architects and nautical engineers had
spotted, came to light in the 1996 Vendée Globe when four
boats capsized and would not right themselves. It resulted in
a complete review of safety in the Open 60s, and regulations
brought in shortly after required new builds to pass an
inversion test. The IMOCA 60 boats now are put through
the most rigorous tests before they can receive their certificate, which has led to a dramatic improvement in safety
standards.

Certainly these keels are cutting-edge and seem to be
forever 'works in progress', as we saw with the canting keels
on the VOR 70s in the last Volvo race, which created no
end of problems and shattered dreams.

I had had to change my keel because of cracks in the steel
structure, but one cannot help wondering whether the design
and construction has been taken just a little too far and if
maybe there should be a rethink to ensure a more robust
solution. These boats are built for round-the-world racing,

not racing around buoys, and the margin for error needs to be larger for this sort of event.

This failure also meant that those of us still in the race needed to look at our own keel arrangements, to check how secure they were. The problem was that none of us could give a satisfactory answer. The distance between the top of the keel and the pivot point is less than a metre, and below the pivot point is 4 metres of keel and then the bulb. The top of the keel, where the hydraulic rams are attached, is vulnerable to high strains all around its structure. But we are sailors, not engineers or designers, and therefore not qualified to say whether what we have is safe or not – although inevitably, at the back of our minds, there is always that nagging question: 'What happens if . . .'

The *Hugo Boss* keel was less than a year old, which is why the failure came as such a shock. Alex's boat was one of the best prepared for the 2006 Velux 5 Oceans race, and *Hugo Boss* was not a new or experimental boat. It was a well-tried one, with plenty of miles beneath its keel, so for the keel to break something was either slowly weakening or there must have been a sudden abnormal strain. We will never know the answer to that now.

It came as a great relief to hear that the rescue had been completed and Alex was safe, and I knew it wouldn't be long before he was out racing again. He was already planning on building a new boat.

The episode was another rescue in the annals of the race. It was part of a tradition that included the rescue of Tony Lush, who was picked up by fellow American Francis Stokes after his boat pitch-poled and sank between Africa and Australia, and Englishman Richard Broadhead beating back for three days to rescue Jacques de Roux, both in the 1982 race. In 1991 Bertie Reed picked up fellow South African John Martin after his boat hit an iceberg on the approach to Cape Horn. It is an axiom in these races that assistance will come from another competitor, and – apart from some excellent operations by the Royal Australian Navy – it usually has.

But for Mike and Alex, the drama of the hazardous rescue was not yet over. Mike takes up the story:

Six hours after the transfer, Ecover *was moving well again, the wind had built to match our reduced sailplan and we were seeing speeds of 15 to 20 knots. Still conditions were such that the boat was very much in control – I loaded the aft ballast – but moments later a squall hit us from astern. The wind jumped up from 25 knots, and sleet and snow accompanied a truly icy blast from Antarctica. The boat heeled over to 20 degrees so we altered the pilot to come down 10, released the vang (which had no load), and moved towards the mainsheet to take the pressure off the boat.*

Nothing unusual here but as I went to take hold of the sheet, something made me look up the rig and I was stunned when I saw this big explosion. It came from above the main spreader and sent a shower of carbon shards into the clouds. There was then a terrible grinding bang, which is a sound every skipper dreads. The mast had broken and my Velux 5 Oceans race was effectively over.

We were completely blown away. We could not believe all that had just gone down – it was too bizarre. Instead of rushing headlong into this new development, we ate the meal we had been preparing, then started a marathon 12-hour ordeal of cutting away the broken sections of Ecover's *beautiful mast and setting the boat up to continue sailing.*

This was mind-numbingly hard and disappointing. For me the competitive race was over. For Alex there was the loss of his boat and a totally misplaced feeling of guilt. But the work to make the boat safe and sailable remained. Alex volunteered to go aloft and spent a treacherous hour dangling with 20 feet of mast crashing around him. More squalls, more snow and an icy deck made working hugely difficult and dangerous. But working together, we achieved what would have ironically been completely impossible alone, and as dark descended on an extraordinary 48 hours I hoisted the staysail and we altered our course once more away from Fremantle and towards Cape Town in South Africa.

The weather is foul. There is 35 to 40 knots of searingly cold wind with icy squalls which have given both of us the first stages of frostbite in our fingers. We are resting, eating, sleeping and chatting about the future. Right now, we have few concerns other than the immediate ones.

We may have lost an expensive mast, we may also have lost our place in this race, but I would not trade any of it for what we have gained in getting Alex off Hugo Boss. Right now we might all be looking at a far more tragic outcome than a lump of broken carbon mast.

The two of them sorted out a jury rig and headed for Cape Town. We knew Alex was out of the event, and though we all hoped Mike might get his spare mast shipped out so he could rejoin the race, it seemed right now that in the space of one day we had lost two of the top three boats in the race. This left Bernard in a league of his own, and the rest of us wondering what we could do to cause an upset.

7. The Southern Ocean

As Mike and Alex headed towards Cape Town, the wind where I was began to back to the north-east and I was able to make some good headway towards the south. But I was soon faced with a difficult decision.

I needed to get further south and into the stronger westerly winds, but to do this I had to get the spinnaker up. Normally this would have posed no problem whatsoever. But the unreliability of the autopilots put me off. If they failed when I was flying 350 square metres of spinnaker, the results could be serious for me and the boat. I took what I thought was the safe option and stowed the kite away.

These attempts at self-preservation were in vain, though admittedly the results were not exactly serious. As I was stumbling about on deck that night, the mainsail swung across just as my bare foot landed on the main sheet, which tightened like a winched cable and ripped the nail off my left big toe.

From the amount of blood that spurted out around the deck, it was as if my leg had been completely severed. It was a mess, and it soon became clear that the nail had to be completely removed. I snipped it away with a pair of wire cutters – the next best thing to clippers – then cleaned the wound with whisky and bandaged it up. It did not hurt so much as create an inconvenience, but it healed well and soon ceased to be a concern.

I have been lucky with illness or injury at sea over the

years. When I started out on *Suhaili* in 1967, I was suffering
a severe attack of jaundice. I felt terrible. My skin was waxy
and yellow and my eyes and urine were both yellow, but
there wasn't much I could do apart from rest and drink
plenty of fluids. I did not go to a doctor as I knew the only
cure was rest, and I needed to get away. It flushed itself out
after a couple of weeks and I was fine. This time, I also
started out with a handicap – on the way to Bilbao before
the start of the race, I fractured my coccyx when I lost my
footing in the cockpit and fell down hard. It was the first
time ever in my life I had broken a bone – which is remarkable, considering some of my activities over the years – but
again, it was fine after a month or so.

After a month at sea I was at 30 degrees south, still 600
miles from the Southern Ocean. I saw Tristran da Cunha
on the charts a couple of days later, though it was 55 miles
away so there was no chance of a sighting. This was the
fourth time I had passed the island and still I have yet to set
eyes on it. Like St Helena and Ascension Island, Tristan da
Cunha, said to be the world's most isolated settlement, has
close associations with my former employers, the shipping
company British East India Company, though it has not
been used as a stopping point on the Europe to Far East
cargo route since 1869, when the Suez Canal was opened.

From those early days of commercial activity, however, a
small population of British citizens developed. They all had
to be evacuated to Southampton in 1961 when the volcano
erupted, but many returned and today there are about 300
living there, all descending from original settlers. Apparently,
there are seventy families sharing just eight surnames, including Glass, the first family to settle there in 1816. They
earn their living by tending cattle, growing potatoes or catch-

ing crayfish – or the Tristan rock lobster, as it is known. Last year, they celebrated the 500th anniversary of the island's discovery – it was first sighted in 1506 by a Portuguese chap called Tristao da Cunha, though he never bothered to actually step foot on the island, possibly because even now the waters around the island are so shallow at low tide – around 1.3 metres – that it is impossible to get a boat anywhere near.

It is quite small, less that half the size of the Isle of Wight, and is home to ten species of bird that are found nowhere else on the planet and which, like many species of seabird, face extinction. It is said that around 100,000 albatross drown each year, chasing bait on the billion hooks that are put out by international fishing vessels, and since they only ever produce one chick every two years it is easy to see why the species is so endangered.

The island is not exactly a tourist destination – no airport, no landing stage, no restaurants, and 66 inches of rain each year – though there are three guest houses and a shop, so if ever I were to find myself in close proximity in a shallow-draught boat, I would definitely go and explore.

I continued south-east to get to the Roaring Forties more quickly, because there the wind could be expected to be westerly most of the time and of good strength, but it was not until 1 December that *Saga Insurance* crossed the Greenwich Meridian and the 40th parallel and could officially be described as being in the Roaring Forties of the Southern Ocean.

The name was coined during the days when sailing ships came down to these latitudes on their way to Australia and New Zealand and from there, around Cape Horn, to Europe. With high pressure to the north and low pressure to the south in the southern hemisphere, the winds are predominantly from the west; they became stronger as one moves closer to the centre of the depressions and weaker as one approaches the high pressure.

The secret was to avoid either extreme and ideally keep in about 25 to 30 knots of westerly wind so a high speed could be maintained without the waves becoming large enough to force me to ease up.

In the days before satellite communications, it wasn't so easy to choose one's weather. The only indicator had been the barometer, and this would only tell when you had got too close to a depression, by which time it was too late to do anything about it. Today you can download weather files with predictions for up to ten days ahead, and choose a route that best suits the boat. This has made sailing in the Southern Ocean safer and faster.

Now we were into cooler conditions, which I relished, but there was a lot of rain about so everything was damp. It was still too warm to put on the heater, which would have dried things out, so damp things remained damp. Tough.

The day I had to wave goodbye to the last few drops of my precious whisky was a bad day. It had taken four and a half weeks to consume four bottles, which seems pretty abstemious. When working out my supplies, I had not allowed for medicinal usage, and when it came to cleaning and dressing the toe I decided my nursing efforts deserved to be rewarded with a tot. Then it seemed silly to leave a few scanty dregs in the bottom of the bottle, and it would have been a tragedy if the cork had come out and caused a spillage. Better to drink what was left and avoid a potential disaster.

The toe seemed fine although a little more sensitive,

probably because the nerves were sorting themselves out. It was still coated in several layers of antiseptic cream and safely nestled inside a sock inside a boot, so it was well protected for the moment and not causing me any trouble.

My speeds up to that point had been disappointing – single-figure territory mainly – but I soon began to get nice strong winds from the west and decided it was safe to change course to the south-east.

As we picked up the westerlies we began to get surges of up to 20 knots, but our average for the twenty-four hours was just over 10 knots. Every sailor tends to look at their top speeds, their surge or surfing speeds, as these are the exciting bits. In practice of course these are short-lived and misleading. I knew this phenomenon perfectly well, but the attractive surges did not stop me hoping for a higher average.

With these higher speeds came some worrying noises that I had not noticed before. I heard a new sound of rushing water as we reached high speed surges, which I thought might be the source of leaking in the sail locker. But when I looked, I could see no rising water levels there. Over the next two days I searched everywhere for the source of the leak, before finally coming to the conclusion that the water must be coming through a hole in the keel box.

Where the IMOCA measurer had pushed the keel right over, beyond the 40 degrees I think, the filler that is intended to keep the gap between keel and hull as small as possible had broken away. It was like a hose when we surged, and I could see it through the inspection hatch. All sorts of things start to vibrate, including the keel and rudders and in view of what had happened recently to Alex and Mike I began to wonder whether these vibrations were possibly doing damage.

Also there was always the danger that when surfing, a wave would slew the boat as she was rushing forward. If that occurred a broach was quite likely, and that could lead to a lot of damage. With all these ifs, buts and maybes going through my mind while the boat was wound up, and the worry that the autopilot might fail at any time, I found it hard to totally relax.

As we desperately tried to get south into the stronger winds, I needed as much weather information as I could find to help me maintain these good speeds. I sat down at the chart table and started loading up the weather program, but all of a sudden it started coming up with unfamiliar messages and refusing me access. It demanded that I generate a 'rescue license', or 'activate the software', which was not something I'd had to do before. I tried rebooting, but to no effect. The barrier would not go away, and there was no working around it since it demanded a key number that I didn't have. Neither did anyone else, in fact.

I gave up. No weather information. It was two days before someone came up with the idea that I should try removing the dongle – the small piece of hardware connected to the computer that authenticates the software – and reboot. This worked, but by then I had lost two days of weather information and, in all likelihood, the opportunity to make up some miles on the others up front.

I was in fourth place, still more than 5,000 miles from Fremantle and 4,000 miles behind Bernard, who was having to deal with Force 10 winds on the approach to the Australian west coast. Mike was still officially in third place but a few hours away from arriving in Cape Town, where he would decide whether to continue or not. Both Dalton and Unai were 500 miles away, but both seemed to be catching up.

This was the most frustrating night of the voyage so far. How was I expected to know that the removal of the dongle would solve the problem? I had never been told that and it was not in any instruction manual. It was not something the experts mentioned when they installed the program. Instead they told me how much I would like it and how easy it was to operate.

I reckoned this failure cost me about 400 miles, as that is what Dalton gained while I sailed straight into a small high that I had not known was going to develop. I averaged 5.5 knots for two days while he sailed round it.

It made me hanker for the old days, when there was none of this wizardry to confound us. We may not have known what weather was coming, but we could rely on the barometer, and just looking at the wind direction and clouds gave us a clue as to what was on the horizon. Now, when the clever programs we have become dependent on don't work, which is quite often, we waste hours trying to get them to operate, often with no success at all, and lose out to others whose programs are still functioning.

But one of the challenges of this experience was getting to grips with all the modern technology. However much I wished at that moment that I could uninvent these new systems, I was fully aware that my reason for being where I was, was to participate in the modern scene. It was sorted. Time to move on.

We all had to stay north of a waypoint that had been added by the race organisers to prevent us all diving further south where the winds were more favourable. It was put in to keep us closer to southern Africa and away from the likelihood of ice, so we were not about to complain, though I was desperate for more wind and found it rather depressing listening to slatting sails and chasing every wisp of wind to try and create movement.

Everyone else was making progress and the leaders were averaging 10 knots more than us. This was where I missed the windex, the little wind arrow at the masthead which blew off soon after leaving La Coruña. It allowed me to see exactly what the wind was really doing, whereas the electronic instruments were damped. I was also missing a nice mainsail shape, which we had not had since the battens broke.

No one enters the Southern Ocean without a certain amount of trepidation. The Roaring Forties earned their name from the ferocity of the westerly gales and storms that roar through them throughout the year – obviously more so in winter than summer, but they can still appear in mid-summer. When they do blow they are likely to build up a far larger sea than almost anywhere else on the planet. The reason is simple. The Southern Ocean is the only ocean that continues uninterrupted all the way around the world. Every other ocean has land to east and west of it, but, except for a constriction at Cape Horn, nothing bounds the Southern Ocean to east and west.

Its boundaries to the north are the southern tips of Africa, Australia and South America, and Antarctica to the south. This lack of land barriers means that there is nothing to stop a depression carrying on for a greater distance than anywhere else, which can have the effect of building up much larger seas.

A 30-metre-high wave is not unusual in these storms, and when one of those waves heaps up and starts to break at its crest, a small boat in its path is very vulnerable. My first experience of these waves had come in *Suhaili*, when I saw one looming astern. I slammed the hatch and sat down below, braced against anything I could jam myself against. The wave crashed over us and *Suhaili* began to rush forward, but luckily I had streamed long warps astern and they braked her. Moments later she shook the water off and carried on, but if left me quite shaken.

These rogue waves have to be seen to be believed. Someone once likened them to the white cliffs of Dover, and indeed some of them in the Southern Ocean are the same height as a ten-storey building. Research data taken from offshore oil platforms has shown that they occur more frequently than was thought, and it is now considered possible they were the cause of the loss of a number of vessels over the years. I would not like to have to face too many waves like that whatever ship I was in, and the idea of encountering one in an Open 60 did not fill me with enthusiasm.

But it felt good to get going on the long 5,000-mile run across the bottom of the world, through the second most deserted part of the globe, to Fremantle – 'running our Easting down', as it used to be known in the days of square riggers.

The only inhabited parts of this area are a South African base on Marion Island and small research stations on the French-owned Crozet and Kerguelen Islands further on. Apart from that the region is only inhabited by bird life, including the giant albatross and the tiny petrel. Whales used to abound but I have not seen one here for nearly forty years, and so far had not seen any on this trip. In some ways, after our collision with a whale on the way to Canada, this was a relief, but it is sad to think that they have been so reduced by overhunting.

When the first Southern Ocean gale started to blow, I welcomed it as I was desperate to get moving properly again. Unlike the storm in the Bay of Biscay, this time we were running away from the wind, and waves and the autopilots would be responsible for holding us downwind and down-wave. To slew sideways across the front of a wave was asking for trouble. There was every chance we would be rolled and lose the mast.

Knowing the lightness and speed of the Open 60, the considered view is that you should keep up enough sail to run fast, but how fast was a safe fast?

I had had no experience of sailing one of these machines in these conditions, so everything I did was experimental. I reduced sail to a fully reefed mainsail and storm jib, but even that seemed a bit much at times.

Generally, though, we were underpowered. You could feel it even though she was handling well and making about 10 knots. This was the price that had to be paid for learning, and I was content for the time being to let her run on like this as there was less risk if the autopilot failed.

On *Enza*, a 92-foot catamaran which weighed the same as *Saga Insurance,* we had been able to outrun the waves with ease. In fact the greatest danger we faced was from going so fast – we would overtake the wave in front and pile into the rear face of the one beyond. We did that once as Peter Blake was coming on deck and the boat de-accelerated from 28 knots to a dead halt in a split second. Peter was flung back two metres and hit his back nastily on the chart table. We had him confined to his bunk in considerable pain for ten days, and later discovered he had chipped a vertebrae.

On *Suhaili*, which weighed the same as *Enza* and *Saga Insurance* but was only 32 feet long as opposed to 92 and 60 feet respectively, this had not been an option. Initially I had just taken down all sail, but she tended to lie beam on to the wind and waves, and on one occasion a wave hit so heavily I thought she would break up if I continued like that. After some thought I put out a long rope astern in a bight, so its ends were made fast aboard and its loop extended some 300 feet behind us. This acted as an easy sea anchor, and she had swung round stern to wind on it immediately.

From then on this was how I handled all bad weather, but that is relative as well. What is bad weather for a small boat is perfectly manageable for a larger one. This is another of the reasons why the larger boats in use these days make such faster passages.

In the 1977 Whitbread race, with *Heath's Condor*, on the leg from Cape Town to Auckland we had tried to outrun the waves, but she was not a directionally stable boat and tended to slew round broadside on to the oncoming waves once she gathered speed and then go onto her side. We kept breaking spinnaker guys, and as I was the only member of the crew who knew how to splice wire I found myself spending a lot of time below working at the vice. Eventually all of them needed resplicing so I got the Genoa and Yankee set goosewinged, one out on either side, instead of a spinnaker, and the result was dramatic.

The boat became very easy to steer just off downwind, and during the next twenty-four hours we covered nearly 20 more miles under what the young crew referred to as my 'grandfather' rig. Both Peter Blake and I were a lot happier with the new arrangement, and we took line honours for the leg, a day ahead of *Great Britain II*, so we can't have had it all wrong. What was even better was that since the boat was handling so well I could now let all the crew steer, rather than just the five experienced helmsmen we had been using before.

Peter was mate on that trip. His next circumnavigation would be as skipper of his own boat and he eventually went on to win every leg in the 1989 Whitbread race, which was something no one else ever did. He then added the America's Cup to his considerable list of trophies and accolades.

In this race, Bernard looked like he too would be adding some silverware to his burgeoning collection. After forty-two days and twenty-three hours at sea, he crossed the finish line in Fremantle to be met on the pontoons by a group of local aborigines, who danced for him and played their didgeridoos. He had sailed an excellent leg, though 700 miles from the end he had run into a storm that was just as bad as the one in Biscay, with winds that averaged 45 knots over a twelve-hour period but topped out at 70.

In the middle of all this, Bernard found that a halyard, which had broken the day before, had tied itself in a knot with the mainsail halyard. He had no option but to climb the 'bloody' mast, as he put it, to cut it free, which took some guts.

But Bernard had become renowned for his guts, despite being very small and quite wiry. He had built *Cheminées Poujoulat* himself, quite literally with his own bare hands, and launched her in 2000. When he started the Velux 5 Oceans, he knew the boat well and had a very good record with her. In 2002, he won the Around Alone despite having to make a pit stop in the Falklands to fix a problem with his canting keel. He had taken the forty-eight hour penalty and then opened up the throttle to take line honours at the end of the leg in Brazil.

Two years later, he participated in the 2004 Transat and

was racing in during the second half of the race when a series of depressions swept through the fleet, dismasting two of the leading boats and causing Bernard's keel to detach completely. *Cheminées Poujoulat* turned upside down when he was 400 miles from the coast of Newfoundland. The incident caused great alarm, since we had not seen an Open 60 inversion since the late 90s, when stability problems led to three capsizes, all of them in the Southern Ocean, during the 1996–7 Vendée Globe. Fortunately, this proved to be something completely different, but for Bernard the result was the same. He was picked up by a tanker and reluctantly taken off to St John's, Newfoundland.

A week later he returned and, amazingly, located and salvaged the boat. Typically, he volunteered to make the dangerous dive beneath the boat to cut away the mast and rigging, which said much about his courage and determination.

I had been immensely impressed by Bernard in the 2002 Around Alone race, and once again he was proving to be a formidable opponent. He is quiet, very organised and efficient, and a very steely competitor, although he had suffered a series of setbacks in the previous four years. His keel issues in the Transat ruled him out of the Vendée Globe later that year, and in the Calais Round Britain race in 2005 he was again forced to retire after damaging his daggerboard in a collision.

He was a member of Bruno Peyron's crew on the multi-hull *Orange II* which hurled round the world in 2006 in fifty days and sixteen hours to take the Jules Verne Trophy, knocking almost fifteen days off our time in *Enza*.

Going into this race, I felt Bernard had the bit between his teeth as far as proving himself in *Cheminées Poujoulat*, and for that reason, and because he is one of the toughest professionals in the business, I felt he would be the man the others had to beat.

On the same day that Bernard won the first leg, Mike announced his retirement from the race. *Ecover* had arrived in Cape Town under jury rig, and after a few beers and a steak Mike had sat down with his team and sponsors to work out the costings involved in shipping in another mast, which were considerable. He was also worried about being so far behind the rest of the fleet, which not only ruled him out of contention for a podium place but placed him in a degree of danger since there would be no support nearby if he were to get into further difficulty. It must have been a difficult decision for him, but he had to do what he felt was best, and after such a traumatic time rescuing Alex and then seeing his own boat fail, no one could blame him for opting out.

I still had 4,000 miles to go, but having spent a few days in the Southern Ocean was running comfortably and fast before a Force 7 wind of 30 knots and feeling in control.

But suddenly, for no apparent reason, the boat slowed. I leaped up on deck to see what the problem was. All the sails were setting properly, which was baffling. Then I noticed a rope trailing astern. I looked round to see what might have gone over the side, but all my ropes were coiled where I had left them. I took another look aft and realised I was looking at a fishing line of about 25 mm diameter which had caught on the keel or rudders. No wonder our speeds were right down.

I switched on the hydraulic rams on the keel and swung it over so I could see the bulb from the deck, and sure enough, there was the line caught round the keel just above the bulb.

Immediately I dropped the sails to try and keep the boat still and tied a knife to a length of batten to give me the reach I needed to free the line. This proved quite impossible as, although the boat had no sail set, she was still drifting in the 30-knot winds and the batten had too much resistance.

Next, I attached a plastic water bottle to a line and pushed it down beneath the fishing line so I would be able to lasso it and winch it up to the surface, where I could cut it. Again this did not work, although I thought it might later when the wind and seas subsided. So then I tried tying a line to a bent piece of metal, which I lowered and hooked round the fishing line.

This caught, and I began to winch the line to the surface, but the weight was too great for the hook, which unfortunately straightened out. I had a kedge anchor which would have been strong enough, but I was worried that if I used that, with the boat rolling sharply I might put one of the anchor flukes through the hull.

These attempts took all day. We were effectively anchored until I could get the line free, and although the wind was easing it was now getting dark. My concern was that after Alex Thomson's keel had broken, mine might do the same, as it was not designed to take the strain of effectively being an anchor bollard aggravated by the boat's rolling. I made a meal and poured myself a drink to focus my thoughts.

If the wind continued to ease, one of the methods I had tried might work. If it didn't, I had to try something more radical, which was to go into the water with a knife – and this, the more I thought about it, was what I was going to have to do.

I curled up in my sleeping bag for some rest, but did not get off to sleep. I was too apprehensive about what I was about to undertake.

But as soon as it became light, I pulled out my Henri-Lloyd one-piece wet-weather gear, which was meant to be waterproof, and put it on over a set of thermal underwear. The survival suit, which we all carried, offered more protection but it was also more buoyant, which would have prevented me from diving. The water temperature was 4 degrees Celsius, which was pretty cold, so I knew I had to get a few things in place before I went in, otherwise I would be getting myself into a lot of trouble.

The main danger was that my exposed hands would cease to function if I remained in the water for too long, so I had to make it easy for myself to get back on board. In the 1977 Whitbread, one of our crew on *Condor* went over the side, and as we were recovering him a line also went overboard and got tangled around the propeller. On that occasion I had a wet suit which kept my body warm, but my hands and face had frozen very quickly, to the extent that I had no feeling in my fingers after a couple of minutes and could not use them. If that happened this time, I was worried about how I would pull myself back on board. But the job had to be done. We could not remain stuck like this indefinitely and if another gale came along, we might well lose the keel or, at the very worst, be smashed up.

I ran the tail of the main sheet out through the grab handle by the escape hatch in the transom, so it was close to the water, and then tied it round my waist. Gingerly I went over the stern and dropped into the sea.

It was cold but not freezing. The suit made movement difficult, but slowly I swam out to where I could see the fishing line near the surface and dived down. I made no headway at all, mainly because there was too much air trapped in the suit.

Back at the surface, I put my fingers under the neck seal, released air from inside the suit, and then dived down again. This time I made more progress but still could not get close to the line.

I swam further from the boat, to the full extent of the main sheet, which was about 60 feet, plus a further 40 feet on the messenger I had brought with me. I then noticed that one part of the fishing line had broken, but because it was wrapped so tightly around the other part it would not slip free.

I dived again and this time managed to get hold of the tail of the broken line. I rested on the surface for a minute while I got my breath back, and was able to look at my poor boat rolling heavily about 100 feet away. She appeared very small in the immensity of the ocean.

Three albatrosses flew in close circles around me. The countless stories I had heard of seamen who had fallen overside being attacked by these huge birds started to resonate through my head. I didn't want these three to see me as a potential lunch option. Their beaks look vicious, and any bird that has a 3-metre wingspan has to be considered dangerous in its own element. Clearly, this was not the place to dawdle, so I swam back to the full extent of the main sheet, tied the messenger to the freed fishing line, and climbed back on the boat, which was fairly straightforward since my hands were still mobile.

I winched in the messenger until the end of the line came inboard and this, I was relieved to see, brought the main part of the fishing line with it. I cut it with a hacksaw. There was still rope around the keel which could foul the rudders, so I started to unwind the fishing line until it was possible to pull it clear of the keel.

Finally we were free, after almost twenty hours of being tethered. Before going below to get out of the suit, which had kept me dry throughout, I set the mainsail and jib and got back to racing.

We had lost about 230 miles and I wanted to regain those as quickly as possible. Lady Luck, however, was not being kind. I had carried on working on my broken battens, repairing them as they broke and having to fix them again as each repair failed. Each time we lost miles, since the mainsail had to be dropped before I could extricate the battens from their pockets. I finally achieved a more reliable fix, with long splints lashed across the broken parts, but I was running out of bits of batten and eventually had to make a decision as to which ones the sail could best do without.

By the next day I was rested and feeling a bit more positive, but while I was stopped Dalton had passed me. I needed to get moving to correct that.

It was a lovely day, with a strong robust wind from the north-west. The trouble was that if the boat swung about towards the wind, the wind would become stronger. This had happened early on and the autopilot opted out because the strain was too great.

This, I thought, was not a failure of the autopilot, but a matter of putting the boat beyond its load limits – and this was down to sail balance, which was my call. The answer was to reduce sail, but before I did that I thought I'd steer for a bit myself. A 'bit' turned into seven hours.

The difference between me and the autopilot was that I

was able to anticipate. I could also see when we were going to run straight down the waves and risk pushing the bow of the boat into the wave in front.

When this happened, a tsunami of water would crash down the deck. So I steered her slightly off downwave, positioning her more across the waves. This meant I was lengthening the gap between wave crests and reducing the risk of 'burrowing'. Anyway, I sat there steering happily, making good progress and thoroughly enjoying myself in a Force 7 with building seas.

The news came through that Kojiro had also finished the leg. His time was a little over forty-six days, which was a magnificent effort in a boat almost as old as mine. Others may have started the race with faster boats but you have to finish, and that is what Koji had done.

He was making a second appearance in the race, having competed in the 2002–3 Around Alone where he showed himself to be a gutsy and competitive performer. In that race he was sailing a 40-footer but as soon as the race was finished he had returned to Japan and set about collecting sponsorship, ideally to build a new Open 60 but, if not, to charter or buy an older one. In the end he bought the old *Temenos*, a well-tried boat that had finished fifth in the 2000 Vendée Globe race, and prepared her methodically for the race.

He had originally worked as a fisherman but started to build up his considerable sailing experience when he joined the shore crew of the legendary Tokyo taxi driver, Yukoh Tada, a class winner in the first BOC Challenge in 1982. After Tada's death Kojiro refitted the boat, renamed it *Spirit of Yukoh* and in 1994 sailed it solo non-stop around the world in 176 days. He had taken part in a number of other competitive sailing events, always showing huge determination coupled with professionalism and a delightful manner.

Although the age of Kojiro's boat meant he was never rated as a favourite to win, the others knew he would be after them. By finishing three days after Bernard and beating both Mike and Alex, he proved that he was indeed a serious contender. I was pleased for him, but that emotion was overshadowed by my disappointment at being so far behind when the front runners stepped ashore.

I was now beginning to doubt I would get to Fremantle by Christmas, so the gap between us was going to be close to three weeks.

That was too much to expect to be able to close during the rest of the race. Kojiro probably had second overall in the bag, provided he did not break anything. I envied him his additional time in Fremantle. I could have used that, not just for repairs but for a bit of a rest. Dalton was now some 80 miles ahead of me and Unai 800 behind.

The batten repairs were beginning to fray again. One bit of broken batten had poked out from the middle of the sail through its pocket – and was likely to catch the runners at any time and tear the sail further.

In the next gale it did just that. As the wind rose, I decided to take in the first reef as a precaution, because I had had two failures of the autopilot in the previous thirty-six hours and didn't like to keep too much sail up. But the sail jammed, and when I shone the torch up the mast I discovered one of the broken battens had extended out through a hole in its pocket halfway between the luff and leech and was caught behind a shroud.

The sail could not be lowered, so I had to rehoist the sail and haul it in on the sheet to get the batten clear, then drop it quickly before it had time to think about getting jammed again.

This was potentially very serious. A jammed mainsail could cause real problems in a squall and make the boat uncontrollable. Once set with one reef in the main and the jib up, we went eastwards nicely and began to recover some lost ground, but not for long.

We were roughly the equivalent position relative to the equator as Nantes in France, but that night brought us snow and hail accompanied by wind squalls exceeding 40 knots. The first arrived just after midnight and flung us right over. The autopilot tried but could not hold her and she gybed with a frightening crash.

The damaged battens that held the mainsail's shape were now split into even smaller pieces. I struggled to the mast and let go the main halyard, but another section of batten had caught round a runner and the sail refused to come down.

It took more than an hour to deal with that. I took in the jib and for a while kept under main alone as the squalls came at about hourly intervals.

It is impossible to race seriously in these conditions because you cannot keep the boat at her best performance. You have to reduce sail for the extreme gusts, but then between the squalls you are short of power. It takes about fifteen minutes to put in or take out a reef, assuming everything goes smoothly. So when squalls are coming through at hourly intervals or less, it is difficult to work out how much sail you need to make sure you can maintain speeds when the wind eases.

With the boat eventually comfortable, I made some tea. I put the cup on the step inside the hatch and wrote up my log book. I could hear the slight hissing rattle that heavy rain makes on the roof, but when I looked round I could see hail coming in through the hatch and into my cup.

We ended up with a light covering of hail and snow all over the boat, which seemed bizarre this close to mid-summer down here, but the wind was a south-westerly coming in from Antarctica.

An hour later we had another vicious squall and I decided to take in the third reef. I eased the halyard again, but once more the sail would not drop. This time a slider had come off the track and jammed behind the Lazy-Jacks that hold up the boom. It took more than an hour to clear, during which we had another white visitation and it turned extremely cold.

Once comfortable, we ran before the gale with three reefs in the mainsail and the Solent set. My speed varied between 8 and 18 knots, depending on the squall situation. This was fine and everything was under control, but I was regretting my decision not to call in at Cape Town and obtain new battens. Without sufficient material to repair all of them, I had to decide, when conditions improved, which ones were essential as opposed to desirable.

The next day provided the opportunity, and I spent twenty-one hours sorting out the problem. We could sail, but not efficiently, and I resented each mile lost because of the poor shape of the mainsail.

But at least I had removed the danger of the sail jamming, and I was relieved to have completed the job when I did because the next day brought another series of very violent squalls.

This was the nastiest squall to date, though it hadn't looked any different when I saw it approaching. The boat luffed up and heeled over 60 degrees, and the noise was deafening, with the howling of the wind being drowned by the clatter and crashing of the sails. The helm was hard over and the sheets eased but she still would not obey. I hung on to a winch in the cockpit for dear life, looking away from the wind to prevent the hail from stinging my eyes. I could not protect my hands and the hail felt as if it was flaying the skin off them and my face. I was grateful for the protection of a beard. I could see the surface of the sea slightly flattened and white with hail and spindrift.

I glanced at the wind strength. It was 55 knots, and within a few moments, and to no one's great surprise, the auto-pilot gave up under the strain. It could do no more. With all the sails flapping, I decided there was nothing more to be done until the gust passed.

In the meantime I was still hanging grimly on to my winch. The squall passed after what was probably no more than a couple of minutes but seemed an age. The pelting hail and wind eased and the boat began to come more upright and then finally responded to the helm. Then she swung down-wind and we were under some sort of control again.

There was a price to pay, though. The shaking of the mast in the squall by the thrashing sails had dislodged the masthead wind-sender. It fell down, held by its cable, which did not last for long. There was no question of going aloft to fix it, because it had smashed itself to pieces in minutes.

So now I had no wind information – which meant I had as much instrumentation on *Saga Insurance* as I had had on *Suhaili* thirty-eight years previously. I did the same now as I had then, which was to go round the boat tying on short lengths of wool that would fly with the wind and give me some idea of direction if nothing else.

That was the most powerful squall in a day of repeated squalls, and if they were going to continue at that strength the large headsail had to go. It was too powerful, and hauled the bow round into the wind.

I went forward, hoisted the storm jib and then turned downwind to roll up the Solent sail. The surges with the gusts were less urgent, and I wondered at what point the gale would cease to build or whether I would end up having to drop the mainsail and ease right down to just the storm jib, but we were not there yet.

My speeds were down a bit. It was a pity, but the boat felt more comfortable and she was much less liable to luff up, decreasing the potential for damage.

This race was about getting to the finish line. If you can get there faster than the others that is a bonus, but first you have to finish. The Southern Ocean is the toughest test of a man and boat there is. To come through it when it is in a vile mood such as this, you have to forget racing and just think about survival.

I had learned that the key to survival was to get the boat so she felt comfortable and not over-pressed, then wait for conditions to improve without sustaining damage. Damage takes time to rectify, and that is when races are lost. Once the boat was comfortable I could relax and even get some sleep, knowing if things changed the different motion would awaken me.

Looking at the seas, I realised that thirty-eight years ago I would have been under a tiny storm jib, and now I had nearly 700 feet of warp streamed out astern in those conditions. It is the difference of the type of boat and size. *Saga Insurance* is the same weight as *Suhaili*, but being so much faster she was safer if she ran with the waves. *Suhaili* could never have done that, so there was no choice but to get her stable to the waves and just sit tight until the bad weather had passed through. In those conditions I used to get my best sleep. There was nothing else I could do.

We passed about 50 miles south of Marion Island and Prince Edward Island during the night. This was the fifth time I had passed but I have never seen either. The South Africans have a research station on Marion. The next islands were the Crozets, a French territory which I sighted at about 20 miles to my north. The whole place is pretty barren, since the strong winds exceeding 50 knots on more than a hundred days every year have stripped the land of all its vegetation. No one lives there apart from the fellows who operate the research station.

The climate is interesting and indicative of the weather to be expected in the Southern Ocean, with some 20 metres of rain a year. Temperatures range from 3.61 C in winter to a sweltering 7.91 C in summer, and most years the sun shines for around sixty hours. Penguins and seals breed there, which provides food for killer whales, and pigs and goats were introduced at one stage but have since been exterminated. In the past sailors have become stranded there through shipwreck, but it is possible to survive. One crew lasted seven months before being rescued.

Mice were introduced by sealers a century ago, and in 1949 five cats were introduced to deal with the mice. By 1977 the cat population had reached 3,700, and by the time a campaign of extermination had commenced the petrel population had almost disappeared. But the good news is

that there are now four types of albatross that use the islands
as a breeding ground. The chicks are the size of Staffordshire
bull terriers.

The seabirds provided me with plenty of entertainment
because they were always around the boat, ranging from the
giant wandering albatross down to the inches-long storm
petrel. At times there were more than a hundred wheeling
around the boat, the albatrosses gliding effortlessly in their
constant search for food while the smaller birds darted
about inches from the wave tops with one leg extended
downwards, acting as a sensor to keep them clear of the
surface of the sea.

The squalls eased overnight, but the barometer showed no
signs of rising until mid-morning on the 11 December, when
the wind increased to a Force 8 from the north-west, a good
direction as I could steer due east, which suited my plans. I
had increased sail when the wind eased but took it in again
as it reached gale force, in case there was another squall. In
a way these strong winds were a good thing as I didn't need
much mainsail, and I could not set more than the third reef
anyway because of broken battens.

The good news was that the north-westerlies did not
bring hail, which meant that getting around on deck was not
so hazardous. Hail makes the deck slippery and I didn't like
skidding, as I had the other morning when it was covered
with the stuff.

I had actually closed the access hatch the previous night
for the first time and debated putting on the cabin heater.
But the heater used diesel, which was needed for the generator, so I did some deep breathing exercises to warm up
instead.

Most days, with the heavy rain squalls, I was able to collect fresh water, but there was too much sea spray around so the water was undrinkable on this occasion. As I still had 12 gallons of fresh water left and, on average, my consumption was a litre a day, I was not worried by this.

One of my major worries at the time was that I could not find any more instant coffee amongst my stores, so had to change to beef tea as an alternative. Fortunately I still had plenty of real tea. My supplies were based on an arrival in Fremantle on 14 December or thereabouts, so there were bound to be some shortages as we crawled our way towards the finish.

Slowly I ran my easting down – the old description for making one's way eastwards. The longitude crept up, not as fast as I would have liked, but it slowly increased. I had set my heart on arriving in Fremantle in time for the third Ashes Test match between England and Australia at the WACA in Perth, but there was now no chance of that. Saga Insurance had kindly found me some tickets for the match, which, considering they were as rare as hen's teeth, was some achievement. But when the first ball was bowled I was still 2,500 miles away, which was not close enough even to pick it up on the radio.

On the 16 December I passed north of the Kerguelen Islands, another French territory where there is a small base, which must be one of the most isolated and cut-off places on earth. Efforts were made to introduce sheep to the islands a hundred years ago but they failed, and the only successful commercial activity was the hunting of elephant seals until the stocks became so diminished it was no longer profitable.

Lying at 49 degrees south latitude, three degrees further south than Prince Edward Island, the Kerguelen Islands

were a mark of the course and we were required to leave
them to our south. This was to keep us from going too far
south, where rescue would be very difficult. This had
become an issue in round-the-world races ever since Tony
Bullimore lost his keel and had to be rescued by the Australian Navy. There is a requirement to have rescue services
available, but that does not mean their task has to be made
difficult. They are a welcome safety net, but one best unused.

With the passage taking so much longer than expected, I
was becoming a bit concerned that I had enough diesel fuel
to keep the Volvo engine going. As this was my most
effective source of battery charging, if I did run short of fuel
there would be no autopilot or communications, except for
very short periods when the solar panels produced a few
amps of charge, which was insufficient for continuous usage.
I could hand-steer, of course, to reduce electrical consumption, and because I enjoyed it I was already spending quite
long periods at the helm – but any enjoyment would quickly
fade if it became a necessity.

Kerguelen could offer a small quantity of fuel if necessary,
but I hoped I would have enough to see me through to
Christmas and decided not to stop, although I was curious
to see what the islands looked like.

Graham Dalton did stop there since, like me, he seemed
to be having a string of problems and he needed to make
repairs. He was running short of fuel and needed to repair
a torn headsail, but the forty-eight-hour penalty meant that
he was unlikely to reach Australia until New Year's Eve.

It was proving to be a difficult race for the fifty-four-
year-old Kiwi, who is the elder brother of Grant. He had
dreamed of sailing solo around the world ever since he
watched Francis Chichester complete his circumnavigation

in 1967, and was influenced by a teacher at school who told him 'The dreams you will have as boys will be the strongest of your life; never let them fade.'

He did not let the dream fade. In the 2002 Around Alone race he competed in a new Open 60 sponsored by HSBC but was dismasted after rounding Cape Horn. He sold that boat, but clearly felt the race was unfinished business because he put together a new project for an Open 50, named *A Southern Man AGD*. Although the only 50-footer in the fleet, Dalton reckoned that having a boat 10 foot smaller than the others could give him an advantage in some circumstances. The sail sizes were smaller and therefore easier to handle, so he would be able to sail more efficiently.

He was doing the race in memory of his son Tony, who tragically died of cancer in December 2006 at the age of twenty-two. It was an emotional journey for him. Having lost my wife Sue to cancer three years ago, I knew exactly what he was going through.

Graham's decision to stop at Kerguelen meant I moved up into third place overall, with 1,200 miles to go. There was now nothing between us and Australia. I had deliberately avoided looking at Fremantle while it seemed so many miles away, but now it became my next objective.

To reach it, I had either to go through the high-pressure system to our north, or duck under it until I was south of Cape Leeuwin, where I could expect a more favourable wind. The latter seemed the obvious choice but downloading the weather onto the computer and then asking the program to choose the quickest route told me that the high would move and give me a speedier arrival if I went north now.

Assuming the program to be more clever than me, I

headed north. It turned out to be a mistake. I had assumed that the program was based on an average Open 60's performance; what I had not appreciated was that when the computer weather program was installed, it had been told to collect data from my instruments, which would create a polar diagram that would show the boat's performance for every relative wind direction. Unfortunately the installer had not asked me about this. If he had, I would have pointed out that with a rotating mast the readings would not be accurate.

The result was the program chose a course that had us sailing directly into the wind, something I did not notice for three days, and by then it was too late. I was becalmed.

Inevitably, when the wind did come up, being north of the high, it was from the east, so not only did I have little wind, I had headwinds again. All hope of reaching Fremantle for Christmas vanished.

I spent Christmas Day feeling quite relaxed. Lunch was boil-in-the-bag chicken tikka masala followed by a mini Christmas pudding. Loyal toasts had to be drunk with orange juice, since I had run out of wine and whisky.

I sang along to the Hallelujah Chorus and spoke to my daughter and the grandchildren, who were having a jolly Christmas in Essex. I had not planned to be at sea for Christmas, but they had stowed a present just in case – a book, *Does Anything Eat Wasps?*, which gave me something to read over my orange juice.

I recalled that on Christmas Day thirty-eight years before I'd felt rather anxious about spending that time on my own. I had always either been with my family or had spent it on the British India ships, and it had been sociable and fun. As it was, I had been at sea on my own for six months and was closing in on Cape Horn, which I was sure would provide me with a few new challenges. I drank a toast with whisky, if I remember rightly, and belted out my favourite carols before sitting down to a feast of stewed steak out of a tin with potatoes and peas, washed down by a bottle of wine that Mike had given me. I then gave myself frightful indigestion with a plum duff of my own making.

On the 28 December, with less than 200 miles to go to Fremantle, I tacked deliberately close to land so that I could pick up a radio station and listen to the Boxing Day Test match in Melbourne. It worked a treat, and hearing the voice of Jonathan Agnew, the BBC cricket correspondent, came as a very pleasant surprise, though what he was reporting did not make for happy listening. England were well on their way to a fourth consecutive Ashes defeat and any hopes of salvaging some national pride were long gone.

After a marathon sixty-seven days at sea, I passed north of Rottnest Island and headed in towards the finish line in Fremantle, crossing just after sunset. A fleet of boats were there to greet me. Some of them had brought cigarettes and beer, which was much appreciated.

I had to hand-steer *Saga Insurance* across the line as once again the autopilot had failed. We were third to finish, so we got a podium position, but the gap between second and third was huge and unlikely to be reduced in the subsequent legs.

My new shore crew of Simon Clay (nicknamed 'Lovely') and Pete Cummings boarded the moment I crossed the line and helped me to get the sails down. By this time the only way to drop the mainsail was by using a downhaul taken to a winch. We headed in towards the Fremantle Sailing Club, where a fantastic reception awaited. Bernard and Koji both came to meet me, and Mike and Alex had also flown in to pass on their heartfelt congratulations. I was happy to see them. Thinking about the 'what ifs' in our game is a dangerous exercise, but we were all very relieved that an eventful leg had been concluded with a round of smiles and warm embraces.

I was tired and ready for a break. We had sailed halfway round the world with a series of aggravating problems that should not have happened. Already, Lovely had drawn up a schedule to sort them out, but we only had two weeks to get the boat sorted before the next and even longer leg around Cape Horn to Norfolk, Virginia, USA. Before then, I had some sleep and fun to catch up on.

8. Cape Leeuwin to Cape Horn

With a strong team in place, part professional and part volunteers, we got a lot of work done in Fremantle. We had rented two houses, very close to each other and a short walk from the Fremantle Sailing Club, where the race was being hosted.

The shore crew had been in Fremantle for three weeks by the time I got in, and my new shore manager, Simon Clay, had already planned our programme and had the team ready to start work. He was well organised and thorough, and any Open 60 questions that stumped him were referred to another new crew member, Pete Cummings. Like Lovely, Pete had worked on Mike Golding's *Ecover* campaign for four years, driving the sail development programme. Prior to that Pete had worked with North Sails on Team GBR's Olympic sails design and production in Athens 2004, so came strongly recommended, with excellent contacts in the Open 60 and Open 40 markets, and had a thirst that, like that of the rest of us, knew few bounds.

Pete's wife Katie was responsible for our logistics, so she sourced all our suppliers and made all our purchases while we were in Fremantle. She is only a wee thing but punched above her weight and quickly got things running with almost military precision. This new role of logistics had been a bit of an anathema to me – I had always done my own shopping and organisation, and was not at all convinced that our campaign needed this extra pair of hands. Paying a woman to go shopping, to my mind, was an expense we did not need.

But I had been persuaded, and seeing her in operation, I'm not sure how we would have managed without her. Whatever we asked of her, she delivered speedily and efficiently, whether it was finding a local sail loft that could do a job without charging us a fortune, picking up friends from the airport or sorting out our visas. She saved us a lot of time and money, and after initial resistance I became a convert to the logistics cause.

For the first time I also had some help with my media commitments, as Sophy Williams was with us, having been appointed by my sponsors Saga for the purpose. Her background was in motor sport and sailing, and she quickly had all the media requests organised. It was a hard task, with many demands for interviews, but we managed most of them, just missing one or two that coincided. It was a huge contrast to Bilbao, where I had had no one looking after this aspect and had been overpressured as a result. Sophy fitted in immediately and became a valued member of the team. It was good to have this important function in smart and caring hands.

Dilip was able to get posted to Fremantle by the Indian Navy for the stay as part of his learning experience. He, Tim and Huw, who had all been a vital part of the volunteer team in Gosport, had made it to Australia and were getting as much out of their experience as possible. Huw had been rather shy when we first met, but in Fremantle, living cheek by jowl with extroverts like Lovely and Pete, he began to come out of his shell, and we began to enjoy his quiet, dry and amusing comments.

Most nights we got together in our tiny back yard at the

house and ate dinner cooked by Julia, who from dealing with my nutritional requirements had become team mother. These relaxing evenings together fostered a strong team spirit and brought us all closer.

Back at the start of this whole adventure, when the boat was in Gosport, there was only Tim and I working on her, sanding, scraping and working through my unwritten list of jobs to be done. He was completely inexperienced so had no idea what should be on the work list, how long that list was or what he was getting himself into, which was probably a blessing. He remained forever energetic and enthusiastic. I bought the beers and, being American, Tim was a bit slow in slaking his thirst, but we soon got him up to speed by taking him to the pub every evening after we'd finished working on the boat to wash away the dust. On the evenings when he baulked at the idea of a fourth or fifth pint, I bought it anyway and stood it in line with the others, telling him it was good training for being a sailor, which is what he claimed he wanted to be!

Tim had come to Bilbao and said he wanted to come to Norfolk too, since it was only a few hours drive from where he was brought up. Australia, he thought, was a long way away and too expensive. But in Bilbao, while we were watching the professional teams that Mike and Alex had working for them, he asked me who was coming to Australia to work on my team.

'No one,' I replied. At that time, I simply didn't have the budget for a shore crew.

Tim said later that my reply broke his heart. He was totally committed to our campaign and strongly believed in our mission to demonstrate the indefatigable spirit of us 'elder' members of the human race. So with one eye on that crusade, and another on all the attractive women who seemed to be working with Alex, he decided he would come along, which I was delighted about. By the time he arrived in Fremantle, of course, everything had changed and I had recruited a support crew, but there was still room for Tim. He summed up his feelings about being involved in a note to me:

'I realised that if my experience in Gosport over the summer and in Bilbao was any indication, Fremantle would be an incredible adventure as well. It's not just the sailing and rubbing shoulders with the elite sailors of the world but being part of something so ambitious with a whole bunch of like-minded people.

'We are living an amazing adventure and if I get to be a part of it simply by being a volunteer, I feel I am extremely lucky.'

I appreciated these words. They summed up why we were all involved. We had not had the easiest time of it, but I felt we were all lucky to be there.

Our preparations went remarkably smoothly, so I was able to thoroughly enjoy our stay in Australia, renewing old acquaintances from previous visits and making new ones. The old Whitbread Race used to stop at Fremantle as its Australian port, and the Clipper fleet called in during December 2005 and received the warmest of welcomes. Everyone who lives there seems to have a boat – and what's more, everyone who has a boat uses it whenever they can. In the UK marinas often remain full even when the sun shines on a weekend, but in Fremantle you stand on the waterfront on a Friday afternoon and watch a procession of boats heading towards Rottnest Island, just a few miles offshore, or up the Swan River, leaving the marinas completely empty. They know about sailing there, and having hosted the America's Cup in 1987, they know about staging big-scale yachting events. The legacy of Alan Bond's Australian campaign for the Cup has been far reaching: before 1987, Freo was a sleepy and rather shabby suburb of Perth, but in preparation for the influx of millions who travelled from all over the world to follow the America's Cup, the state government spent around A$50 million on sprucing it up. Now it is a charming, rather bohemian sort of place full of cafés, bars and markets.

I found time to visit a few of those and was intrigued to find that Fremantle isn't just about sailing and cappuccinos. There are four major museums – which struck me as a lot for a place that has only been established for 180 years, but they each tell an interesting story. The prison, complete with a handsome set of gallows, was built by convicts in the 1850s and until 1991 was home to many of Australia's most reviled criminals, Ned Kelly apart. The Army Museum portrays Fremantle's role in the defence of Western Australia up to the Second World War. The exhibits at the Maritime Museum, a splendid new building right at the mouth of the Swan River, revolve around the *Parry Endeavour*, which took solo sailor Jon Sanders three times around the globe, and of course *Australia II*, the racing yacht with the winged keel that became responsible for snatching the America's Cup out of the hands of the United States for the first time ever. Finally, the History Museum, housed in the old asylum, reminds visitors that Fremantle was the first port of call for the colonists and the millions of migrants who arrived in Western Australia by ship and stayed. If you include the Esplanade Hotel, built in 1896 to accommodate visitors cashing in on the gold discoveries during that time, and the silo in North Fremantle that has a big red dingo on the side painted by Sir Alan Bond during his early career as a sign writer, Freo's billing as one of Australia's most culturally important cities starts to make sense.

The wine's not bad either, and we found time to relax and sample a few of the indigenous grapes. Some of this sampling was to celebrate the New Year – Alex Thomson, who decided to use his pre-booked tickets to come to Fremantle, threw a great party for all the teams. I also had a couple of days away with my friends Sharpy and Pippa at their vineyard down near Margaret River, which was totally relaxing.

My complaints about being without any alcohol, particularly whisky, for over a month had produced a very generous response from friends, and while we were in Fremantle no fewer than twenty-eight bottles were delivered. Now I enjoy a dram, but this looked like serious work, almost half a bottle a day, so I carefully went through the offerings and chose a mix of brands which I thought would see me to Norfolk. The surplus went into the container for future consumption.

The programme of work went well, and the day before the start we were in better shape than we had been at any stage of the campaign. We had got all the electronics working, including fitting a new Iridium base station, so I could receive the weather from another source if the Fleet 77 system fell down, and I had time to play around with the systems and get the hang of them.

The damage to the keel caused by the fishing line was repaired and we fitted new Raymarine wind sensors to the masthead. We replaced a small alternator on the Volvo engine with one producing 175 amps, so I could get a speedier charge for the batteries and cut fuel consumption. A brand-new reacher was delivered, which was medium-sized and easily serviceable by one pair of hands. Our sails wizard Dave Swete, who had proved such a supporter in Bilbao, brought it with him from the New Zealand North Loft and settled down with Tim to repair the damage caused by the broken battens on the mainsail.

Huw was given the task of removing all extraneous wiring inside the boat around the nav area, and Tom Green came out from Raymarine in England to sort out the steering problem. He renewed everything associated with the auto-pilots, and to my great delight both worked fine on test.

It looked as if we might be properly prepared for the next leg – but the day before the restart, just hours before I was due to leave on the leg of 14,500 nautical miles to Norfolk, we suffered another crisis that threw our immediate prospects into jeopardy.

As, on that supposedly final day in Fremantle, we came back into the marina after a test sail, a line went over the side and got caught around the propeller. We dropped the anchor and people jumped in to try and clear the line.

We put it on a winch and tried to pull it clear, but it suddenly went slack. One of the volunteer divers came to the surface to report that it looked as if the whole outdrive unit had bent. A second opinion confirmed our worst fears: the outdrive unit was sheared. How had it happened? Perhaps it was a case of too many people aboard and everyone doing something but no one doing anything specific. It was my fault. But there was no point in worrying about how it happened. We were where we were, and our focus now had to be exclusively on finding a solution. I could sail without being able to motor, of course, but the fear was that the damage might extend to within the boat and I might be faced with a dangerous leak.

The race start was only twenty hours away and we knew we were unlikely to be able to fix the problem in time. We could all see a long delay while we sourced a new outdrive, and the first problem was how and where to haul out. With her two 15-foot deck spreaders, *Saga Insurance* would not fit into the hoist dock unless we took the mast down, but that little operation, plus the rerigging afterwards, was a gruelling two-day job.

Josh Hall, the British solo sailor who had first sailed with me back in 1985 aboard *British Airways* and who was in Fremantle working as shore crew for Koji's *Spirit of Yukoh* team, saved the day by suggesting we hauled the boat over with a strop around the keel, as we had done for the IMOCA stability test. This would bring the outdrive well clear of the water: when on her side, only about 60 cm of *Saga Insurance*'s side deck was immersed, so the keel was well clear of the water and the outdrive was in line with the keel. It was the obvious solution, but to haul the boat over, we needed a crane big enough to handle 10 tonnes of boat. There would be plenty of cranes in Perth but it was Saturday evening, slap bang in the middle of the Christmas holidays .

How many cranes would be available for hiring on a Saturday night? How many crane drivers would be free to come down to the yacht club and stay there all night while we completed the repairs? Most of them would be in the pub, if they had any sense.

I wasn't very confident but, as usual, our friends at Fremantle Sailing Club were, and they started ringing round immediately to all the crane companies in the region to see what they could find.

Meanwhile Dilip, as a trained diver, went overside to fasten a strop around the keel bulb which would be picked up by the crane. Pete followed him in to double-check the knot, but surfaced looking perplexed. The knot Dilip tied was not one he had ever seen before, though it was one he said would definitely hold. Dilip just smiled and muttered dryly, 'Indian rope trick', which had us all in stitches.

About two hours later, the first crane arrived with a driver who, as I suspected, had had to be dragged away from his Saturday evening's entertainment. It took a while to set everything up but when we started to take the weight, the crane's back wheels started to rise up off the ground. This crane was not big enough. So the call went out again, this time for a more powerful and heavier crane, and within an hour the staff at Fremantle Sailing Club had found another one which was quickly put in place. By this time a crowd had gathered to watch the drama, and to ensure everyone could see what was happening in the darkness a few sets of floodlights were brought in. It was like a full-blown theatrical production, with Lovely directing proceedings from his perch on the boat or the pontoon and the rest of us acting out our roles, responding to instructions and watching nervously. The sound of carbon fibre creaking as the crane lifted the hull and rolled her sounded sinister, but she went over onto her side without a problem. Now we were able to see what we were up against. The outdrive had really sheared, and was hanging at an awkward angle.

There were two possible ways to fix the problem, the ideal being to reweld the outdrive back together again. But it was made of aluminium and the welders said they could not get the heat to dissipate quickly enough, so this had to be ruled out. The alternative was to bandage around the outdrive over the crack. Nick Clayton, who had been doing all our fibreglass work, arrived to take a look and after a quick examination said he could fix the problem. Without more ado, he set to work. His assurances came as an enormous relief because, for the first time, it offered us the luxury of believing that a start with the rest of the fleet was a possibility.

I went to get some sleep while Lovely and Pete stayed with Nick and the sleepy crane driver until four in the morning, when the job was finally completed. As soon as it was done, the crane eased back, allowing the boat to come upright again, and once the strop was removed we were ready to sail. It was a great success and a tremendous team effort, but we could have done without all that stress and extra work at the last hurdle.

We had the same sort of send-off in Fremantle as we'd had in Bilbao, with interviews on stage and then the 'death walk', as the TV production company APP dubbed it, to the boats. Unai stripped off, dived in and swam to his boat, which proved to be a big hit with the crowds. We said our farewells and slipped our lines. Ahead of us was the longest leg that has ever been attempted in a solo round-the-world race, short of a non-stop circumnavigation, and I was hoping that with a few thousand miles under my belt and a growing confidence in *Saga Insurance*, my speeds over the 14,500 nautical miles to Norfolk, Virginia, would be significantly improved. I had set myself a target of finishing the Velux 5 Oceans in 112 days. I had taken sixty-eight days to complete the first 12,000 miles, and there was no chance of doing the remaining 18,000 in forty-four, but nevertheless I was keen to improve my performance and maintain my podium position through to the end.

I made a good start to the second leg, crossing the start line shortly after the gun and unrolling the jib as I went. Unfortunately Bernard Stamm did even better, crossing about half a boat's length ahead of me. He took off down the short leg to Scarborough, north of Perth, with a quartering breeze showing just how quick his boat is, but I still held second place at the first mark.

Then, once we went hard on the wind after the Scarborough buoy, Unai and Koji stormed past and I found them sailing faster and closer to the wind, which is about as depressing as it gets. I trimmed sails and reduced the rate but could not close. Towards dusk Graham Dalton in *A Southern Man AGD* caught us up and we tacked south within a couple of hundred yards of each other.

On this other tack I found I was slightly faster, which indicated that something was biased somewhere. As darkness fell the wind increased from the south and it became a hard and wet slog, with gradual sail reductions to reduce the loading on the boat.

Towards midnight I decided to get the storm jib out of the sail locker in case it was needed, and I was busy trying to heave it up to the steeply sloping deck when the boat suddenly came into the wind and tacked herself.

I disentangled myself from the mounds of Kevlar, went aft and completed the tack, then tacked her back on the course I wanted. The autopilot had switched to standby and had stopped controlling the rudders, but I assumed that was due to the violent shift in wind direction caused by a wave pushing us round and forcing the boat to tack.

Clipping on my harness, I made my way forward again

and down the hatch to get the storm jib out. This time I succeeded in getting it onto the deck and was hanking it on when, once again, the boat tacked herself. When I crawled back and completed the tack, I noticed the autopilot was on standby again.

Once more I assumed that the steep waves had pushed the bow round, but I decided that if she persisted in tacking like this it might be best to leave her on this tack for a while while I sorted out the jib. After a while I tacked again and stayed in the cockpit to watch what happened next, and sure enough, an hour after midnight, I heard the familiar bleep of the autopilot alarm and saw it switch once more to standby.

I realised this must have caused the earlier tacks but I couldn't work out what was going wrong. When we were in Fremantle, Tom Green from Raymarine, makers of the pilots, had spent hours crouched down in the boiling-hot furnace that *Saga*'s cabin had become in the 40-degree Australian heat, and had pronounced both pilots to be in perfect working order. We had tested them during our trial sail on Saturday and found them to be fine. But here we were, just a few hours into the second leg, and there was clearly something badly wrong.

I changed the pilots over, but within twenty minutes it went to standby again. I could not go on like this. The pilots are essential if one wants to do anything away from the cockpit, including get some sleep. I considered my options, but I really did not have any. I knew that if I went back to Fremantle, I would lose a mandatory forty-eight hours under race rules, because that was the penalty for re-entering port, plus the time lost getting back there, but all that was secondary to sorting out the problem.

While I was thinking about the pros and cons of going back, the pilot switched to standby again. That was it. There was no need to consider the options any longer. Reluctantly I bore away back to Fremantle.

I called Simon and Sophy to tell them what was happening. Simon had been at the 'Thank God They've Gone' party that shore crews always throw when their skippers get back on to the race track. It is a way of letting their hair down after weeks of stress and hard work, and I'm told that alcohol plays quite a major part in this winding-down process. Sophy was on her way to the airport, aiming for an early-morning flight. Both were given a bit of a jolt by my disappointing news and immediately changed their plans to help me.

I started the engine for an hour on the way back to recharge the batteries and put the pilot on again. It seemed to work OK for five hours but then kicked out once more. I rang Simon and asked him to alert the Raymarine agent, Greg Hanson, to our problem and see if he could be there when I got in to sort it out. When I motored back towards Fremantle Simon came out to meet me, together with Greg and Huw, to give the system another trial. Greg jumped aboard, asked the symptoms and without any hesitation said it must be a power problem. He disappeared below.

Within fifteen minutes, he was back up on deck again.

'The problem is the voltage drop to the system because of inadequate wiring,' he said.

He then explained what he meant. The cable linking the batteries to the control boxes was similar to that used to power a bedside lamp and just not big enough to supply additional power when the pilots came under load. Every time the batteries ran a bit low this problem would occur.

This explained a great deal, and thinking of the heavy wires we put between a car battery and a starter motor to carry the power required, it made a lot of sense, but hearing his diagnosis made me absolutely furious.

I couldn't help but think of all the time I had lost because of this piece of crass stupidity, plus the battens broken and the cost of their replacement. This was a highly specialised piece of equipment and we had gone to some trouble to call in the appropriate specialists to fix it. But it served as another reminder that many so called 'experts' are not experts at all and can place a campaign in quite serious jeopardy through sheer incompetence. My only consolation was that perhaps we had at last got to the bottom of the problem and could sort it.

We sailed back to the Fremantle Sailing Club and berthed. Simon told me to get some rest and took over. I went and had a hot shower and collapsed into a very deep sleep. At last my mind was at rest over this longstanding problem with my steering, and it came as an enormous relief. We did a test sail on the Monday and measured the voltage drop. It was now 0.2 volts, down from 1.7 volts, a very encouraging drop.

The next day at around dawn I cleared Customs and motored out. Simon and friends helped hoist the mainsail and I was off again. They followed for a while but the wind was rising and their RIB (rigid inflatable boat) was becoming too frisky so they turned round. We waved goodbye and once more I was on my own. I was sorry to leave Fremantle. It had been a very happy stop. My team had been terrific, and the locals friendly and helpful. I could happily have stayed longer but was conscious of the others already on the track and was itching to get after them. There was also the safety factor: the closer the fleet was grouped the less the distance and time it would take to assist one another if any of us got into trouble. And ahead of us was the hardest and longest leg – this time we would be going deeper south into the Southern Ocean and would be sailing it for longer.

The wind was still from the south but had veered very slightly and gave me a better angle than two days before, so I made reasonable time to Cape Leeuwin, on the south-west corner of Australia. I was not overpushing at this stage as there was no point in getting any damage this early. Going close-hauled to clear the Cape, I rounded it about 3 miles off on the evening of the 18th and re-entered the Southern Ocean. Cape Leeuwin is one of the three capes that need to be left to the north to define a proper circumnavigation, the other two being the Cape of Good Hope and Cape Horn. This was my fourth passage past it: my earlier ones had been with *Suhaili*, *Heath's Condor* and *Enza*. As I rounded the Cape I ran into a lot of shipping. I stayed awake until I thought we were clear of their lanes, but kept the radar alarm on in case any vessels were further off the coast as I headed south-east.

I had lost about sixty-five hours because of my stop so needed to catch up quickly if I was not to get separated from the others by different weather systems again. Unai in *Pakea* had dallied a bit and was paying for it. He had become caught in a developing low in the Great Australian Bight and had a choice of sailing east or south. He went east, which was a mistake and lost time.

Bernard was out of the traps like a bat out of hell in the opening stages of the leg and was already developing a significant lead, with Koji hanging grimly on.

Dalton on *A Southern Man AGD*, like the two leaders, was

heading well south, and that's what I proposed to do as it led into the zone of strong westerly winds which I badly needed if I was going to stay in touch. I set the new medium reacher and for a while we soared along, but the increasing wind meant it wasn't long before I had to think about hauling it in again.

I bore away, set the jib, and began to roll in the reacher on its furler. It came for a while, but became very stiff when halfway furled. I went forward and the problem was obvious. The main sheave of the furler had broken and jammed. We were stuck with 90 square metres of sail aloft and no obvious means to get it down unless one had half a dozen pairs of hands to help. Well, there were no hands to help and I could not leave it up there. I started by easing the halyard, and then put a rope around the part of the thrashing sail I could reach and winched it back to the deck.

I repeated this process a number of times, gradually hauling the sail down and keeping it under control on deck. The whole task took almost four hours before I finally had the sail down and stopped so it could not unfurl, and then I threw it into the sail locker. I was utterly exhausted.

The good news was the sail was undamaged, and I felt that deserved a Headland. But I now had to think about how I could set the large reaching sails again when there was no way of furling them. I settled down with a glass of whisky and thought about the problem. In effect, if I ever had one of the light reaching or running sails set I would have to pull them up loose or gather the luff and leach together and put wool around them to hold them in a 'roll' as I hoisted them. And that would be the easy bit. If I had the sail set when the wind rose I was going to have to go through the same laborious process I had just been through, and maybe I might not be so lucky next time and lose it overside. If this happened and it dragged in the sea, there was no way I could get it back – the weight would be too much for me to hoist aboard and I would have to cut it away. In effect, unless I had a long calm period, and warning when the wind was going to increase, running sails were no longer an option. But these were what I had been counting on to give me a bit of extra edge. It was infuriating to lose competitiveness so early in the leg.

After rounding Cape Leeuwin I had had light weather for five days, nothing more than a Force 4 and all from the west. It was easy, light sailing most of the time, with everything I could set put up within the limitations of the broken furler. It was a good chance to relax a bit, knowing I was going as fast as I could in the circumstances, and enjoy the sailing, and also some of the sights like Comet McNaught, that was showing very brightly each evening after sunset. I did not see the Aurora Australis which had been so impressive thirteen years before when we sailed through this area in *Enza*. This was disappointing, as that had kept me spell-bound for hours, staring at the movement like giant search-lights being shone on the sky.

I continued on a south-easterly course, getting clear of the Great Australian Bight and south of Tasmania. A week after my second start, I was almost up with *Pakea*, which was just 44 miles closer to the leader, but *A Southern Man AGD* was 500 miles ahead, Koji 1,100 and Bernard 1,500. And already there were gremlins at work.

Initially the Fleet 77 system would not lock onto a satellite, and the Iridium phone had shut down and refused to re-ignite itself, despite lengthy calls to the USA using the emergency Iridium plugged into the main aerial. This meant that once again, within less than a week, I was without weather information except for the general shipping forecast coming in from New Zealand, received on the Sat C.

Then the autopilot went to standby again, but this time I was not convinced it was an autopilot problem. It had been working hard, too hard I thought, and I looked for another cause. One thing I was aware of was that the bow seemed to be digging in, as if we had more weight forward. I went forward and checked the compartments but they were dry. Then I took the hatches off the ballast tanks and found both were full. No wonder the poor boat had felt so heavy. I pushed down their valves and drained them both, which removed about 2 tons of ballast water. I assumed that the valves had been leaking.

Saga Insurance felt a lot better immediately the water was drained away, and the autopilot gave no further trouble. The bow was now higher, so we slid along more easily and were taking less water over the foredeck. I was annoyed with myself for not noticing this earlier, and it showed me that I still had a bit to learn about the feel of my boat.

Our first strong winds did not arrive until the end of January. I had some warning of their approach and was slightly nervous as to how well the boat would handle if we got into big seas. She had proved strong in Biscay during the hurricane, but those waves were only 10 metres high.

This depression was forecast to strike in eight hours so I had a nervous wait while the winds gathered strength. I filled the time by making sure everything was secure or lashed, but there wasn't much more to do apart from monitor the instrument panel, watching the pressure drop and the numbers depicting wind and boat speed edge steadily up. It was my curiosity over how these boats handled in big seas that was one of the reasons I was down here, so while I am always a little apprehensive when a gale approaches, part of me was looking forward to the experience.

When the Force 8 gale came she handled it very well, largely down to the autopilots, which did not falter once. The wind backed sharply within the gale as squalls amplified the effect and I turned her off downwind in these gusts, getting some nice surfs.

The main problem turned out to be the big quartering seas which picked up the stern and tended to give a push at the same moment as the waves struck the transom. This created a turning force that threatened to push us across the front of the waves, but the pilot reacted quickly and the boat responded well. She seemed to want to have sail kept on her, so I left as much as I thought prudent, keeping the mainsail although fully reefed, and adjusting headsails between the Solent and storm jib as the conditions varied. She responded even better once I had filled the aft weather-ballast tank. This made a noticeable difference, even if it lowered the freeboard a bit aft. I was very encouraged and thought of the designers at Groupe Finot with affection.

At around midnight I noticed a small tug of de-acceleration, and for a moment thought we had caught another fish net. Bernard had already snagged one on this leg, but had been more fortunate than I had been on the previous leg because after a short while it had freed up and slipped off. This tug was barely noticeable and the boat quickly gathered way again, so I did not give it another thought until next morning, when I noticed a line trailing out astern. I went back to recover it and discovered it was the main life-raft painter. I leaned over the stern to look into the alcove where the raft was normally stored – it was empty. The life raft must have been washed out of its lashings in the gale.

Of course one hopes never to use a life raft, but it's nice to know it's there. The concern now was for the aperture where the life raft had been stowed in the transom. It had a small inspection hatch at its inward end which could hardly be described as stormproof – one heavy wave breaking at the stern might well smash it and then flood the steering compartment.

I decided the best thing I could do was to put some form of barrier in the alcove in front of the hatch to break up the force of a wave. A spare grab bag was filled with everything I could find that was suitable, mainly sponsors' banners and flags from Velux and Saga Insurance. I then lashed the bag into the aperture, put loads of Sikaflex sealant around the hatch and hoped for the best.

I carried a spare life raft as required by the rules, but it was a much lighter one. Hopefully this would not be an issue. The very last thing you want to do is take to a life raft. They are fragile, made of thin rubberised fabric, and get thrown about in big seas far more than the boat. They are also a smaller target for searchers. So the general rule is to wait until you have to step *up* into a life raft before you abandon your boat. Nevertheless it was one less item of safety equipment available, and although I did not lose sleep over its absence, I would much rather have had it with me.

These Open 60s like *Saga Insurance* are one of the few classes that insist on subdivision by watertight bulkheads. Provided those subcompartments stay intact the boat should have plenty of buoyancy even if one compartment gets flooded. The boat is always a safer place to stay than a life raft; it is larger, stronger, and you probably have some of the supplies and equipment accessible you need to preserve your life for longer.

The main life raft is now stowed in the transom, after some well-publicised capsizes where keels had fallen off and the boats overturned. The idea was to be able to access the life raft whichever way up the boat was, and the theory is good. Interestingly, though, when Alex Thomson came to abandon *Hugo Boss* he found he could not extract this main life raft and so had to used his smaller one for the transfer to *Ecover*, so I don't think we have found the ideal stowage position yet.

The Fleet 77 system developed another problem during the following week. It failed to link with the satellites covering the Pacific Ocean, which was now the chosen zone for it. This cut off my link with the internet, an alternative source of weather information since the Iridium base station was still not functioning. The cause of the problem baffled the experts for days but it was eventually concluded that the antenna, which can rotate, was jamming on the inside of the dome. Would I free it? they asked.

I don't think the experts had any idea what it would be like to remove a large unwieldy fibreglass dome in the sort of conditions we get in the Southern Ocean. It is perched right at the stern, in one of the most exposed parts of the boat, and apart from the obvious risks to my own safety – there was a good chance I might overbalance in a bucking boat – there is often spray around. Salt water on delicate electronics would be the death of an expensive bit of equipment.

I managed it once, on a calm day. I found the azimuth

belt was jamming, freed it and got the system going, but the moment I resecured the dome, it jammed again. I assumed the antenna was jamming on the inside of the dome, and this appeared to be another installation problem that I felt I should not be having to deal with.

Its failure was compromising both my performance and my safety, and that made me extremely cross. Then, because things happen in threes, the Maxsea dongle decided to join in the shutdown party. I played with it for a couple of days and decided it was a connection problem. Taking my pocket knife, I gently lifted the terminals with great delicacy – then tried it, and it connected!

It might not be able to download weather but the Maxsea program was useful as an indicator of my position as it was interfaced with the GPS. Despite this very minor success I found the electrics problems all very frustrating. The equipment was all new, it had been fitted by the people who supplied it, and yet it did not work. It was not exactly a recommendation for the electronics industry, but we seem to accept these sort of failures from electronics in a way we would never accept similar problems with, for example, our cars or washing machines.

So now, barely a quarter of the way into the leg, I had lost both means of downloading weather charts. I could still receive the text forecasts, but these are designed for merchant ships and fishermen and do not have the detail that is now essential for full-on competitive racing. This put me at an immediate disadvantage on the race track, as the others were all able to download the very detailed Maxsea charts which tell you exactly what the wind is doing, where its coming from and how strong it is. This allows the skipper to use the weather tactically and choose the best possible route for fast sailing. Not having any of this information put me in a similar position to a blind boxer. I knew there would be a system coming but had no detailed idea of its direction or force. People encouraged me by saying, 'Well, that's all you had last time' – which was perfectly true. In fact in 1968 I did not even have the shipping forecasts. But these well-intended words of comfort ignored the fact that the game has moved on, and one needed the latest equipment to be competitive.

In those days, there was a level playing field: no one had any fancy hardware and skippers relied simply on their experience, knowledge and instincts. Forty years later, where electronic gizmos are standard issue on all racing boats, one's progress depends not only on their proper functioning but also on one's fluency in the new IT language. I was now fluent with the programs, but this was of little use if the equipment would not enable me to obtain the information I needed to use that fluency.

The introduction of masses of electronics has added a completely new requirement to the skills of the modern solo sailor. Whereas 'maintenance' used to come down to one's skills with marlin spike and spanner, now you need to have an understanding of computers and electronics, at least so far as being able to manage basic problems. In my case, I was spending hours each day looking for solutions to electronic problems and half the time I really did not know what I was looking for. In theory, the various items at my disposal, like the GPS, ought to be able to interface, but in practice they frequently jumped out so, for example, my position would not automatically appear on the chart.

All this fiddling around impacted on both my concentration and on the time I should have been spending on sailing the boat. It also tested my patience and left me exasperated, to put it mildly.

But in the middle of all these distractions I heard that Graham Dalton had pulled into Bluff at the southern tip of New Zealand's South Island to repair a split fuel tank. This meant he would have to take the forty-eight hour compulsory stop, which would enable me to catch up with him.

The loss of weather information affected my race almost immediately after Dalton rejoined. We were advised of a deep low approaching from the east. The further south you went, the stronger the winds. Having lost the life raft in the previous gale I saw no point in risking more damage, and apart from anything else, the closer to the centre of the low one got, the larger the waves, which meant a decrease in speed. So I stayed at about 48 degrees south and from the positions being sent to the fleet from race headquaters watched both Unai and Graham dive south of me. I wasn't sure what to make of it, but as it turned out they were right. The low began to fill and never developed into more than a front.

They had Maxsea and knew the detail of what was projected. I didn't and was handicapped. Unai got nearly 300 miles ahead of me on that one piece of information. I knew I could sail faster than either of them in their new boats in similar weather conditions, but a race is not always about sheer boat speed. It is more about sheer boat speed in the right place and in the right direction, and that was something I could no longer be certain about.

Distance is so easily lost when you can't see what is going on, and every mile to recover those losses is a struggle. I was faced with steering slightly north of east or slightly east of south, and I needed to go slightly south of east. There was nothing I could do until the wind changed. Then it eventually came from the south-west, which suited us perfectly, and I began to claw back some of the lost miles. With no other weather indications, it made sense to keep reasonably close to those two and hope they were reading the weather correctly. If nothing else, I would get similar conditions and could then just try to sail better.

At the end of January, with Bernard galloping towards Cape Horn some 2,300 miles ahead of me, I was furling the Solent headsail when I noticed a tear near the foot of the sail by the clew. This was bad news, potentially disastrous. The Solent is a vital part of the sail armoury, next to the mainsail in importance and usage, and if the tear, which was half a metre long, developed into a full-blown rip, which was inevitable, I would be badly crippled.

Later that day the wind eased and I unrolled the sail and tried to put a sticky-back patch over the tear. But it was too damp to stick. I even tried to wipe it down with precious whisky, but that didn't work either, so there was only one thing for it – a sewing job, and one that I expected to be particularly precarious.

I collected a palm and needle, tied my harness to one of the dagger-board mounts so I could lean on it, and went to work sewing up the tear as best I could. It was not pretty – what we used to call Homeward Bounders, stitches made in a hurry – but when the next front was over us, and the wind was beginning to ease, I would need the Solent to give the boat enough power to outsail the waves.

Another reason for keeping a lot of sail set is that as a wave approaches, say typically 5 to 8 metres high, it creates a wind shadow in the trough in front of it and the boat slows. This is exactly when you don't want it to be slow.

When the wave arrives and the boat rises on its forward slope you want to be moving fast. Usually the sails fill again as they poke up above the crest of the wave and the boat moves forward. It needs to do this in a hurry because the top of the wave, if breaking, can break right over the stern.

On a number of occasions I watched, almost in wonder, as a wave seemed poised to smash down on us, but *Saga Insurance* accelerated away just in time. It's rather like riding a bicycle. If you go slow, you are less stable than when you go fast. The boat sounded dangerous as she surged forward but in fact she always felt a lot better.

This was in stark contrast to *Suhaili*. Weighing in at around 10 tonnes, she was much too heavy to accelerate, so it was better to 'moor' her with warps out astern to prevent her rushing down the leading slope of the wave and broaching.

One time I was working on *Suhaili*'s deck and looked astern to see a gigantic breaking wave approach. I knew I could not get into the safety of the cabin before it arrived, and I knew too that if I stayed on deck I would be washed away. I took the only recourse open to me – I climbed the rigging hand over hand until I was 10 feet up. The wave duly smashed over the boat, completely covering her for what seemed like ages but was probably only a few seconds, and got high enough to splash my boots. For that brief moment there was me, two masts, and nothing else in sight for 2,000 miles in every direction except water.

I crossed the International Date Line on 1 February. I wasn't the last of the fleet to do so as I was further east than Dalton, but because he was well south of me at that point he showed ahead of me and closer to the leader.

Crossing the date line meant I had to add another day, so I had two February 1sts. The day starts on this line, so New

Zealand was on the 1 February but east of the line was late on the 31 January. So I went from the 1 February to the 31 January in an instant.

Had I been going west I would have had to lose a day. It is a phenononemon first noted by the survivors of Magellan's circumnavigation, who arrived back to find they were a day behind the people they had left at home.

One of the features on an Open 60, or perhaps it is more accurate to say one of the missing features, is a WC. Drilling holes through the hull is to be avoided as they create a weak point and pose a risk from damage or leaking and create drag, so the inlet and outlet valves required for a WC are a definite no-no. Most of us make do with a special bucket. Provided you are well braced, normal functions do not present a problem, but when the boat is being tossed about in angry seas the whole operation becomes hazardous. Towards the end of the second gale I had used the bucket for a pee and was just getting steady to pass it back on deck when a wave struck us and the boat lurched. Inevitably, some of the contents splashed out onto the cabin deck. I emptied the remainder of the contents overside and then had a frenzied cleaning session. I didn't want the boat smelling like a public lavatory, and as I was preparing food in the cabin, I knew that unless I cleaned up I could be laying myself open to some unwelcome developments on the hygiene front.

The British used to be known for keeping their ships clean, often using vinegar over the mess decks as a disinfectant before other products became available. The result was that we lost fewer men to disease than anyone else. It's a lesson to be remembered.

I used the same bucket system with *Suhaili*, since I shut

off all her hull valves before setting out to avoid any possible problems, but this type of unfortunate spill never happened aboard her. Instead, something even worse happened: I dropped my second to last cigarette into that same bucket! This taught me not to attempt multitasking.

On 4 February I declared a Headland, as it was the fiftieth anniversary of my first going to sea. I was seventeen when I joined my first ship, *Chindwara*, in the Royal Albert Docks. I had spent two weeks the previous summer on HMS *Vanguard*, Britain's last battleship, as a Junior Seaman RNVR, as insurance that if I received my national service call-up I would be able to do it in the Navy. We spent the time moored up in Devonport living with more than 1,000 other seamen aboard.

Bernard Stamm had developed a huge lead of more than 1,800 miles over second-placed *Spirit of Yukoh* when he rounded Cape Horn, just twenty-four days after leaving Fremantle. It is much harder to stay motivated when the margin is so enormous, but I don't think Bernard knows how to ease up when racing and he never lost his focus for a minute. All the time he was considering his weather and tactical options to make sure that he and his boat arrived first in Norfolk, looking and feeling like new.

Kojiro, in turn, was 1,000 miles ahead of me, and although I had been making up a few miles a day on him, it was nothing like enough to close the gap by the finish in Norfolk.

Any hopes I had of holding him were dashed the next day when the pin securing the headboard of the mainsail to its three sliders came loose and one of its sliders sheared. There were bits of the fitting up the mast, bits broken and bits missing, which pretty well sums up a diabolical situation.

This was looking really bad. I now could not harden in the mainsail sheet without putting strain on the next slider down, which was not designed to take it. If this then sheared, the weight would go to the next one down, and so on, until I would end up with the mainsail completely detached from the mast.

I knew that there was only one solution, which was for me to go up the mast to recover the bits stuck up there and try to make some sort of repair. This was something I had not had to do in this race so far, and in the prevailing conditions – Force 6 winds gusting Force 7 – I knew that climbing the mast would pose some dangers.

I remember being told that the ideal rolling period on tall ships is eight to nine seconds. If the ship has too much righting moment she rolls faster and this would throw sailors off the yards.

A yacht has more stability, and my rolling period was three to four seconds, which meant I could be thrown about unmercifully the higher I went. However, the problem needed to be addressed. I got out my climbing gear and prepared to go up to recover the cars. I made one attempt but I knew immediately it was not going to work. My left wrist, which was strapped up due to a persistent bout of tendonitis, just would not accept my weight, so I was effectively attempting this manoeuvre one-handed.

It is not too difficult limiting the amount one is thrown around when climbing a mast, but two hands are absolutely essential – one to adjust the jumar clips as you go up, the other to hold yourself steady. My wrist had been a problem since the first leg, and despite treatment in Fremantle had become progressively worse when any pressure was placed on it. I had been winching with my right hand from the start of the leg and was resigned to being one-handed for the rest of it. But this problem with the mainsail could be a critical handicap if I couldn't fix it.

To get aloft I decided I would have to wait until I found calmer conditions, perhaps even anchoring somewhere once I had rounded the Horn, where the relentless swell would not be such an issue. That was still 2,800 miles – or ten to twelve days – away so I would just have to make do by setting the main up to the first reef and tightening its halyard as much as I could to keep as much tension as possible in the luff of the sail.

I don't willingly climb masts. It's dangerous, and especially not advisable when you are on your own. I was a little alarmed when I saw some footage of Alex at the top of his mast with his kite still flying. I may have done that at his age but I would not take the risk now. He is young and still considers himself immortal, as young men should, and that would have given him a real buzz, but I have had too many close shaves over the years to do something like that unless it is absolutely necessary. As you get older you lose a bit of that feeling of immortality.

When I was doing the Admiral's Cup in 1973, I was halfway between the spreaders and the masthead when the boat broached. I felt it coming and clipped onto the shroud, so when the boat went over and swung back I didn't get flung around. After the boat stabilised again I unclipped myself and swung back to the mast and looked down to see everyone looking up, wondering where I was. They thought they had lost me. I remember looking down and saying: 'Do you mind?'

On *Suhaili*, after Cape Horn I was up the mast halfway between the upper spreaders and the masthead to rereeve a halyard when she hit a wave. I went straight out and hit the forestay, then swung back in, right through the shrouds, and ended up stuck behind the mainsail. I just said: 'That's it. I can do without that happening. It's too dangerous. Its silly because I could injure myself. You have to be sensible if you are sailing alone.'

Being up high on a mast does not frighten me at all. This is strange, because my knees turn to jelly if I am at the top of a tall building or if I am 1,000 metres up on the side of a mountain.

In 1992 Chris Bonington and I decided to sail on *Suhaili* to the Arctic Circle, via Iceland and Greenland, to make an attempt on the Cathedral, which at the time was the most challenging unclimbed peak in Greenland. I received just one evening of basic instruction in climbing prior to us starting our ascent, with the Royal Marines in London. Before we started, they gave me an intensive lesson on how to put on a harness, how to tie a prusik knot, how to abseil and how to break a fall, but I knew Chris was worried about how I would cope.

The first stage was 400 metres of a sheer ice wall – one and a half times as high as Canary Wharf – which I coped with without trouble. We got as far as 2,400 metres but the final 200 metres looked far more complicated than we had thought and we were running out of time so we had to abort. I relished the physical challenge but, to my surprise, struggled with vertigo. Chris and the other mountaineer, Jim Lowther, who was also very experienced, stood happily on ledges at that height, whereas I would be on my stomach a couple of yards back, inching unwillingly towards the edge.

Interestingly, I found I wanted to use my arms to ensure my stability when climbing, as I was used to doing in sailing, but mountaineers mainly used their legs and feet, which did not come naturally to me.

For now, the mast remained out of bounds, but I discovered I wasn't the only one reporting problems. Unai in *Pakea* had lost both his masthead and stern wind-senders and had split his headsail, while Dalton in *A Southern Man AGD* said, somewhat mysteriously, that he would 'lose out badly' on the next leg.

This suggested to me that he had lost his reaching or running sails, but there was no way of knowing for sure. Koji had problems with his aft ballast-tank valves and was unable to use them, which was a major disadvantage in big seas. I too had a damaged valve, on my aft port tank, which had started leaking badly. A bandage of soft rope and grease had fixed the leak, but I couldn't use that valve without letting in a lot of water into the compartment where all my stores were stowed.

I was eating well, mainly making up a pot mess from various tins of food, but occasionally being more adventurous – as when I had a lethal fry-up of potatoes, onions and salami sausage. If the boat was being thrown about I tended to have a freeze-dried meal, which was easier to prepare, but I like the adventure of cooking for myself as you can never tell exactly how the meal is going to taste. As we went further south I deliberately ate more to give my body the energy to keep warmer. I still had not used the diesel heater.

At this stage Unai made a telling comment that he was not going to head further south for the moment, which indicated to me that he was expecting stronger winds down there. This was valuable information, but at the time the wind wouldn't allow me to go further that way anyway.

The three of us now had strong winds for five days and

I was determined to close in on the other two. I was certainly sailing the boat harder this leg as I got a better feel for her, but the same applied to Unai and Dalton also. I slowly overhauled Dalton and closed to within 30 miles of Unai, but as I moved further east I lost the New Zealand shipping forecasts, the only weather information I could receive, because I could not pick up any reports from Chile. To compound the problem, race headquarters found they could not send us the race positions for some reason so, for thirty-six hours, I had no idea where the other two were.

While I was blind, they both went south again, whereas I took a more direct route, thinking they were doing the same. We were all slightly restrained by another wayline, which had been inserted by the race organisers to keep us clear of any ice hazards.

Although I kept ahead of Dalton, Unai got away again, putting some 30 more miles between us in a day. It was heartbreaking. You sail as hard as you can, with your nerves on edge sometimes, but it gains you nothing if the boat is not in the right place. Unai had no jib and I could not set my full mainsail or the reachers, so we were both slightly crippled, although this mattered less all the time we had the strong winds, when we could not have used those extra headsails anyway.

My objective now was to get ahead of Unai before Cape Horn. It seemed increasingly likely that I would have to pull in somewhere around there, maybe Ushaia or Port Stanley, so that I could sort out the headboard, collect a new furler for the reachers, and get the two malfunctioning satellite systems back working. The more miles I could put between him and me by the Horn the less I would have to recover after a stop.

One of the reasons for needing weather information so badly was that there were two areas ahead in the Atlantic where knowing where the winds were could make a huge difference. These were the variables between the Roaring Forties and the south-east trades of the South Atlantic, and the doldrums. Accurate weather could save days in those sectors, so a forty-eight-hour compulsory penalty stop might be a cheap price to pay for proper information again and it would reduce my dependency on luck. I made contact with Simon and Sophy and told them of my thoughts.

Fortunately Saga agreed to fly Simon out to meet me, bringing the spares we needed for the electronics as well as a new headboard fitting and furler, which we would fit once we were in port.

Finally, 800 miles from the Horn, I got ahead of Unai. I had hung onto the jib for a day, right at its limits, but it paid off with a day's run of 282 miles. This was also the day that Graham Dalton announced he had broken two fingers. I did not like to think about that. It was not just the pain; it was the serious inconvenience and the effect on safety. He made another comment that did interest me. He could no longer put on gloves.

I come from the school of Bill Tilman, the hardy British mountaineer and sailor, and avoid wearing gloves if at all possible. It's not just a grip issue. Gloves can catch in things, but I find that if I leave my hands bare in cold climates, they respond by pumping more blood through themselves. Everyone thinks you are more butch and hardy, but in fact you are not suffering at all. That said, there is nothing worse than just sitting bare-handed when you are not doing anything. That's when your hands do get cold, so I don't mind crew having gloves for those occasions and will sometimes even wear them myself when just sitting doing nothing in the cockpit.

The next four days were spent edging out very slightly on Unai. Simon and I were looking for the best place to make a pit stop. We looked at Port Stanley, which was on the route and not difficult to get to, but the lack of regular flights eventually ruled it out so we had no choice but to go to Ushuaia, an Argentine port some 60 miles up the Beagle Channel – named after HMS *Beagle*, the ship that took the young Charles Darwin on the voyage where he developed his ideas of the origin of the species. I had visited Ushuaia by air some years before but my knowledge of the Beagle Channel had been limited to looking at charts. I had a shock coming.

First I had to round the Horn, the Everest of the sea. It would be my third rounding of the Cape, and, being realistic, probably my last. I don't really like closing doors, I like to keep my options open, but I cannot see what opportunity might arise to allow me another rounding.

It made me a little sad to think I would not come this way again, probably, but at the same time this is not a place you want to hang around for long and the relief when it bears west is huge. You only have to look at a chart of this southern tip of South America to see the effect of millions of years of battering. The land has been worn down and seems to be cringing away to the south-east, away from the ceaseless battering from the Southern Ocean. This is no place to find yourself on a lee shore, and a safe margin south of the Horn is advisable. As with *Suhaili* thirty-eight years before, I made a landfall on the Diego Ramirez island group, which gives a safe offing. The wind was Force 7 and from the south-south-west and I was worried that if it backed more to the south it would have been a hard beat to get round, so plenty of sea room seemed prudent.

In fact the wind did back, but I had sufficient space in hand and was able to clear the Cape by 8 miles, a safe margin, at 13.26 hours on 18 February. The swell was huge and the waves aggressive so it was a rolling, wet rounding. The Cape itself was frequently hidden by dark rain squalls, which added to the brooding atmosphere.

It was easy to imagine what an awful place this must have been to the seamen on the square riggers. I saw the two 'horns' of rock that stick out to the south, but the name was given to the Cape by the Dutchman Schouton, who named it after Hoorn in the Netherlands, I believe. It was anglicised to Horn. I looked at it with mixed feelings and was glad to see it bearing west. Once round, I declared a Headland, and opened up Aunt Aileen's superb fruit cake. It proved to have been worth waiting for. She had made me one for my voyage thirty-eight years before, and decided that this was now a tradition – though since she is now a hundred, she left the baking of it to her sister, my aunt Maureen.

The weather rounding the Cape was fairly typical, but not extreme. In fact I was quite surprised at how few serious gales we had during the transit of the Southern Ocean, an opinion shared by my fellow competitors. This seems to have been a benign year for weather in the Southern Ocean, or global warming is having an increasing effect. In *Suhaili* the big fronts had rolled in about every five to seven days with winds of Force 10 or more, and frequently I was forced into survival conditions.

The week before my first rounding, in January 1969, there seemed to be a string of problems that conspired to make the experience a typically uncomfortable one. First my mainsail ripped into two pieces, then I spilled boiling-hot porridge over my hands and burned them, causing big blisters; then the radio continued to receive but not transmit and the jib forestay broke, which meant I had to crawl out to the end of the bowsprit to retrieve the ends, then splice up a new stay, and finally crawl back to the end of the bowsprit to fit the replacement. All of these issues had to be sorted while I was battling against the sort of gale-force winds and steep seas that one normally associates with Cape Horn; and when I actually got off the Cape I was flat becalmed for eight hours in the last place anyone wants to hang around. I could make out the two tower rocks, and a crystal-clear imprint was left on my memory.

I was relieved to complete that first rounding. Twenty-five years later, when I visited again in the 92-foot *Enza*, the storm was sufficiently strong for us to hand the mainsail and we were propelled solely by the windage of the mast, rigging and main boom. After the instruments registered the top end of a Force 10 and a full storm, they imploded, which was a relief in some ways because we could no longer see the numbers.

On *Enza* we experienced an easterly gale, which was the last thing we wanted since it slowed us right down and the boat had to be held close to the wind. The waves were big and we were being thrown about as if we were a toy in a playbox. We were around a hundred miles out to sea that time, so saw nothing of the most feared landmark on the maritime horizon – but again, we were mightily relieved when it had been passed.

This time in the approach to Cape Horn I experienced only two full gales and nothing stronger, and never saw those huge toppling waves I remember so clearly from thirty-eight years before. I doubt we had had waves more than 10 to 12 metres at any time on this voyage. Admittedly *Suhaili* had entered the Southern Ocean at the beginning of September, the equivalent of March in northern latitudes, so it was still winter, but she rounded Cape Horn on 17 January. We were a month later, and the difference was marked.

Another thing I noticed was that the weather was a lot warmer this time. Yes, I had had hail on a number of occasions and snow twice, but the biting cold which I remember from before was just not there. I had fitted a small diesel heater to *Saga Insurance* to help keep things warm and dry below, but I ended up using it only once, and then for a mere fifteen minutes. Whether this is all down to climate change I don't know. Maybe this was just a quiet year. I saw no ice. I hadn't from *Suhaili* either, but the race rules kept us well north in this race.

When the race has been run with no restrictions on route, there have been incidents of yachts hitting ice, as with John Martin in 1990. He had had to be rescued by fellow South African Bertie Read, so everyone accepts the logic of routing the boats north and away from danger.

We saw ice in the Whitbread in 1977 and on *Enza* in 1994, but we went well south on both those occasions. It makes a difference when you have crew and can keep a good lookout by eye, because ice does not make a good radar target as a rule.

Unai, Dalton and I all rounded the Horn within a few hours of each other. I was first, just a few miles ahead of Unai, and *A Southern Man AGD* was about 50 miles behind. For Unai, it was his first time. I'm not sure he enjoyed it especially, and certainly not the strong gusts of the Antarctic winds on the approach to the Cape.

9. The Worst Weeks

Once Cape Horn was bearing west of north, I headed towards the entrance to the Beagle Channel to begin the 60-mile passage to Ushuaia. The channel marks the boundary between Chile and Argentina, and I had been advised not to cut between two Chilean islands since I was bound for an Argentine port, so I headed up to round Nuevo Island to port, which is Chilean and marks the southern entrance to the channel.

In fact both sides of the boundary appeared pretty relaxed about foreign yachts sailing through their parts of the channel. It was still blowing a gale, and the island gave no lee from the wind and only had a slight damping effect on the waves. As I rounded the island and turned west, we began a hard beat in a very short, lumpy sea with dark rain clouds every twenty minutes or so hitting with higher gusts of wind.

On the Raymarine plotter I soon realised we were making too much leeway, so I held my breath and hardened in the mainsail, hoping the uppermost slide would hold. I had to hope the sliders would stay attached to the track or we could end up either having to make a very difficult tack in a high but short sea, or wear round downwind while there was still room to make the manoeuvre, if we were to avoid being pushed onto the Argentine shore. In the gloom, spray and rain we slammed our way north of west as close to the wind as I could. It was purgatory. Whoever decided that hell had to be hot and dry?

I had a rendezvous with a tow boat off Picton Island but had to get there first, as there was no way they could have passed a tow line in those conditions. It was too dangerous to bring the boats close enough to be able to pass a heaving line, and even if we managed that and then sent across a tow line, we would have needed a very long one to avoid the snatching that occurs when boats get on separate waves and out of sync. Then I got lucky and got a 20-degree favourable wind shift for thirty minutes, which gave me the space I needed. I kept hard on the wind and then with a bit more sea room I headed up towards Picton. I made contact with the tow boat but then the line suddenly went dead. Their Iridium phone ran out of power and my VHF had a very limited range. They were still some way off and out of sight. This loss of communications was the last thing I needed. I was now making 10 knots up an unknown channel in the dark, with no idea what to expect.

If we could not make contact I could heave to, by dropping the sails or putting them aback, while I waited hopefully for the tow boat to find me; but if they did not materialize, I would have no choice but to turn and head east back the way I had come to open sea, and either wait for daylight or forget about Ushuaia as a stop.

Then a light appeared to port. I could not make it out but it appeared to be keeping pace. It came closer and, to my immense relief, identified itself as my tow. Now all we had to do was get a line across, which was never going to be easy in that wind. They yelled across that I ought to sail in towards the land. I didn't like it, and manoeuvring was far from easy, but I had to trust these strangers so I tacked and headed inshore. Then, as I got to within a mile of the island, the wind suddenly dropped away entirely and we were able to take on crew and the tow line.

Seldom have I felt so relieved. You can soon tell if people know what they are doing and the tow team were obviously competent, so once we were under tow we had a stiff whisky and I was ordered to rest, my first break for forty hours.

We arrived in Ushuaia at daybreak and moored with some difficulty and loss of skin as the wind was gusting nicely. Ushuaia, the world's most southernmost city, lies in the shadow of a range of mountains. Snow had fallen on their upper surfaces during the night, which made it appear very picturesque, something I appreciated once we were safely moored.

The town itself was full of bustle. It was becoming known as a tourist spot for cruise passengers on their way to Antarctica or rail travellers wanting a taste of Tren del Fin del Mundo, the 'end of the earth' train. It was still expanding and, having a curiosity for remote places I would like to have had a look round, but there was no time for sightseeing.

Simon Clay had arrived with our spares. His trip had been a nightmare: all his baggage had been left behind in Madrid, which meant a delay in Buenos Aires while another plane brought it out. Fortunately he had allowed for some time in hand.

An engineer arrived immediately to sort out the problem with the Fleet 77 satellite system, which turned out to be just a jammed azimuth drive belt, and we got to work on fitting a new Iridium base station. We also put a new head car on the mainsail, assisted by the crew of the yacht *Zephyrus* who were refitting before heading for Antarctica.

On Tuesday, 20 February we tidied up the boat and that

afternoon, not wishing to lose time or daylight, I set off
down the dreaded Beagle Channel and back to the open sea
again.

Having missed it during the inward passage because it
was dark and I was asleep, I was interested in seeing the
channel on the way out. High hills or mountains on either
side funnel the wind down it – this is not the place to be
single-handed. At times, the wind was a manageable 10
knots from the south-south-west. At others it was 33 knots,
which made one or two of the passages where we had to turn
south-east quite interesting. But the scenery was breath-
taking. Argentina is to the north, Chile to the south, and in
places the channel narrows to under a mile. There was more
traffic than I expected, including a few small cruise liners
which were using Ushuaia as a base for trips to the Antarctic.
Most responded to a wave with a toot on their sirens.

I progressed eastwards and it was becoming dark as I
approached Picton Island again, but here the channel
widened and life became easier. I reached Nuevo Island
eleven hours from Ushuaia and restarted racing, some five
hours over the forty-eight-hour limit.

The immediate decision was whether to go inside Staten
Island or sail further east and round it. The tides for the Le
Maire Strait between the island and Tierra del Fuego were
pretty strong and set up some nasty overfalls, but at the
time I was due to pass by they looked neutral, so I went for
the Strait, which I had never seen before.

We were still rolling heavily in large seas as we entered
the Strait but the sea started to flatten once within it, and
coming out on the north side was like coming into a totally
different climate. The dark clouds receded and for the first

time for a month there was not that huge rolling Southern Ocean swell. With a wind north of west we headed off at 11 knots for the south-east corner of the Falkland Islands. I was clear of the Southern Ocean, perhaps for the last time – but who knows.

While I had been losing time in Ushuaia, the rest of the fleet had been making good progress. Bernard was almost up to the equator, a good 1,900 miles ahead of second-placed Koji. Unai was 1,100 miles further behind, and Dalton a further 200 miles astern. I was 300 miles behind them, but then Dalton pulled into Port Stanley to make repairs and I knew I could put him behind me. My objective now, as I sailed towards the Falkland Islands, was to catch Unai.

It was here in 1969 that Bernard Moitessier, sailing like me in the Golden Globe, decided not to turn left towards Europe but to carry straight on, round the Cape of Good Hope and into the Indian Ocean. I rounded Cape Horn on 17 January but did not find out about Moitessier until April, less than two weeks before I finished. In fact most people were unaware of his diversion until he got to Cape Town, because his 'presumed' positions were still being printed in the *Sunday Times*. So at the start of March, he was assumed to be crossing his outward track. He was due in to Plymouth, the *Sunday Times* reported, on 24 April.

Having been sailing alone for more than 300 days, I completely understood Moitessier's decision. He said that he felt 'really sick' at the thought of getting back to the 'snakepit'. I too wasn't at all sure I wanted to return to what we call civilisation. The sea, being a natural environment, is more honest, and my relationship with it was uncomplicated in a way that bordered on compulsive.

Moitessier rounded Cape Horn at the beginning of

February, some three weeks after me. On 18 March he sailed into Cape Town, some 3,500 miles from where he was thought to be – which was in the Atlantic – and sent a message to the *Sunday Times*. 'My intention is to continue the voyage, still non-stop, toward the Pacific islands where there is plenty of sun and more peace than in Europe,' he wrote. 'I am continuing at sea because I am happy at sea and perhaps because I want to save my soul.'

In his log he wrote: 'Do not think I am mad but I have the impression that there is something that resembles not the third dimension, but the fourth ... I am in very good health.'

From a radio programme I heard before the Horn, I knew that Moitessier was still behind, and then he was not sighted off the Falklands until eighteen days after I had passed them, so there were 1,500 miles between us.

My position on 10 February, the day Moitessier's boat *Joshua* was sighted off the Falklands, was well in the Variables and my speed had fallen as a result. Moitessier would have slowed in the Variables and doldrums just as I had, but even if one ignores this and allows him his full average speed of 117 miles a day all the way home from the Falklands, which is not unreasonable, he would in theory still have had two days to go when I got back to Falmouth on 22 April.

This may satisfy a mathematician but no seaman would be so foolish as to say who 'would have been first'. There are too many imponderables at sea. It would have been close, and Bernard would have won the £5,000 prize for being the fastest had he continued, but the prize we all wanted was to be first.

A year after I finished, someone came up with the idea that the record for the solo non-stop circumnavigation belonged to the person who crossed his outward track first. I could have crossed my outward track long before Moitessier crossed his, had that been a requirement of the race at the time, but it wasn't. The rule said quite clearly it was 'Port to Port'. But armchair experts can invent anything they like.

Some people say that the Golden Globe was not a proper race. But it was a classical race, just like Scott and Amundsen racing for the South Pole.

The record business is a quagmire, as there are too many people making rules. Someone said I was the oldest to make a circumnavigation, but this was not true. My good friend Minouru Saito went round alone aged seventy-one in 2005. Neither was I the oldest to enter this race. That honour went to Harry Mitchell, who was seventy in 1995 when he went missing about 1,500 miles west of Cape Horn on his 40-footer *Henry Hornblower*.

After clearing the Strait de la Maire I maintained an average speed of 11 knots up to the Falkland Islands and a rendezvous with HMS *Edinburgh*, a Type 42 destroyer that was the last of the class to be built. I saw her going about her business in the morning, in fact my radar alarm found her long before she came in sight. Then her helicopter buzzed me briefly. I was having my own private Navy Day! She came back later and stayed for half an hour before performing a 'whizzy' past me to leeward, a most impressive sight.

The Ministry of Defence were obviously looking after me. A couple of days later I was buzzed by a Royal Air Force Hercules on a maritime patrol, and then a day later another warship bore down on me. She turned out to be HMS *Dumbarton Castle*, a patrol boat that protects the UK's offshore oil and gas installations. She was on her way from

Rio to the Falklands, which had been alerted by HMS *Edinburgh* that I was in the vicinity. In both cases the warships lowered their RIBs so I got a chance to chat to some of the crew.

After HMS *Edinburgh* left I sailed on, hoping to close on Port Stanley, but a large bunch of kelp weed caught the port rudder, forcing me to luff right up and almost stop to shake it clear. I decided to gybe further away from land and the heaps of kelp. Port Stanley has long been on my list of places to see, but will have to remain there since we didn't get near enough to take a look.

In fact we did not entirely avoid kelp. The starboard rudder caught a large bunch and later, when I hoisted a dagger board, a great clump floated clear, fortunately missing the rudders. These Open 60s with their bulb keels and skegless rudders are natural kelp catchers. For these waters, you need a long keel and a rudder hanging from the stern or protected by a skeg, and certainly no bulb or winglets at the bottom of the keel.

We were now coming to one of the most frustrating parts of the Atlantic Ocean, even more so than the doldrums, because they cover a larger area – the Variables of the South Atlantic. They are governed by the St Helena high-pressure zone or South Atlantic high, which randomly conjure up any type of winds and weather from nothing to gale force, clear sunny skies to violent thunderstorms. How we handled this next obstacle would in all likelihood decide the order of the last three places in this leg and perhaps the race itself.

When I sailed through his area in *Suhaili* I took a north-easterly course out into the centre of the South Atlantic, as recommended in *Ocean Passages for the World*. I had eventually broken into the south-east trades, but not before I had recorded a day's run of 9 miles and spent twenty minutes one evening lying on deck listening for a sound, any sound at all. I thought I had gone deaf. It was so calm, there was not even a ripple on the hull. Now, with the modern weather information, I felt I could make a much faster and more efficient passage . . .

I headed north-east while spending much of my time, yet again, trying to sort out a weather-forecasting system. I had been fitted with a new one in Ushuaia but the trouble with it was I had had no time to get accustomed to the glitches that inevitably arose.

So I was left with three-day forecasts only, which were not enough to let me work out what the St Helena high was going to do by the time I reached its vicinity. I resorted to guessing. This proved to be the wrong tactic.

In retrospect I made a huge and disastrous mistake in not following Unai and then trying to outsail him, but the weather GRIB files showed an interesting system of north-westerly winds closer to the coast to the north-west of the centre of the high and I decided to use this to try and sail round him and the centre of the high. No one had mentioned that the main weather model had least information in its database for this zone, but I made that discovery the hard way and it cost me the leg. I even crossed tacks with Dalton by about a mile as he headed north-east and I continued north awaiting the forecasted winds. I called him on the VHF but he did not respond.

The winds never did come round to the north-west, indeed for two days both GRIB forecasts gave them as north-west when I was getting north-easterlies. The difference was catastrophic for my plans. I got stuck between two systems, the forecasted north-westerlies to the north and new south-westerlies to the south, which were not predicted to be this far north.

In this patch of calms we lost valuable time. But calm areas are not always calm. One night we had a magnificent lightning display and one particular bolt must have landed within 200 metres of us – there was only a half-second delay between one huge flash and the ensuing thunderclap. This was accompanied by torrential rain and a sudden squall of wind up to 27 knots which had veered 45 degrees. The autopilot could not cope with that, and having been nicely balanced for 18 to 20 knots, she tacked herself.

I got her back round and changed down from the Solent to the storm jib, and as I finished that the wind dropped. I decided to wait before doing anything as there was still lightning and dark clouds all around, illuminated by a nearly full moon in between the clouds. I had no idea whether we might have another squall so I left her with limited sail for the time being. I sat on my favourite perch in these circumstances, the top step of the companionway, from where I could see the green illuminated instrument repeaters at the chart table yet jump on deck in a hurry if necessary.

Any hope of catching Dalton disappeared when I got caught between the two weather systems. It had started with a deluge before dawn with a big wind squall and wind shift, followed by another wind shift back and then the next squall. This went on right the way through until the following morning. One minute I would be sailing east, the next the wind had backed 120 degrees and I was aback.

There were nine deluges, most of them heavy, enough to wipe out the wind. In all I had to gybe four times and tack eight. I made seven sail changes in the next twenty-four hours, but by the end of it my gains were negligible. This effectively meant I missed the weather window that became available to the others and was forced to sail east for two and a half days while they were all sailing north towards the finish line.

When the sky began to clear I waited three hours and then set more sail. The wind was back east of north again, but we could not go on headings towards Uruguay. The GRIB files were not registering what was really happening, so my best bet seemed to be to take a course as close to the rhumb line as I could to Cabo Frio on the coast of Brazil and try and get into the easterly trade winds.

The lack of sleep and constant need to deal with a boat that frequently tacked itself as it lost steerage way began to take its toll on me physically. I managed seven hours sleep in eighty hours, nothing like enough if one is to remain efficient, and I knew it. I cancelled all media and video requests to free rest time.

I skipped meals so that I could rest, which I knew full well was a stupid thing to do, because inevitably my body became run-down and my skin erupted into a mass of tiny little boils that itched annoyingly all over my right leg and arm. Why they didn't break out on my left side, I have no idea. I treated them by taking antibiotics and eating properly, but they were daily reminders of my flagging spirits and it was a fortnight before they had entirely disappeared.

I would have been better without the weather files and sticking to the old sailing-ship routes which took one further east. Yet again, I was forced to conclude that too much technology is not always the right solution, especially when it turns out to be unreliable. The only consolation was that with so much fresh water available, I was able to wash everything, including myself.

We did close in on Dalton as he worked his way through the high. At one time we were down to just 100 miles apart, but we might as well have been on different planets. His wind was enabling him to get north, while mine, from the north-north-east, gave me the choice of heading east or not much north of west. He made it into the trades after a struggle and was away. I was still pinned down going east, with the added obstacle of a new high developing, whereas he, like Unai, was going north towards the finish and there was nothing I could do about it.

Having missed that weather window all I could do was try and edge towards where the winds were or hope they might come back towards me as the high moved about. In fact I was unlucky on both counts. It was a week before I eventually reached the trades, by which time I was too far behind to be anything but an also-ran in this leg, and probably doomed to finish last in Bilbao as well.

These were probably the worst weeks of racing I have ever experienced. The sheer frustration of just not quite getting into the trades, which for four days were moving away as fast as I was moving towards them, was taunting me in a very sadistic manner. The one weather file I could now get was usually inaccurate and I eventually stopped downloading it.

To stop myself going mad I convinced myself I was not in a race. I stopped checking the race positions, and resigned myself to getting the boat to Norfolk as quickly as I could.

Reports from the other boats showed them in completely different winds and making good progress north. Bernard finished the leg on 4 March, 2,900 miles ahead of Koji. Unai had broken clear of the Variables and was tearing up the Brazilian coast, and Dalton was slightly south of me but 7 degrees east, a much more favourable position, which gave him winds from the east, whereas I had them from north-east, which would not let me clear the Brazilian coast to the north.

It had become a lot warmer so I had changed to shorts and a safety harness. Oilies had to be donned and removed carefully, as I had cuts and grazes all over my hands and wrists and every time they caught in a sleeve or cuff, the scabs would be shaved off.

The ones sustained while mooring up in Ushuaia twelve days before looked as if they had occurred yesterday. They were red, raw and bloody. Then I remembered I had not eaten since breakfast, but not feeling like cooking I opened one of the Argentine salami sausages and ended up eating the lot. This was accompanied by a sustaining drink of milk reinforced with a dram of whisky.

Despite my frustration, there were times when I relaxed and enjoyed the weather, which was mainly sunny, and the sparkling blue seas, which are always good for morale. When there were no squalls, I enjoyed some nice steady winds, albeit from the wrong direction. I could console myself with some wonderful sunrises and sunsets, watching the red glow outlining the clouds after sunset. I might not be able to race, but I could still derive some pleasures from being at sea and untroubled by other people.

A pattern had begun to develop. The wind came up at night and died to almost nothing each afternoon. During one of these afternoon calms, when we stopped completely for an hour, I went swimming to keep cooler and clean and also to check the hull. The seawater temperature was over 30 degrees. Before diving in I checked the sea around for the

slightest sign of wind ruffles and put a line out over the
stern, extending 15 metres, as a safety precaution. I might
be frustrated by the situation but I certainly wasn't suicidal!

The lesson is that the Variables can be very variable, and
the model used by NOAA, which every forecaster seems to
use, is flawed for this area north of the Argentine border
through lack of sufficient data. I wish someone had told me
that before I made the decision to try and go around the
high to its north-west. I might still have been in the race.

Weather forecasting is a lottery, as we all know, and much
of it is inaccurate, which is deeply annoying irrespective
of whether you are organising a picnic or trying to win
a round-the-world yacht race. Forecasts vary. Some fore-
casters rely entirely on their computer models, others – and
the French come to mind – use their instincts more. French
meteorologists seem to be prepared to put their heads above
the parapet and tell you what they think. I used to be pretty
good at reading the weather data but I was out of practice
at the start of this race, and since then I had not had forecasts
on a regular basis, never for longer than a week, so it had
been very hard to build up a feel for what was going on.

Few sailors get it right all the time. They either get lucky
or are clever and call it right, but very few people do it
consistently. Someone like Ben Ainslie has a gift for seeing
wind that no one can see. But he does not want to spend
all day calling the weather from up the mast, where he can
best see the signs on the surface of the water.

Eventually we worked our way far enough east to enable
me to tack north on a course that would almost clear the
Brazilian coast, while hoping the wind might turn slightly
favourable. When coming south through these waters the
previous November, I had had south-easterly winds in this

region, which would have suited me beautifully now, but the direction remained obstinately north-east so our course was slowly converging on the coast. The others had had freer winds in this stretch and had romped up the coast, but I was being forced to go hard on the wind. It was frustrating and annoying, but nature is neutral and you just have to learn to accept what it provides. Sometimes it favours you, sometimes not, but we did seem to be having far too many 'nots'.

I knew that unless we got a good veering wind shift we were going to have to tack out again at some stage. The question was when. If I tacked now the course on the other tack would be south of east, pointing perpendicularly away from the objective; however, if I left the tack, the wind might veer and make this eastward tack even less attractive. I decided to tack and held it for seven hours until we began to get headed slightly, which meant the other tack had become a better option.

Those seven hours were agonising. My competitors were speeding towards the destination and I was making no progress that way at all. I was effectively giving them 90 miles. But in the end it turned out to be the right decision. When I tacked back, we could just make north, and over the next two days the wind slowly veered, not enough to clear the coast at that moment but enough to make me feel I was back on the race track and might get a veer.

It felt good to be engaged in a contest once more and for the first time in a while, I downloaded the latest positions and took stock of what had happened while I had been trapped by the Variables.

The others may have had a freer wind up the coast and had made better speeds, but their real advantage came from breaking free of the Variables sooner than I had been able to. But the bad news was that on 13 March Unai was some 1,650 miles closer to Norfolk than me, and Dalton 850 miles closer.

Freed from the prison of the Variables, we were now beginning to move along nicely. There were some 3,000 nautical miles to go; I had no reasonable hope of catching either Unai or Graham; all I could hope to do was shorten the gap. But we had begun to make some decent progress at last.

We recorded our first daily average of over 10 knots for the first time in seventeen days and held it for three days, almost to the equator. I could plot our progress by the noticeable movement each night of the constellation of Orion, which had been to our north, but slowly came over-head and then bore to the south. It was a positive sign. The skies are clearer at sea because there is less background light from cities, and it is even better in the southern hemisphere because there is less land and fewer people using electricity.

My hopes rose of closing the gap with Unai, even though he was making good progress as well, but I gave up a few miles by going well clear of Recife, some 40 miles off the coast. There was more commercial traffic than I had expected along this stretch of ocean and I wanted to keep well clear of it. My radar transponder started bleeping shortly after I had headed north and sure enough, thirty minutes later, a ship came up over the horizon. As I got closer to the easternmost point of Brazil I crossed a busy shipping lane which kept me up for thirty-six hours.

Whether any of these vessels noticed us I don't know, but they gave no indication of having seen us. Ships would come in from starboard, which meant I was the giving-way vessel, and I would have to tack to get clear of them. More dangerous were vessels coming up from astern on a converging course. As the overtaking vessel they should have kept clear of me, but none tried, and once again I was forced on a number of occasions to tack to make a safe clearance. None answered calls on the VHF radio, and I could not help wondering what the watch-keepers were doing and whether they were actually keeping a lookout. There are fewer merchant ships about now than when I sailed *Suhaili* back from India or around the world, and far more yachts making ocean passages, so one would expect shipping to be more on the alert.

Perhaps part of the problem was that they did not expect a yacht to be sailing so fast, although their radar plotters should have been able to tell them our speed. Although tacking for a few minutes was a nuisance and lost me more time, avoiding the vessels was not difficult – and was a better option than hanging on to what might turn out to be a collision course. But it was hard work and very stressful.

I am quite aware that at times I can sound like a grumpy old man, so the news that I had received the 'Seadog of the Year' Award from *The Oldie* magazine was not, initially received too well. But when I found out more about it, I felt honoured. I would have loved to have been at the lunch at Simpson's-in-the-Strand in London to receive the award.

Sir Terry Wogan was the chairman of the judging panel, which also included Jon Snow, Maureen Lipman, Ned Sherrin, Gyles Brandreth and *The Oldie*'s editor, Richard Ingrams. Sara, who accepted the award from Sir Terry on my behalf, later reeled off a list of all the folk who were in attendance. Their names brought home to me how far I was away. I would have enjoyed the opportunity to meet the panel and guests such as Sir John Mortimer and Peter O'Toole, Jeremy Irons, and fellow oldie Leslie Philips, but hopefully I will get the chance at some stage.

I sent through an acceptance speech that Sara read out: 'I had not considered myself even starting the apprenticeship to be considered an Oldie until your message came though. Old to me is eighty-five years, not where I am now in the springtime of my third phase. However, when I looked at the panel I realised that such a collection of talent could not possibly be wrong, so maybe I am old enough to be an Oldie after all. And if one is going to be classified as old, it is nice to have it recognised in this manner. I am sorry I cannot be with you. I am currently racing north off the Brazilian coast and won't be home until May, trying to prove, with indifferent success, that age is no bar to activity. It is with gratitude that I accept this award and regret that I am not there to be able to meet so many who are on my list of those I would like to meet. Thank you.'

I'm not a big reader of magazines but I've always loved *The Oldie*. It does exactly what I have been trying to do with this campaign, which is to make a stand for age over youth, albeit in a rather eccentric way.

Then I heard that Dalton had pulled into Forteleza, a port on the Brazilian north coast, after his rudders were seriously damaged following a collision with something. It was pitch black so he was unsure what he had hit, but the boat had stopped dead in its tracks and Dalton was forced into port.

Sadly, things went from bad to worse when he arrived there. First he was struck down by a bad bout of sickness, and then his boat was burgled with the loss of all his communications equipment. Finally, and worst of all, his keel bulb dropped off.

Despite all this, he refused to give up. His crusade to finish the race in honour of his son Tony burned as brightly as ever, and he resolved to find the keel bulb, get it fixed and carry on, even though it was unlikely, with all the time delays, that he would finish within the designated time as set out by race rules.

As we approached the equator, the wind began to follow predictions and slowly veered. The western side of the Inter-Tropical Convergence Zone, which divides the weather of the two hemispheres, is the thinner edge of a wedge renowned for its calms, its wider sector being on the African side of the ocean. But sometimes the trade winds from each hemisphere will combine and provide an easterly wind right across this zone, and for a few days, as the others made their way north, this is what happened, judging by the speeds being made.

It could not last for ever, of course, and as we came up to the equator the wind ominously began to ease. The doldrums are not always devoid of wind. They can be, but that is rare. They are a zone populated by variable winds, which are usually very light except beneath clouds. You don't spend all your time eking out a knot or two – you tend to spend it watching the clouds and awaiting the sudden squall that often lurks beneath them.

And these squalls can be quite large. I measured one that according to the radar was 9 miles across, and while it was passing overhead the visibility was down to 200 metres, so it was not a good time to be crossing a shipping channel. Fortunately we were running clear of them at the time.

On my sixty-second day at sea, on 17 March, I celebrated

my sixty-eighth birthday by crossing the equator. I tried not to pay any attention to the anniversary though the phone kept ringing and the emails kept landing. I had a glass of whisky and the last of the aunts' cake and that was it. As I said in my log, I don't feel old, though celebrating my birthday in the same week as I received *The Oldie* award dampened any youthful delinquent urges I might have had.

For the next day the wind came stubbornly from the north-north-east, so we were still unable to reach off and make good speed as we had land to clear. The bashing to windward brought on the leak in the sail locker once again, and I had another mammoth baling session to remove almost a ton of water. But slowly, over the next few days, the wind veered, and as we drew level with the Windward Islands we could at last make good speed, averaging between 10 and 13 knots for six days.

When Unai in *Pakea* crossed the finish line on 23 March I was still 1,400 miles behind. If I was going to keep hold of my third place overall, I had to get a wriggle on. In Fremantle I had established a lead over him of five days but that had been whittled away by the two port stops and the lack of progress in the Variables.

If I was to maintain my podium place I needed to make sure that I arrived in Norfolk within that five-day margin, and to do that I needed favourable winds. An east or south-easterly would do nicely. If it assisted me, I could easily cover 1,400 miles within five day; but if the wind blocked me, I calculated the remaining distance could at worst take eight days. On the final leg from Norfolk to Bilbao of just 3,500 nautical miles, this deficit could be impossible to make up.

I almost pulled it off. For three days I managed to keep

up a good average speed heading in the right direction. Then a depression came over to the north of Norfolk, the wind died, and was followed by very light south-westerly winds which slowly veered round to the north-west, just where I needed to go. The wind eventually steadied from the north.

I was just about able to lay the course, but only close-hauled. We bashed on, watching the sea temperature rise to 26 degrees as we crossed into the Gulf Stream. This had a wind-against-tide effect which was lumpy and uncomfortable and slowed us. The only good thing about this was that the waves breaking over the boat were like a lovely warm shower.

My five-day lead over Unai evaporated when I was still 400 miles from the finish. Every minute more between that point and the line was a minute I had to make up in the final leg. As we crept in towards Virginia Beach and the finish line off the entrance to Chesapeake Bay, the weather showed its contempt once more and the wind died. I spent eight agonising hours covering the last 16 miles and arrived just as night was falling. I could barely disguise my disappointment as I crossed the line and handed over the boat to my shore crew.

I had been at sea for seventy-five days and it had been a nightmare – from having to return right at the beginning to fix the autopilots, through losing all communications, then damage to the mainsail, the loss of time going to Ushuaia, followed by the hopeless weather forecasts in the Variables, the reappearance of the doldrums and then the final calms.

True, there had been some wonderful moments along the way. Surfing in the Southern Ocean was exhilarating. Rounding Cape Horn and seeing it clearly for only the second time was memorable, and crashing through sparkling blue seas beneath a warm but not too hot sun was uplifting. But I was glad it was over. I was not physically tired, but mentally I had had enough for the moment. If there had been no more legs to race I would have been happy, because all I wanted was to get away, have a rest and put the past seventy-five days of frustration and disappointment behind me.

The fact is, I wasn't doing very well. I was lying last of the 60-footers, and that was not what I envisaged when I set out.

I didn't feel I had sailed a bad race but my performance had been hampered by computer programs that did not function properly and by poor workmanship. I had completed two legs, which amounted to around 27,000 nautical miles, but had never had the chance to show what I and *Saga Insurance* could do. Racing solo around the world is as much about resolving problems that occur on the way round as it is about sailing well and making good weather and tactical calls. But whichever way you looked at it, I'd had more than my fair share of those problems.

I felt people were looking at me and saying, 'Yes, well, he is getting around the world, but he is not competitive.' For the first time, it occurred to me that people might be saying I was too old to do this and that I was making a fool of myself.

A few days away from *Saga Insurance* would do me good, and I knew myself well enough to know that after a couple of days away from boats and the sea I would be desperate to get back. I still had something to prove. It was not enough that I was still in the race. I wanted to be winning. I had had a good record of winning, and I felt that it was in danger of being shattered. We had two weeks to sort everything out and prepare the boat to show what we were really capable of.

10. The Final Leg

It took me a good few days to recover from my seventy-five days at sea. This was the third longest voyage of my career, but unlike the first two, which were both in *Suhaili* when I was in my twenties, this one had taken its toll on my mental and physical reserves. I have noticed that whereas when I was in my twenties I only needed a day or so to recover from a long voyage, now, closing in on seventy, it takes about five days. Maybe some of this was due to the fact that I had been working solidly since the previous May and I probably needed a proper long break.

If my body was a battery it was running low and needed a recharge. I don't have much difficulty adjusting to uninterrupted sleep, and at the same time I don't need a vast amount either, but one does need to catch up. I slept and ate well to restore strength to my body and began to feel I was returning to normal.

Trousers that had been tight before the race were now hanging loosely around my waist, though my weight remained the same since my arms and shoulders had been pumped up by all the physical work during the previous five months. My legs were weak, which is quite common after a long period at sea, but the boils that had developed on the last leg were healing well, which is always a sign of a return to a healthy body, so I knew I just needed some decent food and some prolonged rest and I would be ready to go again.

When I arrived in Norfolk, I was tired and a bit dispirited.

Too much had gone wrong, and I needed a break away from the boat so I could get myself motivated for the last leg. A part of me felt I had had enough of the race and I wanted to get it over. But there was still everything to fight for and now I wanted to be ready for the last round. The short break did me good. As usual, being away from boats and the sea soon had me wanting to get back to them and enthusiasm was quickly restored.

Norfolk had never hosted a yacht race stopover before but it was ideal for the Velux 5 Oceans due to its location on America's east coast, which has become an obligatory port of call in any round-the-world yacht race for routing, commercial and social reasons. To get there, the fleet had to cross the Chesapeake Bay which is one of the trickiest stretches of water for sailors – the combination of lobster pots, recreational traffic and some flukey winds and tides can can make for unexpected problems.

Norfolk is the world's largest naval base, so everywhere one went there were large slabs of military grey iron looming high out of the water. The US aircraft carriers – and there were three of them there when we arrived – are 1,092 feet, or a fifth of a mile, long, and made the visiting HMS *Ocean*, which at 660 feet is one of the largest ships in the British fleet, look rather puny. Most of the people we met worked for or with the US Navy and the national flag was flying in many of the gardens, which is something you don't see much in England. The race village had been set up in the marina at Waterside Park on the Elizabeth River, a location that allowed visitors to come and see the boats and skippers at close quarters and then disappear into one of the waterfront bars and restaurants to polish off yet another vast plate of food.

Our Norfolk host team of Jim Dixon and deputy Morgan Fletcher Drum went out of their way to make our visit as stress-free as possible, although throughout my time there, I found it difficult to relax and just wanted to get the last 3,500 nautical miles out of the way.

Our Saga team moved into a small rented house near Virginia Beach which became our base for the stay, a half-hour drive from downtown Norfolk, where the boats were berthed at the Waterside Marina.

As in Fremantle I wanted the team together as it keeps up morale and is an excellent way of ensuring that everyone knows what is going on. Julia, who had done such an amazing job in looking after us in Fremantle, ensured that once again we were well fed and hydrated in Norfolk.

There was not a great deal of work to do on the boat, which was just as well as we had just two weeks between my arrival and the restart. The main task, fitting a new outdrive so we could motor, had to be cancelled because we did not have enough time to remove the mast and rigging and haul her out, one of the disadvantages of the deck spreader arrangement on *Saga Insurance*. It would have taken a day to unstep the mast and at least two days to step it and set the rig up again. There was no time to include that in a tight programme and besides, I was happy with the rig as it was. Apart from checking it over I wanted it left alone. I had pushed the boat much harder in the last two weeks and it had held up well.

The sails were sent away to be checked and the engine was serviced. The two laptop computers I used for communications and navigation were showing signs of fatigue. This was hardly surprising. A small boat is not a kind environment for computers: they sat on the nav table, held in place by Velcro, but every time the boat hit a wave it sent a shudder through them as well. When they were not being bashed about, there was always a risk of water getting into them. But they are vital to the modern racer, so if they became unreliable they added to the frustrations and time wasted. One of mine had become seriously unreliable and had to be rebooted every time I asked it to select another program or talk to its partner.

Happily, I took delivery of a new Lenova computer given to me as a birthday present by the manufacturers. I was assured the hard drive was sprung and all my problems would be solved. Tom Cecil from Clipper Ventures loaded all the programs it required and we ran it up a few times before I sailed.

We installed a new life raft in the empty cavity in the transom and tackled the problem of the leaks in the sail locker, which we thought we had traced down to faulty plumbing in the ballast tanks.

There were a few changes to my loyal shore crew, though Simon continued to take charge. He had spent a few years living in Virginia Beach since his father, a retired commander in the Royal Navy, had been stationed at the naval base there and had some useful contacts, on both the business and social fronts.

His deputy for the stopover was Tony Reid, who had been in Bilbao when I was first introduced to them. Swiss, as he was known, had also spent a few years with *Ecover* after a career in telecom sales for one of the big mobile phone operators. As well as knowing a good deal about Open 60s, he also had his own company supplying and installing media equipment to the top end of the marine industry, both on racing yachts and super yachts. I could have done with having him pegged to the chart table during the first leg when my equipment had proved so troublesome.

Having been together in Fremantle, the team had formed a strong bond. Their experience and knowledge was growing, so I had no doubts about leaving them to work on the boat while I recuperated at a friend's house, which was nestled on the edge of a beautiful lake. My band of volunteers, who had started out as green enthusiasts, were now practised boat hands, having devoted many hours to the campaign. Charlotte, a student naval architect who had been with us in Gosport, had travelled to Norfolk even though she should really have been studying in Southampton, and both Tim and Huw were back on board, forever chirpy and committed. The Cummings had returned to their regular jobs and so our logistics were in the hands of Katie Noble, another highly efficient virtuoso shopper.

When it was time to return to work, APP, the TV production company who were making a film of the race, decided it would be a good idea if the astronaut Buzz Aldrin and I met, as I had completed my solo non-stop circumnavigation just three months before he set foot on the moon in 1968. Unfortunately a meeting could not be arranged, but through the marvels of modern communications we were able to have a chat over a video link. Here was someone who would not allow age to restrict his activities, and he told me with relish of a trip he was planning in a Hummer vehicle the next year across Antarctica to the South Pole. It sounded like one of those adventures that every septuagenarian should undertake.

We welcomed another sponsor to the campaign in Norfolk. Old Pulteney Whisky from Wick, on the north-east corner of Scotland, decided to support the remainder of our race, and it was a match that seemed totally appropriate for me! This ensured that I was not going to run out of product for my evening happy hour in future.

All the boats were berthed together and we shared equipment through the fleet as necessary. Bernard Stamm, who had accurately predicted he would complete the second leg in forty-eight days, now had a lead of fourteen days overall on second-placed Kojiro and could only lose the race if all the bad luck dumped on him in the final leg and he failed to finish. Kojiro was thirty-five days ahead of Unai who in turn was forty-two hours ahead of me. There was always the possibility that the remaining miles would produce some close racing on the water, but the only real competition left was between Unai and myself.

By this stage in the race a strong friendship between the skippers, their teams and the organisers had developed, and this included the Velux and race organising teams. This has always been a feature of this particular race and it was encouraging to see a happy tradition maintained.

In my experience, most races never develop like this as the sailors only see each other before the start, which is always pretty frantic, and perhaps at the finish, but in the Velux 5 Oceans the intermediate stops gave an opportunity for the skippers, their families and teams to get to know each other. We worked side by side each day and would often team up in the evenings for social events organised by the host officials. There were ice-hockey matches to watch, dinners to attend, shopping malls to visit – though these didn't make it onto my list of activities.

The atmosphere was relaxed and extremely friendly. I feel sure this is one of the reasons why the race has always been popular. The camaraderie that develops during the stopovers produces some strong and lasting friendships. We saw evidence of that when a group of veterans from the race – including Dave White, who had established the race back in 1978 – staged a reunion. All ten skippers were from North America. All had done one race and some still harboured hopes of doing more; in fact the Canadian Derek Hatfield would have been with us in this race if his brand-new Open 60 had been finished in time. He won Class III (Open 40 class) in the 2002–3 Around Alone and was planning to be on the start line of the 2008 Vendée Globe.

The reunited skippers had had varying degrees of success in their solo sailing careers but they all remained passionate about sailing, and all of them were still actively engaged in racing or cruising even though some were beginning to take it easy due to rheumatic joints or financial pressures. It was a meeting of like minds and spirits and a lot of fun. There is no room for the boastful and arrogant when everyone has shared the same risks and experience. We are intense rivals when racing but in port the camaraderie has a chance to develop and we were able to see the evidence as skippers past and present swapped tales and tips.

This fellowship was threatened by a football game which matched Kojiro and my crews against Bernard and Unai's teams. The game resembled all-in wrestling more than football as Unai's team closed in on me from either side in a tackle that would have meant a red card in any professional game. But my rugby experience proved a match for them. By the finish surprisingly no one had been hurt and everyone was smiling.

The race restart was set for Sunday, 15 April, but as the day grew closer we watched a depression deepen inland and the predictions showed that it was going to arrive over

Norfolk at the precise hour we were due to get going. The race director David Adams called us all together with the Norfolk organisers to discuss the situation. The predictions were rather alarming. Local meteorologists suggested there would be 45 to 50 knots of wind and choppy seas.

While we had all sailed in more severe conditions and knew our boats could cope with them, we realised that getting out of the marina, putting start boats in place and transferring crew was clearly going to be extremely dangerous. In circumstances like that it is easy for one simple thing to go wrong – for a boat to be damaged and require lengthy repair or, at the worst, for someone to get injured or even killed. Our event did not justify that sort of risk. The discussion lasted just twenty minutes; it was focused solely on safety and not commercial considerations, and concluded with a unanimous vote to delay.

This proved to be the right decision, as the weather deteriorated even further. States of emergency were declared in two states and an unprecedented 7.5 inches of rain fell on New York in twenty-four hours.

As compensation for guests who had come to watch the start, a wonderful reception was organised aboard HMS *Ocean*, which was taking time out in Norfolk from its duties patrolling the Caribbean looking for drugs-runners. The two-hour drinks party culminated in Bernard, Koji and I dramatically disappearing upwards on their aircraft lift straight out onto the deck, where it was very wet!

Three days later the weather eased although the wind was now from the north-east, and we made a start in Hampton Roads, in sight of the huge US Navy base in Norfolk.

There had been a chance that Dalton in *A Southern Man AGD* might arrive while we were in Norfolk, but he had to divert yet again, this time to Bermuda, with autopilot problems, which effectively meant he missed the cut-off date for the last leg and was out of the race. It was a sad end to Dalton's adventure. He had entered the previous race but had to withdraw when he broke his mast, and now he had dropped too far back this time.

With the start moved to a weekday, things were quieter than they would have been at the weekend. No big crowds or dramatic send-offs this time as we went down to our boats to be towed out to the start. Unpromisingly, our hull was holed near the stern above the waterline by a cleat as we were towed clear of the berth. We had no wish to miss the start, so Simon immediately got to work with some underwater epoxy, leaning out from a dinghy to apply it.

The four boats crowded together at the weather end of the line as the start gun went and began a hard beat out into Chesapeake Bay. The conditions suited neither me nor my boat, and I was reminded of the saying that ports rot ships and men. My muscles had definitely softened in the two-week break.

Once past the huge naval base I was able to free off slightly down the channel that leads out to sea. Already Bernard was only just visible, while Kojiro was a bit closer and Unai was slowly leaving me behind as the wind eased and I let out more sail.

I was not too worried about the positions at this early stage as once we got going I knew we could speed up. Shipping movements at the entrance to the bay forced me further south and by nightfall I could not see any of the others, who were somewhere ahead and to the north. It was a weary bash into a strong north-easterly, which made the boat shudder as she smashed down into the waves, but I had more confidence in her now and kept her pushing hard, something I would not have considered at the beginning of the race. After 30,000 miles I finally had trust in her strength.

The ability of the Raymarine instruments to read the seawater temperature came in extremely handy in this section of the ocean, as it enabled me to find the Gulf Stream. This great warm oceanic river flows from the Gulf of Mexico around Florida, where it can reach a speed of 4 knots, then up the US east coast to about 40 degrees north, which is about level with New York, where it turns eastwards and later divides, part of it heading towards Spitzbergen in the north of Europe and part of it to Portugal in the south. It is the main reason that northern Europe has a moderate climate. Although its speed declines as it turns eastwards it is still worth half a knot, which one might as well have as not.

The seawater temperature off Chesapeake was 9 degrees Celsius, but during the first night it rose to 24 degrees, which told me I was in the main stream. The difference between the speeds being shown by the boat's log, which measured my speed through the water, and the GPS, which measured my speed over the ground, confirmed that we were gaining some benefit.

With a north-easterly wind and a north running current, the seas became short and lumpy, but I kept bashing away into them until we hit one wave and stopped dead. I was lying on the navigation bench and with the force of the jolt shot forward, so that I was jammed in between the chart table, which was now above my head, and the controls for the canting keel, which were digging into the small of my back. These survived all right but I received a couple of bruises.

By the early hours of the next morning there were ominous sounds of sloshing water coming from the sail compartment. Crawling in, I discovered it half full of water yet again. Worse, the dogs on the watertight door to the next compartment forward were loose, and it had a good foot of water sloshing around in it. I took in sail to ease the pressure on the whole structure.

Where was this water coming from? We had replumbed the ballast-tank pipes in Norfolk and the job looked pretty sound. In any case, when I did ballast one of the tanks there was no leaking as there had been before. The water was coming in at the rate of a cupful every minute when we were heeled over to starboard, which was manageable but not for too long. I eventually came to the conclusion that the problem must be something to do with the starboard dagger board, so I promptly hauled it up.

The leaking eased, which indicated the casing might have a crack in it somewhere, but it wasn't obvious. I baled the water down to an acceptable level but then had to pump perhaps 200 strokes every two hours to keep it there, which took its toll on my energy reserves. This was fine for a short time, but before long I began to feel my strength begin to sap. Pumping and baling had to go on – I had no choice – but they left less time and energy for other things, and I knew it would be advisable to try and find a way of avoiding it before I became too tired to think straight.

I waited for the weather to ease before I could get in with a bucket and bale out properly. This amounted to taking some forty buckets – or 400 kg of water – out of the forward compartment alone. This extra weight held the bow down, which made the foredeck much wetter and changed the feel of the boat since she was obviously deeper in the water at the bow.

I remember this same thing had happened in *Suhaili* in the Arabian Sea in 1965, when we were sailing from Bombay towards Muscat, and I discovered the builder had not put in floors to hold the frames to the keel around the mast. The hull had been opening every time the boat pitched, which meant the water kept on cascading in, so the three of us – me, my brother Chris and a friend, Heinz Fingerhut – had baled for thirty hours non-stop, one of us on deck throwing the contents of the bucket overside, one filling the bucket below and one resting. When the seas eased we had collapsed into our bunks, and it was the water lapping my ears some eight hours later that awoke me. We baled again and then went over the side to ram caulking cotton into the seams, which was successful in reducing the rate of ingress though almost catastrophic when we attracted the attention of five sharks.

When we arrived in Muscat we spent nearly a month getting proper floors made and fitted before continuing our voyage to Africa. At least then the leak had been obvious. Here and now, I had no idea where it was. All I knew was that it could be reduced if I kept the starboard dagger board raised, that it could be controlled but at the expense of a lot of frequent hard work, and that it was distracting me from racing.

In order to try and keep the boat more upright and lift the dagger board higher and also make the sails work more efficiently, I tried to heave the sodden sails over to the higher side of the boat, but they must have weighed 300 kg with the water in them. I got one halfway across the compartment when the boat lurched, throwing the sail, with myself beneath it, back downhill, where I ended up waist-high in water and firmly trapped.

It took me a few minutes to extricate myself, heaving at the sail to release one leg, then the other, until I was able to wriggle clear. It was a consolation that the water was warm, but I was soaked and although I had a change of clothes, I had only brought a very limited wardrobe. The only way to dry wet clothes was by wearing them, and even this was only partially effective, since clothes that have been soaked in salt never dry out properly.

As well as the leak, there was the matter of our lack of progress. We were getting nowhere in the race and were unlikely to do any better until the winds came round and allowed me to reach.

Unai and I were within 12 miles of each other as far as I could tell, but his tracker and Sat C had packed up so he was having to call in to race headquarters with his positions and this caused confusion because the times given varied quite markedly. Bernard and Kojiro, also close-hauled, were pointing higher and slowly getting away from the rest of us, with every chance of getting a little break to allow them north.

This break would not last until I reached that spot, now I had taken my foot off the pedal to reduce the amount of water coming into the sail locker, so my immediate future looked set to feature more days of close-hauled work, which suited my boat less than theirs, while they would merrily speed away with a westerly wind.

But Bernard and Kojiro were not the issue any longer. They had first and second places to lose, not to win. Unai was my objective and beating him in, if possible by the forty-two hours I needed to take third place for the race overall, was my main focus.

At this point Unai suddenly eased sheets and shot away south-eastwards. I considered following, as I was tempted by the easier option of less bashing for the boat and I felt I could cover him. I went through the weather charts carefully, but there was nothing to suggest that he would gain any advantage by heading in that direction. Besides, I was uneasy about going south into that zone between the Azores and Bermuda. Both are frequently the homes of high-pressure systems with very light winds, and there was an increased likelihood of north-easterly winds as one got closer to Europe.

The weather program also showed little change if I continued on my present course, close-hauled due east, and it looked like a small high-pressure system would divide me from Bernard and Kojiro within a couple of days.

I looked at how things were looking to the north. Here the winds were more likely to be from the west, which would provide a more comfortable ride to the constant bashing I was faced with at the moment, and much faster sailing for *Saga Insurance*. But it meant taking the gamble of losing at least a day on everyone else as I made my way north. I would still have to get through the high-pressure system, but I would get through it more quickly if I went north as it was heading east, and once that had passed the westerlies would prevail.

I thought about it for a bit and then tacked. My new course was initially more than 120 degrees from the finish line – in fact I was heading for Halifax in Canada again – but if I could bear the pain of that for a day we would hopefully reap the benefits later. I tried not to think about the downside – that if the gamble failed, I would be throwing away any chance of doing well – and just hoped the weather forecast was right.

Almost twenty-four hours later we were flat becalmed in the centre of the high. Indeed race headquarters got worried and called to see whether I was all right, as they said I had hardly moved between the last two positions. The reason was simply lack of wind, not anything untoward, but it was good to know they were still monitoring us so closely.

It was tiring keeping the boat from drifting aback, which she did frequently as we hardly had steerage way, so I wasn't able to get much sleep, especially as the hydraulic steering ram chose this moment to empty all its oil into the steering flat and ceased to operate. I switched to the electric one and hoped it would last to the finish.

Then, after nearly thirty hours of sailing the 'wrong' course, there was the first indication that a westerly was coming. By lunchtime we were charging along straight for the finish, averaging more than 12 knots. I did not want to go any further north anyway. A large quantity of icebergs were being reported only 400 miles north of us, being brought down by the south-flowing Labrador current, and I had no desire to go anywhere near them.

In the meantime Unai had continued his progress to the south-east and was now some 8 degrees of longitude ahead of me, but also 8 degrees of latitude south. But of that I was not certain, because his position was being given as 200 miles nearer to the finish than me. Sometimes less. It was infuriating not knowing exactly where he was, whereas he, of course, knew where I was.

Bernard and Kojiro had been given a helping hand by

some favourable winds up front and were now some 500 and 400 miles ahead, the three of us in the north all matching each other for speed, about 12 or more knots on average.

I was pushing *Saga Insurance* much harder now. I had confidence in her rig and sails and knew she could take more speed than I had asked of her earlier in the race. It felt terrific to be hurtling through the waves at those speeds, and I was enjoying the sensation that came with this improved performance.

The noise increased too. Hard, sharp screeches as the sheets tightened on a winch drum in a squall had always alarmed me, but the sound of the hull pushing through the water had now become so familiar that I did not need to look at the log to know what speeds we were achieving.

We spent one night averaging 14 knots before a strong north-westerly wind, with surges up to 20 knots. It was deeply fulfilling, glorious sailing. By the time I had had three days of these conditions I was still some 8 degrees north of Unai, but he was now behind me. I had taken a full 8 degrees of longitude out of him in that short period of time and was now 200 miles closer to the finish line than he was, and sailing faster. My gamble appeared to be paying off, but I could not afford to ease up for a moment.

Every yard gained counted towards a position I could be proud of, although at the same time I felt rather sorry for Unai. This is what had happened to me south of Rio de Janeiro, when there was a gut-wrenching feeling that we were losing out but there was nothing we could do about it. My diversion north had enabled me to recover some of the deficit I needed to reduce his overall lead. It was now all down to whether the weather conditions would favour me with another 200 miles over him. It looked like I would beat him in this leg and I thought a lead of 400 miles at the finish would be sufficient to beat him overall.

I was still aching in the arms and legs from the baling, which left me with a tiredness that short spells of sleep were not sufficient to cure. But they were long enough to produce a range of very weird dreams, similar to the ones I had on *Suhaili* all those years before. I was dreaming of people I had known in my past but had not seen for years. For instance, one time I dreamt of our old nanny, Carrie Richards, who had been my mother's nanny before she became ours when we lived in Beckenham. She has been dead for nearly forty years, yet she was as vivid in my dream as if she were right there in front of me.

These types of dreams had been quite common on this voyage, as they had been last time round. On *Suhaili*, I remember the dreams mostly concerned the voyage. It was like my voyage was an eliminating heat and there would be another race after we had all arrived back in Britain. I'm sure these dreams must all mean something but I have no idea what.

The tiredness did bother me a little, however. My slower recovery was about the only advantage I could think of that the youths had over me! The four of us left in the race were all strong and fit, and the differences between our performances had narrowed as those of us with limited Open 60 experience caught up.

We had become used to being bruised; indeed, this was inevitable when the boats were rolling and pitching so heavily. You only have to be caught off balance when not hanging on to something and you go crashing across the boat. The only way to avoid it would be to pad up like an American football player, which would inhibit speed of movement. Cuts, too, are inevitable, particularly on the hands, but these toughen with time at sea and the palms become very hard.

To lighten the boat so she could be driven faster, we had removed anything we thought unnecessary in Norfolk. We reduced the sail wardrobe to just three off-wind sails, cut down the food stocks to twenty days and removed any spares that were not essential. When the skippers discussed how much fuel we were each taking, the others all said about 120 litres, whereas I went with 80. In part this was because I knew my little Volvo engine was highly efficient at keeping my batteries charged with its two big alternators. In all we probably reduced the weight by 700 kg, a useful saving which I hoped would give me a few additional valuable miles.

Transferring diesel from 25-litre containers into the day tank was always interesting, especially when the boat was bouncing about, and I did it with a siphon which made a spill less likely. However there was always a danger that the diesel would splash up, and on one occasion it did, giving me a nice mouthful. I spat it out, washed my mouth with water and tried to remove the smell from my beard and moustache. When that did not work I rubbed whisky around my mouth, which made a great improvement to the aroma assaulting my nose.

I was still only having one nip of whisky a day. But I had left with one bottle of Old Pulteney empty, so I wrote out a message with an offer of a reward for the finder, sealed it in the bottle, using sealing wax to create a better watertight fit around the cork, and threw it overside. Two days later a second bottle was empty and went the same way. I have never done this before and suspect that the chances of either being found are very slight, but you never know. I suspect the currents will direct them towards the coast of Portugal, and if they miss that they will continue towards the Canary Islands.

Although the wind eased and then became a bit flukey with some quite aggressive squalls, I continued to make better time than Unai and by 27 April had increased my lead to 260 miles. At this point Unai obviously decided his southern route was not working for him and began to edge north. Looking at the wind prognosis it seemed he might get similar winds to me for a few days, in which case my lead would not increase by much. I still did not have sufficient lead to be safe; another 150 miles might do it, but we were both dependent on whatever weather came our way and this was out of our control.

I might have had the slightly faster boat, but if the weather turned against me that advantage would be lost. To be certain I needed the weather information – and, as in the previous legs, I suddenly lost it. The Iridium phone packed up, though no one could work out why. Then I lost one of the weather programs I was using, and finally, to cap it all, I lost the other one. I was weather-blind again. I sent an email via Sat C to Tom Cecil in the Clipper office in Gosport, and within an hour had instructions on how to restore the Maxsea system. Well, almost restore it. I could get the weather forecasts all right, but certain other features seemed to have disappeared, such as the link with the GPS. It came as no surprise to find that technology was still proving unreliable right to the end.

On 30 April, my twelfth day at sea, the weather map threw out a small depression that was about to form close to Cape Finisterre, right in my path. Its movement would surely decide the race. If it went north I would get westerlies, which would rush me in to the finish; if it went south I would get easterly winds, and those would probably hand Unai his third place overall.

First and second positions in the 2006–7 Velux 5 Oceans race were decided that afternoon, when both Bernard Stamm and Kojiro finished in Bilbao within forty-three minutes of each other. They had both put their names in the record books. For Bernard, having successfully defended his 2003 title was a remarkable performance and an honour he richly deserved. His whole programme had been marked by efficient preparation and a determined competitiveness with precious few errors.

Kojiro's performance was also astounding, especially when at one stage near the finish he closed the gap to within 4 miles. When one considers his boat was some 2 tons heavier than Bernard's it would have been interesting to see what might have happened in the race overall had he had a lighter boat. He had got better and better as the race went on, and if his plan to get sponsorship for a new boat comes to fruition, he will prove a formidable contender in future solo races.

As Bernard and Kojiro finished I still had some 600 miles to go and Unai 900. There was still everything to race for. That distance could take forty-two hours if the winds went light or came from ahead.

The following day I made good progress for a while, but then the depression began to exert its influence and the wind slowly came round to the east. I was forced away from the direct course for Bilbao, and north-east towards Ushant, while, 300 miles and closing behind me, Unai was surging in with strong westerly winds.

I plotted the wind carefully and hoped that Unai might yet become stalled. I knew full well that no race finishes until the line has been crossed, but it was not looking good.

I beat north-east all night and lost distance, but the forecast indicated the wind could be expected to come round to the north, so I tacked early and followed the wind round so that eventually I was heading directly for Bilbao once more.

My hopes had been raised but were quickly dashed that night when the wind dropped away. The weather had thrown me its final piece of nastiness.

There was no point in railing against it, but it seemed appalling luck that just when I had almost built up sufficient miles to have a chance of regaining third place, I had run straight into headwinds and calms while Unai was coming in with the fresh westerly winds. There was now no chance of beating Unai by the necessary forty-two hours to hold on to a podium position. I had worked hard this leg to close him and felt completely deflated by the circumstances.

Forty years before I would have gone into orbit, screamed and kicked things, but age seems to have calmed me down a bit. In any case I had other issues to deal with. I was coming up to the main shipping routes to Northern Europe and soon my radar detector was sounding full time.

I switched it off, as there were going to be plenty of radars operating near me for the next few hours and I needed to keep a constant visual lookout. I crossed the southbound lane, then the northbound, then the two inshore lanes, and only in the inshore southbound lane did a vessel come close. Under the rules it was for him to avoid me, and I was relieved when he altered course to give a greater clearance.

As Unai beat in towards Cape Finisterre, I drifted slowly towards the finish.

He had been slowed, but the gap between us was now down to just over 150 miles and closing. Looking at the weather, it seemed that a westerly wind might prove stronger closer inshore, so that night I gybed and headed south towards the coast. This also put me in Unai's path, as I had decided I had better cover him. The wind did increase as we got closer to the coast, and by the following morning I was surging in towards the harbour at 14 knots in poor visibility.

I switched on the VHF and soon began to hear messages between the committee and other boats which suggested they were all out on the water waiting for me.

Then, at about 4 miles range, the huge western breakwater to Bilbao harbour came into view. Boats full of journalists now approached, but I had no time to acknowledge them. We were travelling fast and I needed to ensure that we crossed the line between its two marks.

We sped on and eventually crashed over the finish line, a small armada of welcoming boats scattering clear as we came through. But even now I could not relax. The wind was blowing us straight down and onto the beach and it was imperative to slow down quickly.

Simon, Huw and my brothers Chris and Michael jumped on board from an RIB, through Chris very nearly fell in the drink when the transfer did not go entirely to plan. We started to get under control by rolling the jib. Because the outdrive was still faulty we had no engine, so we had a few problems trying to stay clear of all the other boats and there were a few close calls. The wind was blowing, the skies were leaden and grey and the seas were very lumpy, which caused seasickness problems among some of the media boats. Then the tow RIB came alongside and we dropped the mainsail.

It might not have been the sunniest of welcomes but the relief in getting across the finish line was overwhelming. Finally, I could start to relax.

As soon as the pressure was off, I started to enjoy the moment, waving to the crowds on the breakwaters and acknowledging the sirens of the ships in harbour that rang out to greet us.

It took around forty minutes to get into the Getxo Marina and we broke open a bottle or two of Old Pulteney to celebrate. By the time I arrived, the pontoon was sinking under the weight of all the friends and supporters who had travelled to welcome me in. Everywhere I looked there were familiar faces, though Sara and the children were conspicuous by their absence – Sara had written to say that the problems of coordinating the various school commitments of five children with my arrival, for which she had only a vague estimated time, were too complicated. I quite understood and so was not expecting to see her.

The media circus got into full swing even before I arrived, as Sophy fielded calls from the British television and radio stations all wanting live interviews. At around 11.30 a.m., on my arrival, I was presented with a microphone and gave my first interview. Almost six hours later, having completed forty-two interviews, I was, unsurprisingly, utterly exhausted.

I had a quick snooze, then went and met my team and some old friends for my first post-Velux dinner. During the dinner there was a bit of commotion by the door and, to my great surprise, the children trundled in carrying a huge banner bearing the words 'BZ Grandaddy'. I had no idea this had been arranged – according to Sara, my jaw hit the table. They also presented me with a 'hoodie', a gift from *The Oldie* after I won their Old Seadog Award. It was a very special moment and I was thrilled they had been able to make it.

Unai finished twenty-four hours later. I had beaten him for the leg prize, as I had in the first leg, but the gap that developed between us in the second leg had proved too large to bridge. Overall, he pipped me by eighteen hours and seventeen minutes. It was a bitter disappointment to have come so close to beating him, knowing that had it not been for one of the many failures of the weather or autopilots, I could have taken him.

So we were positioned last of the finishers. But events like these are more about getting round the course than posting a position. As the longest race in the calendar, the Velux 5 Oceans is the ultimate test of the sailor and the boat. It is about getting your boat through its trials, repairing it as necessary and making sure you are there at the end. In this respect we had beaten more experienced and better prepared teams like those of Alex Thomson and Mike Golding, who had had to abandon or withdraw, and there was some considerable satisfaction in that.

The final leg had been a series of emotional highs and lows, and I had spent much of the race being frustrated and not feeling that I was racing properly, but the main thing was that I had got round. Although circumstances had not allowed us to show our real paces, *Saga Insurance* had proved herself a good, strong and fast boat. The race was over. The great adventure I had started eleven months before was finished. I had completed my second solo circumnavigation.

Eight days later we sailed into the Solent with the weather proving unfriendly to the last. There were grey skies and grey seas, but as soon as we came round the Needles I felt the sun shine. It was nothing like it had been when I sailed into Falmouth in 1968, when I was met by a crowd that I was told numbered a quarter of a million people. My voyage back then had been a trail blazer, and people were captivated by two aspects of it: the uncertainty over whether sailing non-stop around the world solo was possible and whether, after 312 days on my own, I had gone mad.

I hadn't, thankfully, though there are some who thought I was mad to do it again.

In a final flourish, six of the Clipper yachts, crewed by sponsors and friends, joined me off the East Lepe buoy west of Cowes and escorted *Saga Insurance* to Gosport.

Once again the clouds were low and cheerless, and had this been just another stopover, I would have regarded the Solent simply as a grey rather gloomy stretch of water. But as a runway into my home port, it looked glorious, and I was more than happy to set eyes on familiar landmarks such as Yarmouth on the Isle of Wight and the entrance to the Beaulieu River on the mainland.

As I charged up the West Solent, the flotilla of welcoming boats seemed to get bigger and the helicopters and RIBs started to gather. We were joined by the Royal Navy and the Queen's harbour master, and we gave *Bear of Britain*, the famous Farr 52 racing boat, a run for her money as she went out training with a full crew on board. But today it was *Saga Insurance* which received all the attention. The Clipper carrying all my family, including Sara and the children, drew alongside and I wondered how they were coping with the rough conditions and the swell. They all looked OK, and judging from the chorus of disapproval that went up when I lit a cigarette, they were all loving the occasion.

We received a seven-gun salute from the Royal Yacht Squadron as we passed Cowes, which was a very special moment for me. Picking up the tow into Gunwharf Quay in Portsmouth was a challenge in the choppy waters but eventually we nudged our way into the marina, where we received a rousing reception from family, friends, sponsors and spectators, led by Roger Taylor of the band Queen who had helped start me off all those months ago with a blast of their song 'Don't Stop Me Now'. It was a truly wonderful finish, but after 157 days at sea this time round – which was almost half the time it took me in 1969 – I was happy to be stopped.

Conclusion
'The Sea Has Not Changed'

My objectives in entering the Velux 5 Oceans were threefold. Firstly, I wanted to draw a line in my life after losing my wife Sue in 2003 to late-diagnosed ovarian cancer; secondly, I wanted to see what the Open 60 circuit was like and race one of the boats; thirdly, I felt there was an around-the-world race left in me and I wanted to show that age is not a disadvantage if you don't let it become one.

After knowing Sue since I was eight, growing up together, marrying when I was twenty-two, she twenty, and sharing everything, apart from a seven-year divorce break, for the next forty-two years, life without her was something I had difficulty dealing with. I had become so used to talking everything through with her and sharing ideas; many of them she rightly condemned, but she gave me an opinion I valued and usually followed. She had shared all the bad times, when business partners double-crossed us and then turned nasty. She was the one who was tapped on the shoulder when the writs arrived, as I was usually out. I have never forgiven the perpetrators of those bad times, not because I was unable to deal with them legally, but because before we got to that stage Sue had been put through so much. Initially, after her funeral, I was in shock, then numbed, and that numbed feeling lasted for more than two years. Mourning is a desperate time, when, in addition to the feeling of loneliness, you regret all the things you never got round to doing together.

The mourning had to be brought to a close at some point, because life had to go on, whether I liked it or not. I was still on the planet, and I had a daughter and her family who had meant so much to us, and still did to me, and who deserved attention, not least because of the support they had given me. I was still feeling Sue's loss badly right up to the time I bought the boat, two and a half years after her death, and this continued for a while into the race. But slowly the need to concentrate on the race and the dangers of the sea, something I had done since the age of seventeen, and getting back into the rhythm of the sea, reassured me. I was back to my home, to my greater security, and it gave me the comfort I had looked for. During the race I thought of Sue a lot, but as the race progressed I found that the feeling of hurt was lessening. Perhaps because of my need to keep a focus on what was going on in my little isolated world, perhaps because of being back in my own secure environment, perhaps because the passage of time can tend to dull the sense of guilt and remorse, perhaps simply because time is a great healer. I don't know. But I found myself beginning to put a new perspective on where I now was. You can never abandon the memory of a person who has given their life to you, shared the good and bad times, as Sue did, loyally and unselfishly. She will always be close to me, even though she has gone from me forever. Maybe we shall meet again, I hope so; but even if we cannot, she would have accepted that whichever of us was left behind would have to get on with life without the other. The race gave me time to think these things through and become easy about a future.

*

The world of solo ocean racing has advanced enormously since 1968. I had been on the periphery of the Open 60 scene, but not in it. The changes I observed were dramatic – it was rather like comparing the era of the biplane with that of Concorde. Ever since 1968–9, when we showed it was possible to sail solo non-stop around the world but no one knew what was the ideal boat for the job, this new class of Open 60s has developed. The design over the past ten years has become standardised to a considerable extent: 60 feet long, with a wide and shallow hull and very large sail area. Rotating masts and canting keels with narrow fins and large lead bulbs at the bottom have followed. It is still a development class, with the boats becoming lighter and faster, using state-of-the-art technology with composite materials. Even though *Saga Insurance* was nine years old when I bought her, and some 2.5 tons heavier than the new boats, she had been ahead of her time when built. I still felt as excited at being a part of the new era as the Wright Brothers would have been had they been given a chance to fly a supersonic jet

But to be competitive with the newer boats I had to be fully race-ready, and the one obvious factor about my whole programme was that it started too late. We only had three months from buying the boat until the start. During that time it was necessary to qualify, by sailing across the Atlantic and back on a voyage of not less than 2,000 miles between ports. This came first, as it had to be completed to enter the race, and it also gave me a chance to get to know the boat a bit and find out what needed doing to her for the race. Then we had to do a major refit. The programme was always going to be tight; it allowed little time for bedding everything in and checking everything was working.

The preparation depended on knowing what needed to be done and things coming together when we needed them. We lost some time as we learned what needed doing and how to do it – like removing the keel and fitting its replacement – but more valuable time was lost being let down by suppliers, delivery teams, and people just not doing work properly or on time. Those delays deprived us of the time needed to try everything out, get to know new systems and test everything thoroughly. This would have exposed some, probably not all, of the problems that were to bedevil me during the race and that ultimately cost me a great deal of time and, in the end, race position.

This became a serious issue in Bilbao, where we were still trying to get the boat ready when people descended very late with new equipment and new computer programs. In the end I just could not absorb so much information in such a short period. I spent days at sea after the race started trying to get to grips with the equipment, often with no success. With hindsight we needed a minimum of five months, not three, to get the boat qualified and ready, and even then more time with the computer programs would have been useful.

This compounded as the race progressed. The problems that developed as a result of late preparation caused delays at sea, which meant we had less time in port to catch up.

The other very significant factor was my lack of awareness of how the whole Open 60 scene had moved on. All the boats bar us had professional preparateurs and considerable budgets, and their skippers were professionals with no other distractions. My total costs for the whole event, including the cost of the boat, were less than half Kojiro's budget and a quarter of Alex Thomson and Mike Golding's. Although

Alex, Mike and Josh Hall, who was looking after Kojiro, were generous with their help, what we lacked on our team was someone with up-to-date experience of the boats and the new racing scene. We only got that later, in Fremantle, when funds permitted.

There were continuous problems with computer programs, and computers too for that matter. The expert arrives with the program, which he tells you is easy. He installs it, runs though it and goes away. What he has not told you is how to deal with the program when it goes wrong, which it is almost certain to do. The result is you spend vast amounts of time trying to sort out a comparatively simple problem, or one that seems simple once it has been explained.

A typical example was the Maxsea program, which suddenly decided it needed me to register. For three vital days I could not get weather, and so missed a high-pressure system that cost me 400 miles. Pleas for assistance went unanswered, until another user of the system told me to remove and replace the dongle. That simple operation solved the problem. The program was not actually saying it wanted my registration details, but that it had lost contact with the dongle. But if no one has told you about this problem and its solution, how are you expected to discover it on your own?

The other tendency is for an expert to look at your programs, tell you he has a better and easier one, and proceed to install it. This is dangerous. You have now lost the program you were beginning to understand and have a whole new range of glitches to overcome. The programs need to be installed well in advance, with quite a lot of time allowed for getting used to them, and an expert at the end of a phone line. Only when there has been time to absorb these programs do they become really useful. Without this they can take vast quantities of time and mental effort which should be used for racing or resting.

Having a fractured coccyx was not the most comfortable way to set off on a circumnavigation and certainly hindered me in the early days. I found lifting heavy weights like sails hurt for the first couple of weeks, but then this eased and by the end of the first leg I had forgotten it had happened. The sprain or whatever it was that affected my left wrist was more of a problem than my coccyx. It lasted for almost three months and, despite the attentions of a physiotherapist in Fremantle, did not really disappear until the last leg. We never worked out what caused it. The salt-water sores that developed towards the end of the second leg were a result of being tired and run down. I took penicillin to deal with these and once I got to Norfolk, rest and good food soon cured them completely. Apart from penicillin and Savlon, I did not use any other medicines.

From a strength and sleep deprivation point of view, I found I could keep going as long as I was at sea, but once I reached port and the demand was no longer there I did need longer to recover than I had when younger. In my twenties and thirties, after a good night's sleep I was usually up and ready to go. I could still do that now if I had to, but I would not be at my best. I needed something like five days to catch up on sleep and allow my body to recover. Once the race was over I suddenly found myself vulnerable to colds, and caught a bad one that would not go away for a fortnight. This is not unusual. While I still *had* to sail I sailed aggressively, unaware of the drain on my reserves. There had to be a payback at some stage and it came once I felt I could relax after the race.

When we returned from the Jules Verne in *Enza* after seventy-five days of a 5,000-calorie-a-day diet, my cholesterol was at 9.8. I felt very fit at the time; I was 7 kg heavier but this was muscle. This time on my return my cholesterol was at 5.8 when I got back, actually down a little from the last time it was checked. My weight was 2 kg less than when I sailed, but my waist was 30 cm less and my shoulders had bulked out. As always after a long period at sea my legs had lost muscle, and it took time to build them up again by taking good walks. I suspect my calorific intake did not exceed 3,000 calories a day this time, and I never felt hungry.

I know this is an event where finishing is primary, and in that respect I beat those who pulled out, but I did not enjoy coming last of the finishers. At the beginning I was out of practice, after an almost six-year break, and it took time to get myself up to speed.

I was never worried by being alone. I have always found that I am perfectly content on my own at sea, ever since I set out with *Suhaili* in the Golden Globe. When a journalist asked me how I was going to cope with the loneliness I told him I would know after the first fortnight. If I couldn't cope I would be back in port by then. But I think I have become less dependent on company at sea since then. Seventy-five days of solitary confinement, which was the length of the second leg of the race, was not a problem from a human point of view; I was quite content. I think the previous three years of living alone after Sue died had also made me less bothered by loneliness. I enjoy the feeling of freedom and the ability to be totally selfish and do exactly what I want, when I want. But I can also enjoy sailing with a crew just as much, so I don't feel I have to be alone at sea.

I am probably unusual in that I do not really want to

communicate much when I am at sea. If I used the satellite phone twice a day there had to be an emergency. I enjoy not being bothered, almost being out of touch. Many other solo sailors are seldom off the phone, and it makes me wonder why they sail single-handed in the first place. Email was different, as I could deal with that when I chose, but we set up a separate email address for me that was only known to a very small group, so I avoided all the unnecessary emails that would have been a distraction. Even so, spam was creeping in towards the end and adverts for Viagra started to pop up, which seemed particularly unnecessary and inappropriate to my situation!

My relationship with the sea undoubtedly helped. Having made it my career from the age of seventeen, I do not feel threatened by it. I can swim in the middle of an ocean without a thought. I am probably most content when at sea in my own boat; I feel at home there and enjoy the feeling of freedom and satisfaction that I am responsible for my own life and safety and not dependent on anyone else. If I have crew with me then I include them in my sphere of responsibility. Of course I can be frightened by a rogue wave and will make every effort possible to avoid bad weather, but that is just being sensible. I would certainly prefer to face a storm well out at sea than close to a shore. I still believe that the Merchant Navy training gave me the right approach to the sea: never take it for granted and assume, when planning a voyage, that the worst can happen. Above all we were taught that the essence of good seamanship was safety. Avoid unnecessary risks. It is easy to be daring, but if one thing goes wrong that dare can turn into a disaster. A few seconds of showing off can so easily turn into a lifetime of regret. The crew are safe so long as the boat is safe. Risk the boat and you risk the crew's lives. I have never lost a crew member. I have had two fall overside but with good crew teamwork we got them back. I don't ever want the loss of a crew member on my conscience.

An Open 60 campaign has become a team effort these days, and any sailor needs the back-up and support that a team can provide. My team was unusual in that it was a combination of professionals and volunteers from Fremantle onwards, but this worked well. Simon had a large team at his disposal. They had varying experience and ability, but they had enormous enthusiasm and you can always achieve more when enthusiasm is present. The volunteers did not mind how menial or dirty a job was, they knew it was necessary and just got on with it. Simon, Pete and Tony provided the professional expertise. It made sense to focus their abilities on the more complicated problems, but the volunteers got to assist in these tasks and learned a great deal. We started with enthusiasm and little experience; we finished still with enthusiasm but by the end the team had much more knowledge to draw upon. Bringing the team together for meals in port in the evening definitely helped to foster a keen sense of team membership, which stood us in good stead from a work point of view and gave us all the feeling of belonging to a happy and close-knit family. By the finish we had become a 'family' of friends. I may have been at the sharp end and the one who got the publicity, but it could not have worked without that family behind me.

The team support is not only essential in port with the overhaul and maintenance; it is still required when the boat is at sea. You need someone ashore who can chase up solutions to problems with equipment – as I had with the communications – that occur while you are away sailing, and plan the next refit and obtain all the supplies and spares required. Having someone like Simon in my team, to whom I could give such a problem and leave him to chase up the solution, made a huge difference. I could not have chased up solutions to my computer program problems while at sea. In this respect the modern sailor is not really a 'loner'. In order to be competitive all the single-handers these days use their teams for continuous support.

No one in their right mind goes to sea if there is a gale forecast. But if you spend a lot of time at sea you are bound to run into bad weather from time to time. The first gale you meet is frightening, the second less so. Fear is of the unknown, so if you meet a lot of gales after a while you learn that you can survive them and how best to do so and they become less frightening. This does not mean you know it all, though. A hurricane, as we had the day after the start, is always a threat, and while I was not frightened by it, I was concerned that I was handling the boat properly. I have always thought that one of the most useful things to have before you go to sea is a sense of apprehension. Assume you are going to run into bad weather and go through the boat ensuring it is ready for the worst possible scenario. Make sure your course gives you sea room or funk holes if you need to run for shelter. Then if you do run into bad weather, you are ready for it. If you don't run into bad weather, well, at least you had the confidence of knowing the boat was prepared.

When I reached the finish line in Bilbao I was ready to stop. *Saga Insurance* had been a very exciting boat to sail and as I got to know her better, and sail faster as a result, I became happier. I had enjoyed the pure sailing side of the race, but not the frustrations that came from poor computer

programs and unreliable equipment. The constant break-
downs in the communications and computer programs had
worn me down far more than the changing of sails or dealing
with leaks in the sail locker.

Going around solo a second time was not difficult, despite
the gap of thirty-eight years. The race track had not changed,
nor had the weather. I had been down in the Southern
Ocean three times in the intervening years in any case, so
did not feel a stranger there. The real difference was in the
technology, not in what nature had to offer. Technology
cannot get you out of difficulty when you are in a storm,
but it can help you to avoid it. It also allows us to get
weather information that was not available to us in the
1960s, which has helped dramatically to reduce times for
circumnavigations – when it works. This is probably the
biggest difference between then and now. The sea has not
changed.

The number of people who have sailed around the world
is still just 170 – fewer than the number who have gone into
space, and a twentieth of the number who have climbed
Mount Everest. A solo round-the-world race or voyage is
still one of the most difficult and hazardous challenges
available to man.

The Velux 5 Oceans race in 2006–7 was a turning point
in the series that had started as the BOC Challenge in
1982. The hurricane at the start brought enormous media
coverage, and this attention did not diminish. The result was
a success for the sponsor, the race organiser and the boat
sponsors and skippers. The fleet was small, in part because
the sponsor was not announced until quite late and people
inevitably wondered whether the race was going to happen.
There may not have been many competitors, but the compe-

tition was as intense as it had ever been. Skippers and sponsors need time to prepare for events and inevitably will make their plans around those that are definitely going to happen. The Velux also has the misfortune to coincide with the French Route de Rhum transatlantic race, which is naturally important to French sponsors. But the Velux has always been a more international event than any of the others, and this is where its future still lies. The race stopover countries provide additional opportunities for sponsors to promote themselves to a wider market. The value of the media coverage achieved by my own entry alone was some £15 million, a huge figure in promotional terms.

On balance I enjoyed the Velux 5 Oceans race – I always enjoy that feeling of freedom you get at sea – but felt frustrated by little things in the racing. One of my happiest recollections is of the team supporting me for this venture and the camaraderie that has built up. Those friendships will, I am sure, endure. My worst memory, apart from that awful period in the South Atlantic when the weather predictions were all over the place, is the passage into the Beagle Channel.

As a voyage, yes, I am glad I did it. It gave me an insight into the Formula One scene which is the Open 60s circuit and a chance to experience sailing at this level. I never doubted I could get round, but I wanted to be competitive, and this was not to be the case. In many ways it was only after I had sailed around the world in the Velux 5 Oceans that I was at last ready to race.

Should I have done the race? I don't know. I do know that if I wanted to do the race this was my last chance, as in four years' time I probably cannot expect to be so fit and capable.

The race, from a personal point of view, was not a success, which has been very disappointing. I knew I was going to be seen as 'the old guy' and people would make excuses for me on that account, which I found condescending and very annoying. But I didn't need those views in pure racing terms. I felt badly let down by the support I received from certain sectors of the boating industry, which left me floundering. When I had things working I was competitive, but all too often I was struggling with problems that should never have been there. I always believed I would get around the world this time – getting around, ultimately, was down to seamanship – but I had hoped to be more competitive.

Having completed the race, I have no desire to continue in the Open 60 circuit. It has been interesting and informative, but it is very different to the type and style of racing that appeals to me now.

Would I do this again? No. This was my last realistic chance to be competitive on the solo circuit, and it certainly sharpened me up. But I do not feel a desire, like my good friend Minouru Saito, to go round solo again. He did it two years ago and is planning to go again at seventy-four years of age. If I go again it will be in a cruiser, to see places I've enjoyed in the past and others I have always wanted to see.

Looking ahead, however, I am sure that I will remain actively involved with racing. I really do not mind what I race so long as it is a level playing field. As a sport sailing is like athletics – there are as many different types of event, from match racing like the America's Cup, through fleet racing on handicap, dinghy racing and the solo and short-handed circuit, whether in mono- or multihulls, and there are always records to break. I am much more attuned to the long-distance, short-handed side of the sport, but not averse to a fully crewed race provided I have a competent and congenial crew. Whatever the future holds, I cannot visualise a life without a boat, or a voyage to sail her on.

Acknowledgements

Whilst the sailor may be out on the oceans alone, these days there is a crew of people who have helped to put the boat there and look after affairs at home, without which a modern race would be impossible. I was incredibly lucky to have the support of willing amateurs and professionals alike who shared one obvious trait, enthusiasm.

Obviously it is not possible to write a book and focus on racing at the same time, so whilst I did some writing at sea, Kate Laven collated this with the overall picture and background so that this book could be produced in a remarkably short time frame.

David Stubley and Frederik Ulfsaeter were responsible for putting together the sponsorship arrangements with Saga Insurance and Aynsley Jardin was our link there.

My daughter, Sara Hales, looked after my personal affairs whilst I was away.

Before the race, I was given enormous support by members of the Little Ship Club, most notably Richard Griffiths, Peter Newberry and Pat Walsh, plus Greg North, Martin Jerome, Juan Coetzer, Charlotte Rigg, Tim Ettridge, Commander Dilip Donde, Indian Navy, and Huw Fernie.

The boat support team was fundamental under the leadership of Simon Clay, with support from Tony Reid and Peter Cummings, Katie Nible and Katie Cummings. Julia Stuart looked after the nutrition for the voyage and also took charge of the team's homes when we were in port. Sophy

Williams joined me during the first leg and removed the burden of co-ordinating the media arrangements. David Swete joined us in Bilbao and again in Fremantle from North Sails and ensured that my sails were in perfect racing trim at each start. Without this team, the voyage would never have happened.

Index

He just wanted a decent book to read ...

Not too much to ask, is it? It was in 1935 when Allen Lane, Managing Director of Bodley Head Publishers, stood on a platform at Exeter railway station looking for something good to read on his journey back to London. His choice was limited to popular magazines and poor-quality paperbacks – the same choice faced every day by the vast majority of readers, few of whom could afford hardbacks. Lane's disappointment and subsequent anger at the range of books generally available led him to found a company – and change the world.

'We believed in the existence in this country of a vast reading public for intelligent books at a low price, and staked everything on it'
Sir Allen Lane, 1902–1970, founder of Penguin Books

The quality paperback had arrived – and not just in bookshops. Lane was adamant that his Penguins should appear in chain stores and tobacconists, and should cost no more than a packet of cigarettes.

Reading habits (and cigarette prices) have changed since 1935, but Penguin still believes in publishing the best books for everybody to enjoy. We still believe that good design costs no more than bad design, and we still believe that quality books published passionately and responsibly make the world a better place.

So wherever you see the little bird – whether it's on a piece of prize-winning literary fiction or a celebrity autobiography, political tour de force or historical masterpiece, a serial-killer thriller, reference book, world classic or a piece of pure escapism – you can bet that it represents the very best that the genre has to offer.

Whatever you like to read – trust Penguin.